ARAB WOMEN IN THE MIDDLE AGES

SHIRLEY GUTHRIE

ARAB WOMEN IN THE MIDDLE AGES
Private Lives and Public Roles

Saqi Books

For Charles

British Library Cataloguing-in-Publication Data
A catalogue record for this book is available from the
British Library

ISBN 0 86356 773 8 (hb)

Saqi Books
26 Westbourne Grove
London W2 5RH
www.saqibooks.com

Contents

Note and Acknowledgements

All Arabic terms have been verified from Lane's *Arabic-English Lexicon*, which was based principally on medieval dictionaries of classical Arabic. The transliteration is a simplified form of the *Encyclopedia of Islam*, retaining only the '*ayn* and *hamza*, and substituting *d* for *dj*.

My sources were necessarily selective and make no claim to be definitive. My grateful thanks go to André Gaspard for his enthusiasm and belief in this project, to Mai Ghoussoub for her helpful guidance and suggestions, and to Alfred Goldman for reading the manuscript and constructive comments. Finally, I am indebted to Charles Guthrie, without whose understanding and encouragement this work could not have been completed.

Introduction

My aim was to present an alternative vision of Arab women to counter western perceptions distorted by the lens of Orientalism and historical experience. This is an in-depth study of issues affecting women's life in all its dimensions, centred as it was on the patriarchal family unit where the interests of the individual were subordinated to the greater good of the extended family and clan. Arranged marriage, notions of honour and shame, the control of female sexuality and the seclusion of women are difficult and sensitive issues for a non-Arab to explore, and the depth and variety of this field and the diverse geographical locations present a host of problems.

One must ask whether it is possible to posit a model of a unified Muslim society? Within some one hundred years, the Muslim world embraced converts from diverse ethnic strands, who outnumbered the Arabs, but Arabic was the lingua franca of religion and cultural expression. The oldest surviving of the four law schools, that of al-Malik of Medina, was the closest to the lifestyle of the Prophet; it reflected the mores of pastoralists and was predictably conservative. In Iraq, the liberal Hanifi rite was the most influential branch. The two other schools were the Shafi'i in Cairo and the Hanbali which prevailed elsewhere in the Muslim world. In time, many of the jurists, who were non-Arab, interpreted Qur'anic prescriptions concerning women in light of their own value systems. Their varying pronouncements reflected accommodation to local custom and practice, thus attitudes to female seclusion, costume, propriety and suchlike varied from country to country.

Women were more socially active when Islam was largely confined to the Arabian Peninsula, but later restrictions were outweighed by women's rights of inheritance, for example, recognised in law. Relations between men and women in the culture of the Near East had been firmly delineated from time immemorial prior to Islam; they were preserved in the countryside but, as canon law evolved, were modified for city life. It is arguable that women's later status was in many ways undermined in the assimilation to the social mores of the converted societies.

This study is restricted largely to Arab women of the eastern Muslim world on several counts. Orientalism and the splendours of the art of Iran and the Ottomans have inspired studies of women in these areas. Arab manuscript painting is much less well known. I have previously drawn on extensive examination of thirteenth- and fourteenth-century illustrated *Maqamat* manuscripts from Iraq, which provided a rich source of information on contemporary social life; where relevant, they are referred to as visual evidence. Arabic is a difficult language and it is one aspect frequently neglected by western commentators. Language is the key to people and society, and access to medieval dictionaries revealed much valuable supplementary material.

My sources were wide and drawn from the world of learning - the religious and political elite - and include the tenth-century geographer al-Muqaddasi and Ibn Khallikan's thirteenth biographical dictionary. The harangues of Ibn al-Hajj came from fourteenth-century Cairo, a bastion of Maliki orthodoxy frequently undermined by women's public behaviour. Al-Maqrizi's fifteenth century history of Egypt was also highly informative. But these were men who wrote for a highly-literate male bourgeois audience representing a social order based on the superior power of men and little concerned with the needs and aspirations of common people. Their often-negative views, and those of theologians, were redressed to some extent by chroniclers such as al-Jahiz, a man of letters and satirist and the judge al-Tanukhi, who compiled anecdotage. They were keen observers of social life in all its nuances, and they cast a refreshing, human slant upon the habits and characteristics of their time.

Although women were largely excluded from the political process, pious women, compilers and transmitters of *hadith*, made their mark and were highly respected. The Prophet's wives and others in the early community were frequently mentioned and exemplars for women everywhere. The philosopher al-Ghazali expressed strong views on sexuality in the eleventh century; while many of these addressed the perceived needs of men, there nevertheless seemed to be some understanding of the female condition. Ibn Battuta's reports from foreign lands were useful in highlighting divergent lifestyles from the Islamic norm. Al-Sakhawi's fifteenth-century biographical dictionary, *The Brilliant Light (Al-daw al-lami')* contained entries for many women famous for their piety and learning, but it is striking that, while the careers of their sons are worthy of mention, their daughters were referred to only by name. On a lighter note, Arab proverbs and folk tales, Ibn Daniyal's shadow plays and *The One Thousand and One Nights* threw light on the common people, while medical and pharmaceutical records demonstrated that women were pro-active in the control of their own fertility. Finally, the poetry of Arab women in Iraq and al-Andalus across the centuries lent an authentic voice which transcended town, country or desert and drew them together in common cause

Sources were also chosen to substantiate a suggested ubiquity of experience in the Muslim world. The mosque and ritual prayers, the *suq*, the *hammam*, dress for men and women conforming to tradition and religious prescription, cookery recipes (with regional variations) and so forth were all highly visible entities in the urban experience. The material is not definitive, but tends to confirm that a common culture, bound by the Arabic language, did evolve.

It is to be hoped that this work will appeal to a wide audience, provoke further thought and stimulate an increasingly interdisciplinary approach to the study of Arab women, in whatever period. My interest in their lives stems from residence and friendships forged in Bahrain, travel in the Middle East, as well as the inspiration of my Arabic teacher and friend, the late Taha Husayn.

CHAPTER 1

Marriage and the Home

Marriage

Al-Ghazali, acknowledging the benefits to men of marriage, which relieves the mind and heart of the man from the burden of looking after the home, and of being occupied with cooking, sweeping, cleaning utensils and arranging for the necessities of life posited one eleventh-century male viewpoint reflecting the urban bias of traditional Islamic culture.[1] Thus a husband would not find 'most of his time wasted, and would not be able to devote himself to work and to knowledge'. He also conceded that 'A good woman, capable of setting things to rights in the home', was 'an invaluable aid to religious holiness.' This conservatism reflected his role as the arbiter of Sunni orthodoxy, would have appealed in periods of social dislocation, and was perhaps a response to it. Nevertheless, despite the noblest of all her tasks being to produce and raise children, a woman's everyday domestic role was seldom acknowledged in Arabic literature, where women were frequently portrayed as the playthings of men.

The patriarchal nature of Muslim society and the value attached to lineage ensured that men formulated the rules for marriage. Family and political alliances and economic interests for the collective good came into play at the expense of individual feelings, and first cousin marriage was preferred, since it kept wealth – in whatever form – in the family. It also ensured, as in the biblical levirate marriage, that women and children were not left destitute on the death of the breadwinner; this was an ever-present possibility. However, some women were married off outside the tribe for economic or political expediency as weaker tribes forged alliances for protection with more powerful neighbours. In these circumstances, there was little element of choice for the marriage partners and the girl was frequently married between the ages of ten to twelve years, before puberty, to circumvent her exercising her prerogative on the age of consent. Her's was a small still voice, if heard at all. To be fair, a young man equally had little say.

Despite the prestige and trappings of the court, arranged marriage for political reasons was equally unappealing for Maysun bint Bahdal, the Christian wife of the Caliph Mu'awiya and mother of his successor, Yazid. Maysun longed for her own kin:

> I'd rather be in the company of my proud and fine-figured cousin than with the bloated foreign mass. My simple country life appeals to me more than this soft living. All I want is to be in my country home, indeed it is a noble home.[2]

Honour was all and the young woman bore the burden as its repository. It is arguable that honour, that is, the regulation of female sexuality as it impinges on the male, was easier to establish and maintain when marriage was kept within the family. Male relatives could guarantee in unequivocal terms a girl's virginity and family honour. These related to her 'worth' and relegated her in a sense to a commodity, at the same time severely restricting her freedom of movement in society at large. The least hint of sexual impropriety, real or imagined, besmirched the males of the family, and the behaviour and fertility of the married woman was carefully monitored. Men were quick to apportion total blame in sexual matters to women. However, the penalty for wrongfully slandering a woman, thus impugning the family, was rigorously meted out in line with Qur'anic condemnation.[3] Patrilocal marriage ensured that a mother-in-law was also assigned a particularly powerful role, as monitor and guarantor of family honour and a major influence on her son.

Life for many a young new bride, moving to her husband's family home was a daunting situation, exacerbated by her ever-present mother-in-law, an oft-maligned figure in most societies, but nonetheless an extremely powerful matriarch. Where girls had been contracted to marry their first cousins, their mothers-in-law were their aunts, whom they had known since childhood. This could produce its own tensions. Further, because of the close kinship ties, there was ever the possibility of interference from their own parents. On the other hand, many girls would find comfort in easy familiarity and intimate knowledge of a bridegroom and family known from their earliest days.

Marriage for women was monogamous. Their spouses, however, were allowed serial marriage or concubines, and for many women the spectre of another wife must have loomed large. It would indeed be unusual if the appearance of another wife in her home did not place great psychological pressure on the repudiated wife; this would be intensified when children followed, and many would have found the strains unbearable. Sons and daughters, the extended family on both sides, even servants, would find their own loyalties confused. Financial factors and the future custody of her children would necessarily come under scrutiny. A new wife and her children and the children of concubines were all entitled to material support, as well as a share in the man's estate, and the children of his first family would see their birthright literally diminishing before their eyes. Divorce was probably not an option for many, woman or man, as there was too much at stake financially, and there was little a woman in those circumstances could do.[4]

Despite the very harsh penalties and dangers in transgressing sexual codes, there are many references to adultery in Arabic literature. It was therefore patently possible for women to enter into extramarital sexual liaisons, wherever and however they conducted them, in spite of family vigilance. In these circumstances, the veil would offer the perfect guarantee of anonymity. How did these women make the acquaintance of their paramours, if they were not in some way related to them? When did they have the opportunity to be seen unveiled in the first place? The simplest explanation might be that the men were friends of their husbands who had visited their own homes as guests, and somehow they must have glimpsed each other. Perhaps servants were brought in as go-betweens, although it is most unlikely that other women in the same household could have risked being implicated. Is it possible that women became romantically involved with their brothers-in-law? These were men with very close acquaintance and opportunity. The Umayyad ruler Walid evidently took to heart the proverb, 'Be good to your own wife and you can have your neighbour's', for he inadvertently caught a glimpse of his sister in law and promptly fell in love. Walid, unlike most men, could act with impunity.

Marriage contracts

Affluent women were frequently wealthy in their own right and some were well able to lay down ground rules in their marriages; their hand was strengthened when the match was advantageous for the groom's family, for whatever reason. However, unlike women in the lower strata of society, they did not appear personally in court to defend their cases, and left this to (male) agents. Their husbands, who often had the diversions of concubines or other wives, possibly considered it a matter of 'peace at any price'.

It appears from the ample evidence in Ibn al-Attar's *Book of Contract and Seals* (*Kitab al-watha'iq wa'l-sijillat*), a textbook laying out sample agreements, that some Muslim women, particularly in tenth-century al-Andalus and north Africa (Ifriqiya), in theory enjoyed considerable licence to dictate their own terms in marriage contracts, through binding conditional clauses. For example, one bride stipulated monogamy, for 'should he commit aught of the above, (taking another wife or concubine) then matters are in her own hands, and she may repulse the intruding woman by contract'.[5] In some cases women even enjoyed the right to demand a divorce. Others found it necessary to include visits to their families, which suggests that many husbands even withheld their permission for something so fundamental to a girl's emotional wellbeing, and to preclude relocation elsewhere of the marital home. The prevailing Maliki legal rite was extremely conservative, but it was tempered in these instances by the fact that society was an amalgam of Arabs, Christians and Jews. Berbers, European mercenaries and local custom also came into play.

Given the enormous distances involved and the great inconvenience, if not hardship, one can only marvel that travel for many men featured so prominently in the medieval period. This obviously had great implications for women, and another contract insisted that:

> The girl's spouse might not absent himself nigh or far for more than six months – save to discharge the pilgrimage incumbent upon his soul, for which he may then absent himself three years . . . the meanwhile thereof to see to her upkeep, and to her clothing, and to her dwelling.[6]

There was often a downside to the acquisition of a comfortable lifestyle, for example for the wives of merchants engaged in long-haul trade. The high price of the imported commodities reflected the time, the arduous journey, and the constant possibility of shipwreck, attack by marauding bands or the succumbing to the rigours of climate and travel, and if the husband came back safely, the wife's lifestyle was enhanced. For many women, anxiety that their husbands might take a foreign wife, however temporarily, and the possibility of abandonment, was ever-present. The burden of day-to-day responsibility for the children fell squarely on the wife's shoulders. In the father's absence there might well have been disputes with their grandparents regarding their upbringing. What happened in the case of a young wife? Was she supported emotionally and financially by her in-laws? The ultimate price she probably paid during her husband's prolonged absence was severe restrictions on her movement outside his father's home and contact with men other than the family. Even wives of pilgrims were not immune to the taking of wives on the journey; Ibn Battuta did so on two occasions en route to Mecca from Tunis.

Thirteenth-century marriage contracts in north Africa reflected local custom, also precluding another wife or concubine. Women could initiate divorce proceedings on the grounds of a husband's mental incompetence, impotence or his withholding of marital rights, but only through a court of law or by mutual agreement. On the other hand, a man needed only to utter his intent before witnesses, without offering any reason. In practice, families generally counselled reconciliation in the first instance.

Marriage contracts also included detailed trousseaux inventories and gifts to the bride from her own family, as well as the dowry (*mahr*), which was for her sole use and benefit. Expensive textiles, possibly heirlooms but certainly an investment, were carefully recorded, and several writers noted that women at court possessed extremely costly carpets. Members of the Jewish community were no less prudent. The betrothal document of the daughter of a Jewish trader dated 11 November, 1146, mentioned a textile gift to her of a 'real Tabari from Tabaristan', and this pre-empted later substitution with an inferior product, if not an outright imitation.[7] Embroidered furnishing fabrics from Susanjird, in Persia, were also noted.

Such attention to detail was highly relevant in the event of divorce, as families sought to recover costly items gifted on marriage. All of these formed part of the inventory of a well-to-do household and entailed legal obligations in the event of marriage breakdown. They also served as the guarantee of a financial hedge for a woman facing an uncertain future. The girl's male guardian could also stipulate a 'postponed' (*mu'ajjal*) portion of the dowry, to be paid by the husband should he initiate divorce.[8] However, it should not be imagined that all women were so empowered, that marriage contracts redressing the balance in favour of women were acceptable throughout the Muslim world in all eras, or that husbands necessarily adhered to the conditions. One presumes that contracts were drawn up by families with some means, therefore with something worthwhile to lose, and these factors suggest that the possibility of divorce in this class and the incidence of inter-family disputes was great. This might have been one factor in the bias towards marriage within the family. One must conclude that many young women entered into marriage not in the slightest starry-eyed and already anticipating these problems.

Berber women evidently commanded great respect from men and exacted some authority over them. Around the year 1352 among Berber tribes, no caravan could pass through their territory 'without a guarantee of their protection, and for this purpose a woman's guarantee is of more value than a man's'. It is telling that their husbands wore a face veil.[9] Ibn Battuta had been similarly impressed by the degree of respect which Turkish men accorded their women, noting that 'among the Turks and the Tatars their wives hold a high position'. Indeed he considered that women even held 'a more dignified position'. One ruler's wife received him courteously, while another consort personally poured his drink, but they were hardly representative of society as a whole.[10] The preoccupation with male honour and strict, even oppresive seclusion, persisted into the eighteenth century, for the marriage contract of the daughter of one Ottoman official described her as 'the pride of the guarded women (mukhadarat), the ornament of the venerable, the exalted veil, the inviolable temple'.[11] This is a testament to male pride, but seems also to demonstrate their respect for the virtuous wife. However, this exaggerated respect in no way precluded the introduction of another wife or concubine, and one modern account of personal childhood experiences in such a household remains valid for women throughout the ages:

> The nature and consequences of the suffering of a wife who lawfully shares a husband with a second and equal partner in the same house differs both in degree and in kind from that of the woman who shares him with a temporary mistress.[12]

Seclusion and honour

In theory, the most effective way of preserving family honour was to ensure that the woman had no contact with other men; for those who did leave their homes, suitable clothing was prescribed, and this is extensively discussed in Chapter 5. One ingenious if impractical solution of the jurists was, 'Leave the women unclothed, and they will remain at home'.[13] Many men in tenth-century Baghdad who adhered to the extremely conservative Hanbali law school also strongly disapproved of women going into the public domain, but it would be erroneous to imagine that all Arab women were secluded in their homes. At the turn of the eleventh century al-Hakim, himself apparently no paragon, forbade shoemakers to make women's shoes, so that they would not leave their homes, while in the fourteenth-century Ibn al-Hajj announced that:

> Some of the pious elders (may God be pleased with them) have said that a woman should leave her house on three occasions only: when she is conducted to the house of her bridegroom, on the death of her parents, and when she goes to her own grave.

The branch of the law in Egypt followed Malik of Medina. It was the oldest surviving corpus, the most closely associated with the Prophet's lifetime and extremely conservative. One can therefore understand the need to have such onerous conditions and issues of personal freedom as interpreted by theologians clarified by an independently-spirited woman in the contract prior to marriage.

The above situation was relevant for some Arab women, but when travelling in the western Sahara, Ibn Battuta, while impressed by the assiduousness in devotion of the Muslim negroes of Mali, observed that among their 'bad qualities' was the local custom whereby:

> The women servants, slave-girls, and young girls go about in front of everyone naked, without a stitch of clothing on them. Women go into the sultan's presence naked and without coverings, and his daughters also go about naked.[14]

He was predictably shocked that even a Maliki judge (*qadi*) (who incidentally had been to Mecca) received him with a beautiful young woman in his home. This licence was not the preserve of men, for women there also openly enjoyed 'friends' and 'companions' of the opposite sex. In the absence of veils, Ibn Battuta was able to comment that these Massufa women were 'of surpassing beauty'. He evidently relished pretty girls, or at least the opportunities to see them, and pronounced Yemeni women, who uninhibitedly bade their husbands farewell as they set out on their travels, 'exceedingly beautiful'.[15] He carefully recorded that the people of Yemen 'closely resemble the people of northwest Africa in their customs', thus confirming the durability of local custom and practice and their incorporation into diverse societies following the advent of Islam.

Generally speaking, the higher the social class of the woman in Arab lands, the more likely she was to be excluded from appearing in public and potential contact with strange men. In theory, upper-class females might have had plenty of time for education. Unfortunately, many probably did not have the opportunity, and lived the lives of birds in cages, however gilded. Maryam bint Abu Ya'qub al-Shilbi, (died 1020) who was born in Silves, southern Portugal, became tutor to high-born women in Seville. Maryam had scant respect for them and their secluded lifestyle, and asked scathingly:

> What is there to hope for in a cobwebbed woman of seventy seven? She babies her way to her stick and staggers like a chained convict.[16]

Maryam's cloistered charges apparently had little imagination or education, and one might have expected some relaxation of strict Islamic social rules in al-Andalus by that time, given the rate of intermarriage. That was an older generation, of course, who may have been resistant to change.

Given the emphasis on morality, there was a great collective interest in the control of public space, and streets were defined on gender lines. Men usually walked down the middle, while women kept to the sides. The issues of wearing the veil and costume are explored in Chapter 5. No respectable woman risked being seen even glancing at male passers-by which left her open to accusations of some sort of 'encounter'. From the male standpoint, women were viewed as temptresses and, as the repositories of family honour, had to be avoided at all costs.

While visiting Persia, Ibn Battuta was struck by the large number of women in the streets of Shiraz, and commented, 'I have never seen in any land so great an assembly of women'. Their 'strange custom' was to go to the mosque every Monday, Thursday and Friday, 'one or two thousand of them, carrying fans with which they fan themselves on account of the great heat.' He could not fail to be impressed by this public display of piety, but implied that women elsewhere in the Muslim lands of his travels did not necessarily attend public prayers in the mosque. It seems that in early Islam it was common for women to exercise their right to attend the mosque, where the sexes were segregated and the wearing of perfume discouraged. Orthodox Jewish women to this day worship in the gallery.

However, there may have been many women who were only too happy not to brave cluttered streets in their finery. A thirteenth-century visitor mentioned his forays into the byways of Old Cairo, where 'joy abandoned me' and Simon Simeonis, writing in 1332, also painted a dire picture of Cairo's tortuous mean streets. According to one foreign visitor to Tunis, upper and middle class males, in particular, merchants, 'never suffer themselves to be borne on their own legs, but ride horses';[17] women travelled only on the back of a donkey. Yet around the same period, Baghdadi women and men were openly promenading on two of the city's bridges in the evenings.[18] This had evidently been a popular diversion for centuries, since Ibn Jubayr spoke of the 'numberless' people, women and men, who crossed over the Tigris between different quarters night and day 'in recreation'.[19] The degree of seclusion apparently varied between social classes and local customs in the different Muslim lands, according to theological responses to particular social circumstances.

It would not be surprising if some women felt intimidated by the dark alleyways and the close proximity to strange men, many of whom were hostile to their public presence, and chose only to venture over the threshold of their homes on rare occasions; in these cases they possibly felt that their long robes and veils offered some anonymity, if not protection. They might have done well to heed the rantings of Ibn al-Hajj against donkey drivers. He sarcastically referred to their over-familiarity with women and to shocking scenes which apparently took place in the streets. As al-Maqrizi later pointed out, there was also periodic disorder, even looting, in the Cairo markets. These factors led to calls to ban females, and some edicts may have been less misogynistic than well-intentioned and for the protection of women. Male honour, of course, was also protected since a violated woman shamed a whole family.

Women undoubtedly found their own ways to circumvent periodic restrictions on their freedom, as they did on so many other occasions when the forceful hand of officialdom literally descended, for example, in Cairo in 1519:

All walking about was forbidden at night, because the Ottomans seized hold of turbans and girdles and lifted women and youths in the streets.[20]

In June 1522 it was decreed there that women were to refrain totally from going to the markets or from riding on a donkey followed by its keeper – donkey drivers had apparently still not overcome the error of their ways over three centuries. Older women alone were exempt (presumably on the grounds that they posed no sexual threat; did elderly men fall into the same category?). Any woman contravening the edict was condemned to be caned, attached by her hair to the tail of a draught horse and dragged along to Cairo.[21]

One imagines that these measures were sufficiently onerous to keep many ordinary women from going out to visit cemeteries or even to attend the funerals of near kin, and Ibn Iyas continued sympathetically:

> The population suffered enormously as a result of these disturbances. Streets were closed after sunset, and the markets remained deserted because of the paucity of passing trade; one would have thought that life itself was absent.[22]

These practices infringing women's liberty must have been particularly painful, and strengthened the resolve among some to rebel, but no reasonable woman could have cavilled at restrictions placed on her during the plague epidemics which were seen as manifestations of Divine Wrath.

All in all, Ibn al-Hajj was remarkably zealous and well-informed, and his writings throw some light on daily life for some Cairene women: Monday – a visit to the tomb of Sayyid Husayn (al-Husayni), then a visit to the *suq* with intention known 'to God alone'. (He intriguingly devoted a special chapter on his shock at the goings-on in cemeteries. Whatever did he mean?) Visiting the shrines of holy people was a popular pastime, and something of a social occasion. However, one had to be ritually pure before entering a mosque or shrine, and menstruation debarred such outings. Small markets sprang up around tombs, and some at least of the vendors must have been women. Thankfully, Ibn Jubayr's visit to the al-Qarafa cemetery in Cairo was more spiritually uplifting. He saw a sight 'wondrous to behold', the tombs of 'fourteen men and five women, upon of each of which was an edifice most well wrought'.[23]

Ibn al-Hajj's greatest bile was directed towards women who sunbathed in skimpy clothing on the banks of the Nile and those who congregated at pools.[24] Tuesday was when women gathered with friends; on Wednesday, they visited Sayyida Nafisa, then pretended they had legitimate business in the market of Old Cairo. Sunday saw a return visit to the market. Eventually, women's access to the *hammam* was restricted to the evening.[25] However, on Thursdays there were more women than men in the markets, and one apparently could hardly move for them. This was the weekend, after all, when affluent women went shopping for jewellery and perfume. Ibn al-Hajj found goings-on such as women conversing animatedly with men reprehensible; he believed this would lead to deplorable consequences. These women probably disagreed vehemently with his opinion that it was up to a husband to buy his wife's jewellery and clothing. Many a dispute as a result of a man daring to forbid his wife such excursions apparently led to great arguments, even separation, but this was not a problem peculiar to Muslim women. Men conceded that for those women who had to go into town out of necessity, the ideal prescription was for old clothes which trailed down to the ground. As we shall see, women's fashions did not always comply with this opinion.

Ibn al-Hajj despised women who dared to go on boats, but this was evidently another popular female pastime. Ibn 'Aqil reported a '*baytiyya* vessel, in good trim' with 'beautiful finery and marvellous woodwork' moored under the balcony of a palace in Baghdad.[26] The name suggests an enclosed superstructure 'like a house' (*bayt*), which would certainly have offered privacy to women passengers. Other handsome boats, such as the *sumayriyya*, possibly of dark wood, and the *zabzab*, a small vessel, also provided a welcome respite from the clamorous city and relief from the searing heat of summer for the leisured classes. For mundane journeys, perhaps family and tomb visits, ordinary women travelled on utilitarian river boats, such as the *balam*, a river boat par excellence, with scroll ornamentation at both ends. It drew little water and was usually poled, although it could be sailed or rowed according to conditions. The *balam* was unlikely to offer women privacy, but some boats were used exclusively by women. Al-Tanukhi's amusing anecdotes included an account by the vizier Hamid ibn al-'Abbas who was on a visit to Ubaydulla in a *harraqa*, a type of river boat usually reserved for their use. It was well draped to ensure privacy and was rowed by white eunuchs. On asking why, the enquirer was advised that it was improper for the crew of such a vessel to be virile.[27] Such faith in the medical profession was somewhat misplaced, since the operation was not invariably successful, and one can only speculate if Ibn al-Hajj was justified in his condemnation.

In 1518 a judge, noticing women chatting to the guards, remarked, 'The women of Cairo are debauching the ruler's soldiers, and they will not be capable of fighting'.[28] Again one sees the blame assigned to women. Several concessions eventually had to be made; again older women were exempt, but others were permitted to go to the bazaars if accompanied by their husbands. It was decreed that women were able to ride neither horses nor mules, but nevertheless the authorities acknowledged the difficulties faced by women who lived and worked in different quarters.

These were very public displays of women's gatherings which demonstrated their solidarity, and one wonders if they were frequently an act of public defiance at the many onerous restrictions which the orthodox authorities sought to impose out of religious zeal? Concubines apparently enjoyed much freer social relations with men than married women; was this because they were playthings and commodities, and easily disposed of when they became fractious or their charms predictably faded?

The city

The population of Baghdad at the end of the tenth century was around the one and a half million mark, and each district was a microcosm of the city at large. Ibn 'Aqil's first-hand account of of the city in the next century described the *Bab al-taq*, as follows:

> I will not describe to you what you might find hard to believe. I will simply give you a description of my own quarter, which is but one of ten, each the size of a Syrian town.[29]

Ibn 'Aqil continued:

> As for its streets, there is one which closely follows the Tigris. On one of its sides, it has palaces overlooking the river, and disposed in such fashion as to spread all the way from the Bridge to the beginning of the Zahir Garden.

He also described al-Karkh, the district on the west bank of the Tigris, and commented on 'The sound of its waterwheels, the quacking of its ducks, the clamour of its soldiers and servants, while the Tigris gently streamed along'.

Even a high-class brothel there was described in the *Thousand and One Nights* as 'A tall and goodly mansion, with a balcony overlooking the river-bank and pierced with a lattice-window'.[30]

A contemporary proverb ran, 'A man's paradise is his home' so gardens would have been a prerequisite in such surroundings, mirroring paradise in their lush greenery and scents, their appeal to the senses of running water, coolness, the interplay of light and shade and, perhaps, reward in the hereafter. One can see the attractions of these most desirable areas of Baghdad, and many women must have aspired to live there, although relatively few were so privileged. Al-Hamadhani parodied a boastful *nouveau riche* tenth-century merchant whose house was in the best part of Baghdad. The proud owner took pains to point out that the copper door handle had been bought from a famous workshop, weighed six pounds, and cost three gold dinars. Such ostentation was far removed from the traditional values of the early Believers. Following a disastrous fire among reed huts in Kufa, the Caliph 'Umar sanctioned rebuilding in stone, but cautioned that no one should build more than three houses, 'Do not vie with each other in building'.[31] Al-Ghazali's treatise *Fitting Conduct in Religion (al-adab fi al-din)* further exhorted the rich to 'maintain a humble bearing, not claiming rights and privileges others do not have, but always giving thanks to God'.[32]

Building costs would vary according to location, the materials used and whether they were available locally. In the fourteenth century, according to Ibn Khaldun, the richer inhabitants of Baghdad:

> Make their walls of stone, which they join together with quicklime. They cover them with paint and plaster and do the utmost to furnish and decorate everything.[33]

The groups who lived in such style were neatly summed up in the time of Harun al-Rashid by his exceedingly powerful vizier Yahya ibn Fadl. They were 'Viziers, distinguished by their wisdom, upper classes elevated by their wealth, middle classes marked by their culture',[34] and embraced the *'ulama'*, the doctors of divine law *(Shari'a)* and merchants who dealt in luxury commodities. Maysun bint Bahdal possibly spoke for a great many unhappy women. For her, the supposed good life at court palled; she would 'rather be in a life-throbbing house than in a tall palace'.[35] There was also a necessarily large bureaucracy and many civil servants. These were the people in work, with high qualifications, whose wives presided over well-regulated households and led fairly leisurely, if sequestered, lifestyles.

The Islamic city was a series of more or less self-contained quarters around the main public area; each had its own local mosque and market which provided the day to day needs of the inhabitants. Ties to district were largely based less on class, rather on kinship and alliance associations to particular tribes from the nomadic past, or on religious affiliation, with no necessary common occupation or profession among the men. Nevertheless some street names in Baghdad indicated particular professions. Perfumiers and dry-goods merchants in the eleventh century resided in the area known as *Darb al-za'faran* (Saffron Lane or Gate), an immediate indicator of prestige and wealth, while judges and notaries tended to reside in *Darb Sulayman*,[36] so many women had neighbours from the same social groupings. Sixteenth-century documents from Aleppo and Damascus suggest communities there numbering around one thousand people, where it is reasonable to assume a certain intimacy and solidarity between the residents.[37]

Houses consisted of several basic types, according to geographical location, largely built of sun-dried brick or stone. Large family compounds, sometimes comprising several buildings, were built around a courtyard; simple houses had large single doorways, while grander houses had two-leaved doors within a pointed archway. Wood was scarce in Egypt and ebony and camphorwood were imported from India. Doors were frequently works of art, with elaborate carving, and sometimes verses of poetry, and in the cases of rented property were listed in the inventory, as they were often stolen. Al-Hamadhani's merchant's door was 'from a single cutting of finest teak! Never eaten by worms, never rotted'[38] and a costly import from the east, and one of al-Jahiz's misers complained:

When there is constant coming and going, opening and closing, bolting and withdrawing of locks, doors get broken . . . When there are lots of children . . . door-nails are torn out, every wood lock is pulled off.[39]

High class houses in Egypt had wooden ceilings painted in the Syrian style, and marble also featured as floor and wall decoration. There was extensive stuccowork; al-Jahiz spoke of 'rooms plastered with gypsum'.

Ibn Jubayr, recalling his visit to Alexandria, wrote that among the wonders of that city:

Was that its buildings below the earth were as substantial as those above and even more ancient and more solid, for the water of the Nile flows through houses and streets from beneath the ground, and wells are linked to one another and so flow into one another.[40]

These were evidently large dwellings and cool refuges in the heat of summer. Al-Tabari noted that in the east 'bundles of long, thick rushes were strewn' about the mansions in summer and 'great blocks of packed snow placed between them'; this obviously depended on income and geographical location. Others in Baghdad resorted to their basements, and many people slept on roof terraces or in well-ventilated spaces, perhaps near a directional wind-catcher, in the height of summer. In winter, smaller rooms, which could be easily heated, functioned as bedrooms.

Foreign visitors to an Arab home nowadays are frequently surprised by the delights inside, beyond the entrance, from a deliberate and fairly unprepossessing exterior of blank walls; of course, this is entirely in keeping with pious injunctions and traditions against public ostentation and superficiality, and privacy for the family. Their exterior facades offer no clue to the lives of the inhabitants ensconced behind walls of silence. The conventions of society and religion dictated the seclusion of women, both indoors and outdoors, and the paradigm for the Muslim household was the courtyard type of home. One is aware on entering a large courtyard house, for example, through a small door set in a much larger entrance, that this represents the transition from the secular world, and that nothing of the private character of the house or its occupants can be hazarded by the visitor or the passer-by. There was frequently a separate women's entrance, set into a different wall from the main doorway.

Western (male) orientalists have long been preoccupied with erotic fantasies centred around the *harim*. In fact the term referred simply to the inner sanctum of the household and its female members. It was out of bounds to men who had no close blood ties, and it stressed the inviolacy of the family. As for these unrelated men, *Sura* 24 reminded them not to enter the dwellings of other men until they had asked their owners' permission and wished them peace.

No outward-facing unscreened windows allowed a view of the interior, neither was it possible for neighbours to overlook any part of the house or yard. An additional factor was security, since access was controlled only by the large locks on external doors. Male social life revolved around the *majlis*, literally the 'sitting-room', always supported by the invisible efforts of women, and many men had exclusively male quarters; in that case, these were separate from the main building.

The upper and middle classes

The rooms of a house were multi-functional, according to the time of day and season of the year and they consisted of private (female) space and public (male) space. The *continuum* of women's daily life, when men were absent at work, was dictated by the sun and household tasks and the pace was dictated by social status.[41] In affluent homes this was fairly leisurely, since patrilocality on marriage ensured that there were many women in the extended household and so tasks could be shared and sociable. Servants and slaves were also employed. For senior wives there was respect and their domestic round was lightened. The household constantly shifted around during the day and seasons following shade from the sun in summer and, conversely, seeking the warmer rooms during the winter. This was in some degree a reflection of Bedouin roots, perhaps long-forgotten. Rooms were at once sitting rooms, dining rooms or bedrooms, allocated according to sex. Women, their family and female friends had the run of the home during the day when the men of the household were absent. The kitchen was women's exclusive domain, and this particular physical division of space and labour according to sex is dealt with at length in Chapter 4.

Despite their comfortable surroundings, women in the upper classes were not necessarily mistresses of their own homes. Larger households could also include other wives and concubines and their children. This element of offering protection was fundamental to the Bedouin values so esteemed by Muslim society at large, and the care of indigent family members was highly compatible with the Prophet's own circumstances. Muhammad lost both his father and mother by the time he was six years of age and was brought up in the household of his paternal grandfather, 'Abd al-Muttalib. *Sura* 93 poignantly asked, 'Did He not find thee an orphan, and shelter thee? Did He not find thee erring and guide thee? Did He not find thee needy, and suffice thee?' Many women, however, and particularly if they were denied the opportunity to venture outside, might have found internecine squabbles and petty rivalries extremely trying. Sisters-in-law could show a solidarity against their mother-in-law, if they dared.

Some women were allowed family visits, and there was a fairly regular procession of hairdressers, seamstresses, peddlers and other tradespeople arriving at the doors. Well-to-do homes probably had bathrooms, so there would have been no great call for the women to visit the public bath-house. At least some of this segment of female society enjoyed much autonomy and were able to dictate how they would spend their days. They must have relied on the women of the extended family, domestic servants or slaves to care for their children and keep the household running smoothly in their absences. Frequent proscriptions prove that large numbers of women did appear in public.

Spacious homes had built-in cupboards or open niches for the storage and display of household items, as demonstrated in contemporary manuscript illustration.[42] These were sometimes decorated with carved wood or terracotta, and in the Saljuq period terracotta ornamentation was centred around Baghdad. Ornaments included lustreware and other glazed pottery, the rock crystal items for which Egypt was noted and fine enamelled glass from Syria. The earliest lustreware pottery was probably made in Iraq, around Baghdad, Kufa and Basra in the early ninth century. Its decorative qualities were very attractive and highly suited to display and to impress visitors. Abu al-Qasim described his masterly lustre pigment as shimmering like the sun and reflecting like red gold. These wares could never have been cheap, for the highly technical production using expensive materials generated a very high wastage rate. The iconography of the court in the decorative arts gave way in the late twelfth century to that of everyday life, evidence perhaps of a new market for the craftsmen. It suggests that a burgeoning self-confident and leisured bourgeoisie functioned as arbiters of taste and testified to the homogeneity of culture in great Muslim cities such as Baghdad, Damascus, Cairo and Qayrawan, as well as in Sicily and al-Andalus.

Increasing prosperity meant that there was a wide variety of practical and decorative items available for the home. *Kohl* containers, mirrors, pen boxes, inkstands, stemmed wine cups, ewer and basin sets and many other items were all fashioned in metal. Decorations included inscriptions, vegetal and floral designs and figural representation, as well as scenes otherwise associated with the court such as drinking, musicians and hunters. Style, ornament and materials obviously varied and reflected local and regional preferences.

Fine metalware objects such as massive candlesticks and pierced brass or copper braziers were features of affluent homes. Candles made of beeswax and even ambergris were used in luxurious settings, and sweet-scented candles of amber weighing eighty pounds each lit up the bridal chamber of Harun al-Rashid's daughter-in-law Buran.[43] But candles were expensive, and oil lamps of various types with cotton wicks provided lighting in the majority of houses. Large copper charcoal braziers provided the heat in winter in the homes of the well-to-do.

In the period around 1100-1300, new metalwork techniques and designs were adopted in order to achieve a shimmering, less purely functional, more decorative product. Again, there is a sense of display and pride in the home by a self-confident group in society. Was this initiated by the women themselves? Even if they did not personally visit the market, women brokers likely peddled such items door-to-door. It goes without saying that in this milieu there would be many servants and slaves, of both sexes, and the males were eunuchs. Well-to-do women called on servants or slavegirls to attend their everyday needs, but they undoubtedly personally supervised the household chores or delegated someone to do so and, having decided on their requirements, sent them to the markets.

Perforated incense burners on tripod feet were cast in brass and inlaid with silver. It was the custom to put words in the mouth, so to speak, of particular objects. For example, one incense burner was inscribed with the verse, 'Within me is the fire of Hell but without floats the perfume of Paradise'.[44] However amusing and apt this verse, its *raison d'être* was more prosaic. One should remember that a huge amount of animals was kept around palace complexes and in the streets. One could not have been unaware of their presence, and women would wish to keep their homes sweet-smelling. There was also the need to repel the attendant insects.

Furnishings

So far as furniture is concerned, the term should not be understood in the western sense. Furnishings were an innovation in the 'Abbasid period. Food was served on a large metal tray (*tabaq*) which was laid on a small table (*khiwan*), often of ebony or other exotic woods. In ninth-century Qayrawan, a man whose father had become a vizier and acquired great riches had 'twin tables of glass conveyed to him from Baghdad, and they did not come into his hands but for one hundred and ninety dinars'.[45] This was an enormous sum, bearing in mind that a dinar was a gold coin. Rugs, cushions and mattresses were easily portable to reflect the different usages of individual rooms according to the time of day, and served the dual functions of furniture for sitting on and as bedding. All these required was a shaking or beating, and bedding was aired thoroughly each day. The bed was a thin canvas mattress stuffed with cotton; bedcovers were of cotton or wool, depending on the season, and there were feather pillows. Urban life for some was far removed from the discomforts of the early community.

A sofa (*diwan*) was ranged around three walls of a room, with cushions and square mattresses strewn around and affluent homes perhaps had a dado of tiled panels. Stuccowork and terracotta ornamentation were also prominent features in these houses of stone or dried brick. Tabaristan upholstery was famous, and found its way to the courts in ninth-century Baghdad; by the tenth century it had become a rather desirable item for the new bourgeoisie bride.

For those women with the means, there was a wide variety of costly fabrics from all corners of the Muslim world. Al-Tha'alibi described Tustari embroidered satins, 'worthy to be mentioned in the same breadth as those of Rum' (Byzantium), and embroidered silks 'of regal quality' from Sus.[46] Prices for furnishings in the era seem to have been largely disregarded by contemporary chroniclers, although occasional details of precious carpets appeared.

Wasit, in Iraq, was well-known for its fine textiles, in particular window and wall curtains, and tapestry-woven carpets.[47] At the end of the Umayyad era a court favourite told how he was summoned by Walid ibn Yazid into a room covered in wall hangings and carpets from Armenia. All of these items were the preserve of the well-to-do, since textiles were expensive. At the end of the tenth century, one Arab geographer mentioned curtains of thirty cubits (a cubit being an arm's length) from Bahnasa, central Egypt, which cost around three hundred dinars. These evidently graced a mansion or palace, but one could pay from five to eight dinars for a fine woollen pair from Bahnasa. Two pairs of Baghdadi silk curtains and a pair made from fine linen from Dabiq in Egypt were also noted. Such valuable items were also specifically mentioned in housing contracts, to preclude their removal by an unscrupulous vendor or tenant, which was evidently a fairly common occurrence. There were various housing options open to this class, and a socially-aspirational wife could have found herself in a comfortable position. For those with no private bathrooms, visits to the *hammam* were *de rigueur*. Grander homes had drainage facilities on a slope.

Houses in Muslim Spain were constructed according to the eastern courtyard prototype, with rooms leading off, and in the towns latrines were installed. Sizes varied, but again exteriors seem to have been rather simple. This was particularly so after the influx of the austere north African Almoravid and Almohad dynasties in the eleventh and twelfth centuries. Rich lustreware in al-Andalus, derived from Almohad techniques and styles, was first made at Malaga, and imitated after the end of the the thirteenth century in Manises (Valencia).[48] In the cities lustreware was widely available, not only for aristocratic households, which suggests that many women in al-Andalus enjoyed a high standard of living. These were bright and highly-attractive pieces which women would treasure and perhaps requested as wedding gifts, since they featured in legacy lists and household inventories. Again, one wonders if the wives in al-Andalus personally purchased household furnishings, ornaments and everyday items for the home.

While the traditional courtyard type of home conformed most comprehensively to the tenets and mores of some sort of 'ideal' family unit in Islamic society, it would be naive to think that all families lived in such a household.

The lower middle class

The lower spectrum of the middle classes probably included the highly skilled artisans, metalworkers in base and precious metals, potters and decorators, manufacturers of lustreware and the like, small shopkeepers and minor functionaries in the civil service and their wives and families. For them, and mirroring their income, there was the option of housing ranging from fairly basic to relatively imposing in size. Well-qualified craftsmen and tradesmen were paid more than unskilled labourers. In the year 1,000 a mason earned thirty-five silver dirhams, approximately one and a half dinars a month, that is, the same as a nurse. An ordinary library employee in Baghdad took home two dinars per month, with additional 'in kind' payments such as bread and fuel. These figures, of course, pall by comparison with some of the obscenely large sums noted in the context of the court, and it is difficult to transpose particular rates quoted between different regions due to currency fluctuations.

Marriage for women in this stratum of society was less subject to family control, since there was little in the way of inherited wealth, and many of their marriages may have been more consensual in nature, especially if they married their cousins, although this might have been a less pressing issue.[49] Houses were smaller and where they could not necessarily afford the family much privacy, socializing for husbands had to take place outside the home. Honour played its part, mitigated by the economics of life, but one wonders if the concept of a virgin bride was possibly correspondingly less important and there was a fairly high incidence of re-marriage?

However, women's lifestyles here were no less circumscribed economically than women in the upper classes, but their freedom to venture beyond the confines of home was frequently less constricted. In the medieval period premature death among men and women and the resulting economic circumstances and orphaned children meant that re-marriage to some extent was economically vital for some women. The incidence of re-marriage, sometimes on more than one occasion, for women from the lower classes was possibly much higher than among the well-to-do.[50] Stepmothers, like mothers-in-law, were frequently universally mistrusted and disliked, and one wonders what problems arose with their step-children.

Homes, then as now in any society, generally mirrored economic circumstances. Ibn Khaldun confirmed that some people built 'A small dwelling or house for themselves and for their children to live in. Their desire goes no farther, because their situation permits them no more. Thus, they restrict themselves to a mere shelter, which is natural to human beings',[51] adding that, between the two extremes of grand and basic houses there were 'innumerable degrees'. Relatively well-to-do wives in this class lived in a degree of comfort compared to those of the masses, whose income, if any, was uncertain and spasmodic, and to those who depended on charity.

Did people in general in this segment of society own their own homes? For many, the Arabic proverb 'weightier than a house's rent'[52] was a grim reality. In 1123 tenants of small homes in the Ja'afariyya district of Baghdad were faced with extortionate demands from the authorities with an increase of six dinars a month from one dinar per month. This report is interesting, if unfortunate for the tenants, for it suggests that municipal authorities owned properties for rental. They possibly formed part of a *waqf* or pious endowment, with the income being ploughed back into a religious foundation. A papyrus document detailed house rentals in Cairo of two or two and a half dinars per annum, and an apartment cost four dinars per annum. This latter seems rather high. Another six-month lease stipulated a rental of one and a half dinars.

One ninth-century rental agreement, according to Hanafi legal rites, stipulated that:

If the proprietor fears that the tenant may be absent at the termination of the let and that his spouse refuses to terminate the tenancy, he is advised to put the tenancy (also) in the name of the spouse.[53]

This seems to be a joint tenancy, and therefore a recognition in law both of the woman's legal responsibility and the suspicion that a husband, once having provided his wife with a home, might be tempted to abandon her there. But would this only have been relevant among more affluent tenants, and an inference that notwithstanding the woman stayed on, she could herself afford the rent?

Even in this class there was disparity in income and many wives of tradesmen and workmen had to work, at home, in a workshop or perhaps as domestic servants, for their men's wages were insufficient. They had aspirations, some earned money in their own right, and they were intrepid enough to appear personally in court to state their cases. It is arguable that these fairly ordinary women upheld the *harim* system of female sequestration and in a sense leavened its burden, if that is what it represented. Women did washing, dyed, spun and wove and repaired old clothes.[54] 'New lamps for old', as in the tale of Aladdin was not necessarily fiction. Hawkers went around the streets, cries ringing out, buying used clothing and rags, and offering an assortment of needles in exchange. Did this indicate a flourishing market for second-hand clothing? Or, given the wide availability of paper, were linen and cotton clothes recycled? No matter, there was a definite element of 'trading-in', which might have proved attractive to poorer women. The official male view was that women patently put some thought into their outdoor costume, wearing their finery and proudly striding out in the middle of the road, mixing with men or even compelling them to pass close by as they skirted the walls of houses, and thus risking being accosted and molestation.

Money was not the sole determinant of social class. Al-Jahiz recalled a doctor, Asad ibn Jani, with few patients and in dire financial straits, who 'was wont to sleep in winter upon a bed of peeled reeds, that the fleas might slip off therefrom for the slipperiness and smoothness thereof'.[55] His mattress also provided insulation from the cold of the earthen floor. It is suggested that any definition of 'class' should take into account aspirations, a thirst for education and a disregard or otherwise of material comforts. Perhaps the good doctor was unmarried, as a wife in that position would likely have attempted to 'keep up appearances'.

Women's neighbours were from all walks of life, and as they went about their daily business they would have met a variety of social contacts. They would have been aware of the latest fashions in furnishing and houseware, and indeed may have set them, with requests for specific items and designs.There was something to suit all purses. Coarse linen towels were imported from Tabaristan, and Merv was famous for its sweeping-brushes, which were taken to other areas 'for giving away as presents'.[56] Women in fairly modest households could also aspire to rugs, and they were employed, with children, on looms in workshops set up by businessmen in the villages. Wool, silk and hair from camels and goats were all used, and carpets were produced in various grades of fineness. The male supervisor sat in front of the loom and outlined a coloured plan of the design, colours and so on.[57] The technique of weaving was rhythmic and directed by a particular chant which mentioned the number of knots and the dyed wool to be used. Perhaps the women devised their own rhymes. The decorative motifs of the subject matter was drawn from nature, plants and animals, epigraphy, scenes of the hunt and so on, and in time the arabesque was extensively used. It is likely that most homes had a prayer rug where women could pray in their personal, sacred space. Designs on prayer rugs were totally abstract and the name of Allah did not appear, to avoid defiling with one's feet. Cheaplypriced curtain fabrics were manufactured in Qurqub in southern Iraq. Strangely enough, given the huge market for elaborate and costly materials, weaving itself was a despised craft. This was tedious, precise work requiring dexterous fingers, and causing eye strain, and resembled the tyranny of a modern production line. Sadly and ironically, the purveyors of luxury textiles prospered hugely.

Lower rise apartments of two or three storeys were sometimes built over shops, often with additional structures of lighter materials. These were presumably multi-occupancy dwellings. Nasr Khusraw, on his travels in Fatimid Egypt, saw buildings up to fourteen storeys high.[58] Higher structures evolved due to economic circumstances in the tenth and twelfth centuries, when individual homes ceased to be the norm, and technological advances from mud mortar to lime mortar enabled the construction of taller, sounder buildings.

Each floor had a gallery, and tenants were obliged to go all the way round, past other people's apartments, to gain entry to their own. The whole complex was based around a large courtyard. In poorer accommodation there were lavatory facilities in the open air on rooftops, which was something of a prerequisite in multi-occupancy homes. Life would be difficult and noisy for the housewives living there; because of the close proximity to neighbours and the coming and going of non-related men, they probably observed the social niceties and veiled themselves. However there was the possibility of friendships and female solidarity in children's upbringing and shared tasks. In the circumstances, windows had to be covered, and the opening had a finely carved wooden or tiled shutter which permitted ventilation and light yet prevented strangers seeing inwards. Very young children could not be left alone on the galleries and they must frequently have been 'under their mothers' feet'. Many a gallery would be enlivened by songbirds in cages from the the bird market (*suq al tuyuriyyin*).

In summer, life would be a constant battle to keep cool and provide sufficient ventilation, and lack of privacy would be trying. There was not for these homes the luxury of a fine fabric, sometimes sprinkled with perfumed liquid such as rosewater, which was suspended below the ceiling to provide ventilation and cool air, but possibly just a rudimentary damp canvas hanging. Another method of cooling water was in very large earthenware storage jars placed n the *mashrabiyya*, an oriel-type of lattice window, hence literally 'place of drinking'. The water, which was situated in a draught, cooled by evaporation, and the most comfortable place was here where, incidentally, women could watch the world go by in privacy. Lacking the luxury of a private well in a courtyard, did women personally fetch and carry the water upstairs, or was this done by water-sellers? Or was water brought in with a system of buckets, pulleys and wheels installed at each floor? Whatever, life was not always easy.

Women from all walks of life crowded the haberdashers' shops to buy embroidery silks, lace, cotton or silk braid, and the like, or cotton or linen to spin. Many sold their finished articles such as embroidered handkerchiefs in the *suq*. A special Needle Makers' Market (*suq al-abbarin*) in Fatimid Cairo catered amply for their needs.[59] They engaged in a variety of trades, and this theme is expanded at length in Chapter 7.

For the woman stepping outside her home, she likely walked to her local *suq* for everyday food, but would have had to travel further afield to the much more varied, yet specialised, main market. Then, as now, each trade or craft was confined to its own area of the *suq*, and perfumiers were kept well away from greasy and foul-smelling crafts such as tanning. Ibn Aqil confirmed that 'the term *suq* consisted not only of shops, but also of dwellings'[60] thus many homes were situated close to the place of work of the householders. The *suq* in Aleppo, 'a town of rare beauty' could apply to the market of any town, where large markets were 'Arranged in long adjacent rows so that you pass from a row of shops of one craft into that of another until you have gone through all the urban industries'.[61]

The lower orders

Arab chroniclers were not overly concerned with the plight of the masses. Right at the bottom of the urban social scale was a huge number of unqualified people, those in the 'despised' trades such as refuse, sewage and tanning, the dispossessed, the immigrant, the criminals, and others who lived off their wits. They were scathingly described by the vizier Yahya ibn Fadl as 'filthy refuse, a torrent of scum, base cattle, none of whom think of anything but their food and drink'.[62] This was very rich indeed coming from a man well used to court intrigues and living and entertaining in great style in his own palace. These poor wretches must have lived in miserable rented accommodation with scant amenities, perhaps hutted and ranged round a common courtyard. Women here would be forced to take any sort of employment; indeed theirs could have been the only source of family income. Landlord-tenant relations in this class were often fraught from the financial point of view, as al-Jahiz's anecdote concerning al-Kindi illustrates:

Many a tenant pushesh off the paying of his rent, and delayeth its due, and so the months gather, then off he escapeth![63]

Tenants undoubtedly made off in haste out of necessity, and one can only speculate on the anguish of a wife and mother in such circumstances. Most landlords preferred whole families, not single men, as tenants, and this implies a migration of men from the countryside in search of employment and the breakdown in traditional notions of the extended family.

Were marital relationships in this group more casual, and less subject to opprobrium? Did men and women cohabit on an informal basis? This was the shifting – and sometimes shiftless – segment of society found in all cultures, even today. Their diet would leave much to be desired; the general level of health could not have been good and the mortality rate for all unacceptably high. Commitment could not, for many – man or woman – have been the norm, and out of financial necessity many women must have entered into relationships with men, however tenuous. They probably rented cheap accommodation which offered the most basic of facilities. All in all, social circumstances may have resulted in a dilution of some ideal of female behaviour and the adoption of a certain moral pragmatism by ordinary people.

Many women in this class were marginalized, and their plight is elaborated in Chapter 8.

The countryside

Despite the fact that a somewhat fragile alliance, based on mutual self-interest, existed between town and country, there is a relative paucity of sources on the day-to-day lives of the peasantry, the most populous segment of society. The Arabic terms used for village are ambiguous and Yaqut's contemporary *Geographical Dictionary* (*Mu'jam al-buldan*) indicated that some Iraqi villages had large populations. Certain 'villages' even had a Friday mosque; in theory, then, they should have had at least ten thousand adults who were obligated to perform the Friday prayer, as well as a public bath for the prescribed rites of purification. The population here had to pull together, again to the extent that some of the traditional norms of Islamic society concerning women in public and veiling were set aside. Village society was generally conservative, shaped more perhaps by custom from time immemorial than theological prescription.

It is arguable that landless peasants enjoyed some degree of mobility in times of hardship, having no special space or social territory, whereas landowners with strong bonds to their property were more constrained. For those who merely worked the land, there was possibly much less family interference on the question of a spouse; these people had nothing substantial financially to offer a potential partner nor to lose in the event of a couple separating or divorcing. It is also arguable that in the absence of veiling and a degree of shared division of labour, young people had more opportunity to become acquainted, even if only from a distance, with members of the opposite sex, and were able to exercise an element of choice of partner. Property, on the other hand, defined a family's place in the community, and was intimately bound up with their honour and esteem. Land was in the gift of the state; it might be granted on a heritable basis, when rules of inheritance ensured that the family, including its women, had a vested interest which had to be protected. Marriage for women in those circumstances was possibly less consensual and between cousins. Land was also granted for a limited period for personal services rendered.

The basic social unit was the peasant household, freeborn or not, and the work of women (and children) was necessary for the greater good of the family. Peasant agriculture depended on family size, so country families were probably larger than the urban average, and better physical health for mother and child in comparison with city dwellers would be relevant here. Good health was a prequisite in the face of the demands of rapacious landlords and the state in the form of taxes or payments in kind (*kharaj*), literally what 'came out' of the land, their crops. Home also included the extended family, who could care for young children while mothers performed manual chores beside their husbands. It would simply not have been practical for women to wear the veil while toiling in the fields or tending animals, but the heads of women and men were covered, from time immemorial in the Near East. Hand in hand with what was arguably an element of freedom compared to their sisters in the city, this was, in a sense, a tacit acknowledgment of their contributions to the family in their own right, and the satisfaction of a job well done. It would be interesting to know if, in the event of families moving to the city, country women readily adopted the veil. Might they have viewed it as an unwelcome sign of oppression? On the other hand, some may have embraced it as a symbol of their supposed elevation in society from peasant to citizen, while others possibly welcomed the anonymity it offered in a strange environment amid close proximity to men.

Peasant women generally worked as hard as the men, as back-ups, and there was necessarily co-operation. They planted, weeded, cared for the cattle and on occasion harnessed the beasts and were engaged in the cultivation of raw flax and wool. Women planted aromatic herbs; this is interesting, since this division of labour facilitated knowledge of herbal remedies otherwise disparagingly dismissed as 'old wives' tales'. They cleaned out the garden beds and uplifted weeds and bramble bushes and assisted with the hatching out of the silkworm eggs. This process is expanded upon in the discussion of silk production in Chapter 5. Women and their daughters picked 'the crops and olives and dates in the orchards and ox-ploughed fields of the people'.[64] July was the harvest season for grain, dates, peas, lentils and so forth. The bulk of the fruits of their labour ripened in autumn. Crops such as banana and citrus trees were covered with matting, presumably against the strong sun or frost. Peaches and pomegranates were autumnal fruits and olives were turning black. Rice, haricots, cumin and other herbs were now ready; these products obviously depended on climate and location. People relied too on their animals for labour. All these tasks were accomplished in addition to women's normal household chores of caring for their children, washing clothes and preparing meals.

Women took milk to sell in the market-place, the *suwayqa al-laban*; the name indicates that this was literally a 'small market'. Was it small because it was run by women and perhaps regarded as of no great account? Such a view would be a great disservice to women and food, for the invaluable role of curdled milk in nutrition is discussed elsewhere here. According to Ibn Sidal, milk and cheese were transported in red earthenware vessels which must have weighed a great deal. It was not unknown for milk to be diluted with water. If it was women who sold the milk, they were obviously well up to the tricks of their male counterparts in the *suq* who adulterated bread, and the dyers who substituted cheap colour-stuffs for expensive dyes such as saffron and indigo.

There was an element of mutual dependency between the countryside and the city. Country dwellers bought the products of urban workers. In order to do this they supplemented the family income by going to the weekly market to sell their chickens, eggs, vegetables. One wonders if there was any element of barter? Women's visits to the city were justified on economic grounds and who would have begrudged them a few personal knick-knacks from the *suq*? If they had any spare time, in the evening they knitted woollens or spun cotton material which they also sold.[65]

The Bedouin

And what of Bedouin women? Their daily life was conditioned by the hostile desert environment, and they were constantly alert to the vagaries of the seasons. Nomads were entirely dependent on their camels, and there was the need for constant moving on to find fresh grazing. Not for the Bedouin woman the comparative luxury of a settled existence, and in such materially-deprived circumstances there was always the danger of human predators. Each family had its own tent within the encampment of the clan, and several kindred clans constituted a tribe. Here first cousin marriage was the norm, but other factors such as political expediency came into play. Early Arab poetry is sufficiently replete with the themes of thwarted star-crossed lovers, disapproving fathers, family honour and such to suggest that marriage in such circumstances was not invariably a happy event. One early poem resignedly reads:

> What a man you gave me, Lord of all givers. He's a nasty old lump of wrinkles with shrivelled fingerbones and a bent back like a croaking crow.[66]

Harsh environmental conditions did nothing to alleviate the situation, yet in such adversity strong marital bonds were forged, and many are the tales of Bedouin women fighting desperately alongside husbands and sons on the field of battle. Other Arab women in other eras were equally indomitable.

Home for the Bedouin women, no less than the town dweller, was simply 'house' (*bayt*). Their homes were portable and constructed from the materials to hand, that is animal hair, hence their name 'people of the hair tents' (*ahl al-wabar*). The tent, like the permanent dwelling of the settled lands, was divided into private female space confined to close family, and the public domain of the men. Its furnishings were literally homespun by the women, and consisted of rugs and hangings and cushions and saddle-bags which doubled as bedding. For Fatima, the Prophet's daughter and her husband 'Ali, the future caliph, a sheepskin served as their bed; when turned smooth side inwards, it doubled as a container for camel fodder, and their pillow was of tanned leather filled with palm-tree fibres.[67]

One could not have been unaware of the highly visible contributions of Bedouin women to their surroundings. They had little in the way of natural resources, and it is evident that the availability of handicrafts is dependent on the seasons, materials available and spare time, and so crafts were largely the product of a sedentary population. Nothing would or could go to waste; needles, combs and ornaments were carved from animal bones and wood, and shuttles were required for the women's rudimentary hand looms. Women were probably involved in making, or at least decorating, such items, which were necessities, not luxuries, and it is likely that their sewing reflected the patterns on rugs and camel-bags and that particular tribes had their own designs. Perhaps the men made the wooden bowls carved from date palm trunks for milking their animals, and buckets for the water wells which were everyday requirements.

Bedouin women were accustomed to toiling and venturing outside their homes, and a commentary on pious tradition sanctioned travellers approaching a Bedouin encampment, even if there were no men present, and the womenfolk provided food. Ibn Battuta confirmed this, recounting how a Berber chief offered him hospitality and his mother and sister 'Came to visit us and saluted us, and his mother used to send us milk after the time of evening-prayer'.[68]

Like her country cousin, the Bedouin woman was involved in very hard physical graft, and the site of her toil was not necessarily close by. Water was life for the Bedouin and their animals, and its provision was incumbent on the women. They fetched it from wells in the desert or oasis in skin bags which they had sewn, and one can only imagine the volume needed for enormous thirsty animals. The well was a visible public place, the site of much female social interaction, and a necessary distraction and alleviation from their literally back-breaking tasks. Fuel had to be gathered and animals fed. Grinding corn, however necessary, was apparently a much loathed, time-consuming and difficult task, given their rudimentary utensils. It was in such times that women came into their own, offering mutual solidarity and encouragement. It is arguable that the Bedouin woman was made of even sterner stuff than her counterparts in the settled lands, and thus ironic that Ibn Khaldun commented that in the desert the Bedouin 'Can satisfy their needs with a minimum of labour, because in their lives they are little used to luxuries and all their requirements'.[69]

Dire circumstances fostered a notion of the right to plunder, and he was also of the opinion that:

Their sustenance lies wherever the shadow of their lances falls. They recognise no limit in taking the possessions of other people. Whenever their eyes fall upon some property, furnishing, or utensils, they take it.[70]

'Property', of course, included unfortunate women who were possibly treated contemptuously by men and women alike in their new social setting. Ibn Khaldun lived in the fourteenth century and his record confirmed that nomadic incursions into the settled lands were a contemporary feature of life.

Bedouin from far-flung oases appeared at the caravan halts en route to Mecca selling sheep, dates, honey, cheese and butter. It is probable that most of the vendors were women, since the men would be guarding the animals and the distant encampment. Even in January, and much to the surprise of Persian pilgrims in the Middle Ages, they were able to supply melons and cucumbers, and it is likely that they had been actively engaged in their cultivation.[71] Pilgrims declared the prices 'exorbitant', but in the circumstances, the Bedouin could surely be excused for taking advantage of market forces for one very brief period each year. Was all this money handed over to the family, or did the women consider some of it a private perk? These women were tough, and had to be, for their diet was of the most basic. Not for them the luxury of the voluptuousness and pale skins vaunted by the poets, and in due course they would welcome the extra pairs of hands of daughters-in-law, some of whom would be nieces, and their grandchildren.

It is difficult to generalize about daily life in the Arab world, given the remove in time and the enormous spread of the Islamic lands. Daily life was set against the city, which accommodated all the requirements of religion and the administrative apparatus of state; the Friday mosque permitted communal worship and provided the facilities for ritual purification and it was there that some unity of Islamic thought, manners and mores in time evolved from the deliberations of the jurists. Economic realities underpinned all sections of the population, however manifested, and the responses of the country dwellers and the nomadic population were suitably pragmatic in spite of the disapprobation of the jurists. Even in the cities, it has been demonstrated that migration from other areas frequently caused traditionally-held Islamic values to be set aside. Customary law came into play in the conquered lands.

There is a common misconception in the west that Arab women were confined to their homes and that on the rare occasions when they were permitted to go out, they were totally swathed and invisible in dark clothing. This perception, which views them as weak creatures under the sway of their husbands, is demonstrably not so. It is true that in particular times and places theological attitudes towards women hardened in response to current social conditions, but women across the whole spectrum of Muslim society have been shown to be tough, resilient, and well able to respond to change.

CHAPTER 2

Fertility, Health and Childcare

Fertility

Motherhood is especially meritorious in Islam, and the Prophet said:

> When a woman conceives by her husband, she is called in heaven a
> martyr (in dignity); and her labour in childbed and her care for her
> children protect her from hell fire.[1]

Tradition also holds that 'Paradise is at the mothers' feet'. Fertility was
therefore something highly prized, and with motherhood, a woman's status
in society was assured, particularly if she bore sons. Paradise beckoned for
those who regarded their children as a joy. The downside of all this means
that a very heavy strain was placed on women who, through no deficiency
on their part, could not bear children. One can imagine the anguish and
shame felt by a woman unable to conceive, for whatever reason, especially
in a society where sons were highly prized. Indeed, did the impetus for easy
divorce stem in part for men's desire for sons? There would, in addition, be
the great fear and shame for women of divorce and abandonment by
husband and family as a source of dishonour. In such circumstances, women
were blamed for their inability to conceive. A *Tradition* tells how a man
came to the Prophet for advice on whether he should marry a wealthy
woman of good social standing, but unable to have children. After much
deliberation, the Prophet counselled, 'Marry the affectionate prolific woman,
for I shall make a display of you before other nations'.[2]

It is fair to say that the infertile husband would not feel entirely guilt-free,
since the absence of the honorific prefix *abu*, 'father of' (a son) ensured that
his state was conspicuous to all, despite any number of wives he might
subsequently take. A modern study of a small rural Egyptian community
revealed that the most traumatic experience for men still was sterility for, as
one man poignantly asked, 'Who would ever know that a man had lived if

he leaves no children to memorialise his life?'[3] The preference given to sons was not a prerogative of Arab societies, and persists elsewhere, for example in China.

Of course most parents feel blessed by their children, but there may be an underlying, if unacknowledged, universal hope that their children will provide an emotional and financial insurance in very old age. For these and other reasons a childless wife in many pre-modern societies shouldered a very heavy burden. Malnutrition must have had a deleterious effect on a woman's fertility, and even the platitude that sterility was 'from God' would be insufficient solace for some.

Aids to conception

A woman's first resort to assist conception was the sampling of everyday remedies current among close confidantes. These would vary according to the ingredients to hand and might have been home-made, or prepared by druggists in the market-place. For example, women used *khitmi*, the marshmallow macerated in hot water, or they inserted *khuzama*, a sweet desert plant as a vaginal suppository to promote pregnancy. '*Khuzama*' is entirely apt, since it is derived from the root verb 'to pierce', which suggests that its properties had ever been known. Although the physician Ibn al-Jawziyya recommended: 'If a woman uses the flour of the spathe (the early formation of the dates) as a pessary before intercourse, this will greatly assist her to conceive,'[4] which had the additional benefit of acting as an aphrodisiac, it is possible that this was in any case a folk remedy. Desperate women would grasp at any suggested method, and there were undoubtedly 'old wives' tales' in wide circulation. Even the ninth-century physician 'Ali ibn Sahl al-Tabari surprisingly said in his *Paradise of Wisdom* (*Kitab firdaws al-hikma*) – with shades of European fairy tales:

> If a woman was once pregnant but is no longer so, she should take a frog from a river, spit in its mouth, and throw it back into the river.[5]

Although this was believed to guarantee further conception, it required a great leap of faith on the part of a anxious woman.

Certain illustrious pious individuals were perceived to be imbued with blessing (*baraka*) and the power to grant specific petitions. Their tombs predictably became the focus of women hoping to conceive, hence the frequent reference to women's outings to cemeteries. Many women would appreciate the communal rituals associated with tomb visits and gain solace from the knowledge that they were not alone in their plight. Miracles might happen. Grateful supplicants returned to perform meritorious religious acts of thanksgiving, such as an offering of money, the provision of food for the poor or water for other pilgrims and they represented beacons of hope for the childless. Women would also experience a sense of liberation in openly expressing anxieties and fears which were otherwise suppressed before the extended family.

Long-held superstitions and old wives' tales surround women's ailments in most cultures. Blood, and its central role in rites of passage, is extensively examined in the context of marginality in society in Chapter 8. Lane mentioned a place in nineteenth-century Cairo for the washing of the bodies of executed criminals, where the water, tainted with blood, was never poured out and where 'Many a woman goes thither . . . to obtain offspring (or to expedite delivery in the case of protracted pregnancy).[6]

It is likely that women also wore amulets and charms to promote fertility.[7]

Since prostitution was widespread (indeed prostitutes were taxed), it would be of interest to find information on sexually-transmitted diseases, and how they affected women, their fertility, and their children.[8]

It is arguable that fertility and its control represented an important source of power for women over men, as well as a source for their manipulation. For example, the larger the family, the less financially viable it would be for a man to take another wife, while the withholding of sexual favours could thwart a man's ambition to produce many sons.

Childbirth

Medical manuals from the ninth century such as Tabari's *Paradise of Wisdom*, al-Razi's extensive *Comprehensive Book* (*al-Hawi*) and al-Baladi's tenth-century compendium, the *Book of Pregnancy and the Care of Infants* (*Kitab al-Habala wa'l-atfal*) dealt at length with pregnancy and midwifery,[9] but these views concerned the mother who had access to a doctor and possibly a midwife, and the means to pay for the service. Midwives also worked in hospitals, but one wonders what happened to women with complications who could not afford official medical care? Was there a charitable element to the hospitals? It is interesting to note that it was some considerable time before obstetrical instruments used in medieval Arab medicine were used in the west.

Ibn al-Hajj deplored the conduct of some midwives in thirteenth and fourteenth-century Egypt who exposed both mothers and infants to danger due to ignoring basic rules of hygiene by 'handling babies with hands covered with blood and other kinds of filth, by wrapping them in unclean cloths, and even by licking them in an effort to clean their bodies.'[10]

When labour started, the mother-to-be was taken to a specially prepared room, accompanied by her female relatives, close friends and neighbours, and the midwife, usually a large prosperous-looking matronly figure, was summoned. She arrived, perched on a mule, and already appraised of the necessary password for the night-watchmen.[11] The midwife (daya) was a respected and valuable member of the community. The fee for the birth was arranged beforehand, but we have no details of rates, which she undoubtedly graded according to the family's means. She first of all examined the patient, then settled her into the birth-chair (kursi al-wilada). This was the prescribed birthing procedure in the east, for there is a reference to birth 'stools' in the Book of Exodus 1. Four helpers took their place, one at each shoulder and two supporting her and with their hands pressed against her back. One typical birth-scene mirrors vividly and accurately the above account, in an early thirteenth-century manuscript of al-Hariri's Maqamat.[12] There the brazier containing chemicals for the fumigation of the genital area and what appears to be a distinctive headdress for the midwife are also clearly seen.

Ibn al-Hajj criticised Egyptian midwives who sought to establish exclusivity over a woman's delivery by claiming that the blood of the mother and newborn child had already stained their hands and that no one else could then be called in. This happened if complications arose or the family was not happy with her care. Midwives were unanimous over this point, which might suggest an element of official regulation of their skills and consultation and co-operation between themselves and doctors. Confirmation of this lies in a record from Ahwaz, in Persia, where midwives had discussed cases where they had frequently delivered infants already suffering from fevers.[13]

Death in childbirth, puerperal fever, usually caused by infection after the birth, and other complications must have been common, especially among the poor. It was extremely dangerous when the placenta could not be expelled, and the mother was given snuff, then an enema. Failure to procure this could result in death by haemmorhage. The concerns of Ibn al-Hajj, not even a physician, were thus well founded. Mothers, grandmothers and midwives likely had their own infusions and remedies, but labour could never have been easy.

Having found a good *daya*, families sensibly tended to retain her in the future, even to hold her in some esteem, a practice which continued up to relatively modern times at least. In nineteenth-century Cairo, on the occasion of a wedding, the family midwife, the bath attendant and the bride's nursemaid were presented with fine textiles and sent out on asses with musicians to the home of the bride's friends, inviting them to accompany her to the *hammam*.[14]

These accounts refer of course to a particular social class, and many women had no option but to turn to practised, unregulated midwives in the community, who may also have resorted to sympathetic magic. Early Arabic medical manuscripts demonstrated a connection between childbirth and the occult. Even Hippocrates recommended that a lodestone be placed in the hand of a pregnant woman to ensure an easy delivery, while in Egypt al-Baladi, another doctor, recommended the careful removal of a coriander plant and hanging the root fibres over the thighs of a woman in labour to facilitate the birth.

Women set store in the power of talismans and amulets. Talismans for a difficult birth quoting the Qur'an were sometimes written in saffron. One, written in ink inside a clean vessel, from *Sura* 84 (*al-Inshiqaq*) read: 'When the sky is split asunder, obeying its Sustainer, as in trust it must: and when the earth is levelled, and casts forth whatever is in it, and becomes empty.'[15]

Water was poured in and it was believed that through the Word the water became imbued with the healing powers of Allah. Some water was sprinkled on her abdomen, and the woman then drank the remainder. Astrology (*'ilm al-nujum*) also played its part in birth rituals, and it may be that pregnancies were induced or delayed according to propitious astrological signs, for example in the case of the births of foreign eastern rulers. There were doubtless magical practices current also among the ignorant and superstitious, despite theological attempts to abolish them as remnants of the 'period of ignorance', with predictably dire results for mother and child and the family at large.

The desire for many sons, for whatever reason, social or economic, was particularly strong. Given the high rate of infant mortality and in spite of custom, might many mothers not have been thankful for a healthy baby, safely delivered, regardless of sex? The Qur'an cautioned:

Wealth and children are an adornment of this world's life: but good deeds, the fruit whereof endures forever, are of far greater merit in thy Sustainer's sight, and a far better source of hope.[16]

At all levels of Arab society the birth of a daughter was heralded with less than joy, and the newly-delivered mother at once knew the sex of her infant by the muted tones of her attendants. After the child was safely delivered, the grandmother was instructed to bring a handful of salt to ward off the evil eye.

An early anonymous Arabic poem prompted by the arrival of a baby girl told how the disappointed father overheard his wife's sad plaint:

Why doesn't Abu Hazm come home instead of staying in the house next door? He's angry it wasn't a boy I bore him, but Allah knows it's not up to me. We only take what's given to us.[17]

Suitably shamed, Abu Hazm kissed his wife and stayed with her and their baby. Another entranced anonymous mother said in wonder, 'My little boy's smell is all lavender. Is every little boy like him, or hasn't anyone given birth before me?'[18]

At the more practical level the Prophet sagely counselled on female children, 'Do not dislike them, for they are the comforters, the dear ones' and, very poignantly, for his only son Ibrahim had died in infancy, 'Love your daughters, for I too am a father of daughters'. His favourite child, of course, was Fatima, who is especially revered in the Shi'a branch of Islam and who married his cousin and eventual successor, 'Ali. One Bashshar ibn Burd guiltily mourned the death of a daughter he had come to love, despite the norms of society:

O my little daughter whom I did not want,
You were hardly five when death took you away.
Then I had loved you so tenderly, that sorrow seemed to break my heart.
Yes, you were better than a son.[19]

In an ideal situation the newborn child was wrapped in a linen cloth, preferably white and not yellow. Midwives had a reputation in the medieval period for appropriating good linen, so poorer families took care not to put out their best baby clothes until she departed.[20] Following the Prophet's example on the birth of his grandson Hasan to his daughter Fatima, the call to prayer, 'God is most great!' followed by the *shahada* or confession of the faith, 'There is no god but God and that Muhammad is his messenger' was whispered in the baby's ear by a male, then repeated.[21] No one was allowed to pass between the fire lit by the midwife to keep away evil spirits and demons and the baby's bed for three days and nights. The infant's mouth was washed out with a piece of cotton soaked in a sacred potion. Sugar, bread and gold were scattered around it – sugar to guarantee goodness and sweetness, bread for long life, and gold so that fortune would smile on the child.

Feasting in some style followed the birth of a son, whereas for a daughter celebrations were somewhat muted. Singers and other musicians were hired by the well-to-do to entertain the guests. Particular religious rites were performed at specific dates after the birth, but the most meritorious took place on the seventh day, when the mother was visited by her female friends. Sometimes the naming of the child was delayed until the seventh day.

The mother was considered ritually impure, usually for a period of forty days, the *nifas*, and then she went to the *hammam*. During this period she was nourished with barley, mutton fat and fruit preserves. Women in affluent circumstances had a fairly lengthy lying-in period, but for many there would be no respite from day to day drudgery. Umm Salma related how, in the early days 'One who gave birth would rest for forty days after childbirth, and one of us would anoint her face with *wars* for freckles'.[22] *Wars* was a unique yellow dyestuff made from a plant from Yemen which resembled sesame. The face-lotion known as *ghumra* was also made from it and was apparently used by brides. One wonders if this was solely for cosmetic purposes, or on account of its reputation as an aphrodisiac? We may see here yet again the association of certain colours, yellow in this case, with rites of passage, which are detailed elsewhere here.

Breast-feeding

Given the climate, the incidence of flies, parasites and dust and in many cases the quality of the water, the first line of defence for a baby, assuming a mother was in a reasonable state of health, was its mother's milk. Ibn al-Quff, among other physicians recognised with theologians that, in modern parlance, 'breast is best', and the theologians agreed. The customary prescribed two-year weaning period therefore constituted good health practice. Although it seems unlikely that any Muslim woman breast-feeding would eat proscribed food, Ibn al-Hajj nevertheless wrote that to do so would result in the child losing 'the *baraka* or blessing of the milk'. Breast-feeding, then, also had religious sanction, and the failure to do so in this respect would have been an additional concern for the new mother. *Murdi'a*, the term for nursing mother (and also for the wet-nurse) had the charming connotations of pleasure and contentment. Whatever her circumstances, a mother probably tried to ensure that her own diet was as sound as possible, for her child's sake. Chick peas were believed to increase the milk flow, (as well as acting as an aphrodisiac), and there were other popular prescribed foods.[23]

What happened to a child in the event of its mother's death or her inability to produce sufficient milk, even her disinclination to feed it? Some mothers in comfortable circumstances might have farmed their infants out to avoid the hard work associated with bringing up a baby, time which they could otherwise spend on themselves and their beautification. If her figure was a concern, breast-feeding was an excellent method of returning to one's former weight in a short time, apart from important gynaecological benefits. The mother had to have her husband's permission to use the services of a wet-nurse, and many children were reared by wet-nurses hired and paid for by fathers for all those reasons.

The wet-nurse (al-murdi'a)

The Qur'an contained sound advice on the care of the foetus, wet-nursing and weaning. Islamic law was quite clear on the position of children fed by the same mother, who were regarded as foster-siblings and therefore came within the class prohibited in marriage. Wet-nurses were available to the upper classes, but to whom could someone with few means turn? Some sort of payment, even in kind, if only to ensure the good health of the wet-nurse, must have been made, and it is likely that there were women known within the local community who were happy to take on the task.

A tale of the Prophet's infancy confirms that wet-nurses hired themselves out:

> Ten women of the Banu Sa'd came to Mecca to look for infants to nurse. All found them, except for Halima bint 'Abdullah. Then the baby Muhammad was brought to her, and she remarked, 'An orphan! And with no money! And what can his mother do?'[24]

Halima, initially reluctant, agreed to take the baby, 'the fairest babe that I ever saw, and he with the greatest *baraka* (blessed virtue)'. The rest is history. Unfortunately, not all wet-nurses matched up to the saintly Halima. Nomads, despite their very basic diet, had the physique of a 'fundamentally sound and healthy' people and chronic disease among them was almost unknown.[25] It was the custom among the more affluent in Meccan society at the time of the Prophet to send children to the Bedouin at a very early age, to 'toughen them up' in the healthier desert climate and to acquire the pure Arabic language. An illustration in an Arabic manuscript dated 1306 in the University of Edinburgh clearly shows a Bedouin wet-nurse at a pre-Islamic fair, with a very large child at the breast; this is not surprising, given the prescribed two-year period.[26]

Certain qualities applicable to wet-nurses were requisite under the law. A healthy young woman aged between twenty-five and thirty-five years old, of equable temperament and good character was the ideal. Any history of abortion and difficult deliveries ruled out good health. The rules of consanguinity were extremely complicated and embraced the woman-foster-child relationship and prohibited her own children from marrying into the foster-child's family. Ideally, a wet-nurse had to be Muslim. It is arguable that wet-nursing widened social relationships; close blood-ties precluding marriage in fact allowed men and women to mix more freely than otherwise possible. These rules were formulated in urban society, but it may be that a more pragmatic approach was applied among country dwellers and nomads, as we have seen in other areas. There was likely an element of reciprocity between women in the extended family and neighbours in times of emergency.

Women in poor circumstances probably turned to wet-nursing to augment family income, and in the belief that they could not conceive while breast-feeding. This was not absolutely guaranteed. There was another important financial consideration. Close kinship ties with the hirer's family ensured that the nurse's own family could expect assistance in times of need. In many cases the health of a wet-nurse's own infant must have been impaired through under-nourishment or increased exposure to disease without the benefits of its own mother's milk. Many foster-children suffered neglect or at least indifference, if economic circumstances alone were a priority for wet-nurses. One tenth-century report cited the death of an infant by overlaying[27] that is, it suffocated in the bed of its wet-nurse (or mother). This happened frequently enough to be common knowledge. It was preferable that the the wet-nurse went to stay at the mother's home and cared for the baby under her personal supervision. This could have been at some inconvenience to the nurse's own domestic arrangements. Apart from the infants, prolonged breast-feeding took its toll on nursing mothers on a restricted diet. The term *murdi'a* implies that the nurse also derived pleasure from the experience, and on many occasions a child was more emotionally bound to the wet-nurse than its own mother.

The hiring and payment of wet-nurses by men was not necessarily altruistic; it represented male control over even such an intimate, female-centred act as breastfeeding, it allowed the resumption of marital relations in the eyes of the law, and might also have been advantageous to a man's family through the bonds of kinship alliance.

Harun al-Rashid's son al-Mu'tasim fathered a daughter by a beautiful and talented singing-girl, who was a slave.[28] Harun's vizier Ja'far married this girl, and the baby was given to a Christian wet-nurse. When the vizierate collapsed, the wet-nurse sold the child as a slave.[29] Another interesting account told how the Egyptian royal *harim* employed wet-nurses. Indeed, on one occasion a nurse even appeared on the throne with her young charge, the little eighteen-month old sultan, Ahmad, who howled throughout the procession.[30] These women enjoyed an enviable social cachet, an element of status, and the consequent foster-brother linkage between their own sons and the scions of 'good' families. However, despite their easy familiarity at a high social level, their own children were precluded from the benefits of marriage.

Weaning was a hazardous transitional period in any infant's life, and a rite of passage. As such, superstition and taboo came into play. The child being weaned was the *fatim*, yet another expressive Arabic name which indicated 'separation' from its mother. When their children were weaned, new mothers would have been well advised to heed the advice of al-Baladi: 'If you want a child to grow tall and straight, with a good complexion, and not turned in on himself, avoid overfeeding.'[31]

This advice, of course, was directed at that segment of society who could afford to consult a physician, and there must have been countless children – and their mothers – who often went hungry.

There was good reason for mothers to be very concerned for their children's wellbeing. Light-hearted banter between guests at a carousing session caused a poet to invoke revealingly: 'May God rain down on your head the plagues of Syria, the fevers of Khaybar, the diseased spleens of Bahrain, the boils of al-Jazira . . . the inflammation of Fars and the ulcers of Balkh!'[32]

The plagues, which occurred for example in Egypt every eight or nine years and were also endemic in Syria, were no respecter of social circumstances. Ibn Battuta reported how, during epidemics, people of all religions assembled at a richly endowed mosque in Damascus, said to contain a rock with the imprints of Moses' foot. It is a cruel irony that the very solidarity of the Muslim family and family visits meant that in desperately worrying times of plague and pestilence the transmission of disease in their community was extremely high.[33] The Christians and Jews kept to their homes until danger passed. Nevertheless, every family was at risk, as lamentation poetry for the loss of whole families revealed.[34] These works were usually written by fathers mourning their sons, but the *Lisan al-'arab* cited a seventh-century poem by al-Ahtal who described what must have been a common and distressing sight:

The waving of the hands of mothers bereft of many children, in mourning on account of them, bewailing the biting cruelty of the daughters of misfortune and afflictions.

Consolation treatises developed as a special genre of literature in Egypt and Syria in the late Middle Ages.[35] They offered comfort and spiritual assurance to bereaved parents, and served to mitigate any official disapproval of what was viewed as inappropriate behaviour, that is, the public expression of grief. It is fair to say that girls were less frequently mentioned than boys. The Prophet's own involuntary reactions at his son's funeral would be a solace to many parents:

And the Prophet went in front of Ibrahim's coffin, then he sat on his grave. Then Ibrahim was brought down to his grave and the Prophet, seeing him laid in the grave, shed tears.[36]

The other mourners were overcome, and were visiby and audibly moved.

Commonplace childhood ailments took their toll to a degree almost unimaginable nowadays, and the poorest ill-nourished children were the most vulnerable. The fevers of teething, for example, frequently resulted in death. For those children who managed to survive a highly dangerous infancy there was still the prospect of a relatively short life. In fact according to medical practitioners, the new born child was, 'weak, fragile, stupid, and can eat only a little' for the first four years of life.[37] In the event, a mother's last refuge for the safety of her child was of course God, and His will.

The evil eye

A child was a blessing from God, and very protected by anxious relatives. Children were believed to be especially vulnerable to the evil eye and other malign unseen forces. According to Ibn Qayyim al-Jawziyya the evil eye was 'Of two sorts: the Eye of humankind and the Eye of the Jinn. Every one with the Eye envies, but not every envious person has the Eye.'

And a poet reportedly said: 'How great is the need of the perfect for a fault which will protect him from the Eye!'[38]

Even today, one should be very careful indeed when admiring an infant not to exclaim 'What a lovely baby!' or words to that effect, merely to murmur '*Ma sha Allah!*' 'What God has willed!', implying admiration and submission to the will of Allah. Superstition played a large part in the life of medieval society, and belief in the 'evil eye' is still current in the Middle East and indeed in many other areas. There was always a warm welcome for female sellers of lucky charms. Talismans were widely used to ward off illness or the evil eye or to effect cures. Sometimes they were written on the patient, apparently near the source of the affliction, at others they were written and worn.

There are injunctions in the Qur'an against magic, and the only amulets with Prophetic sanction are those containing the name of Allah or Qur'anic verse. Women and children wore different types of charms in plain gold, silver or gilt, base metals or leather. If one did not have a miniature of the complete Qur'an, then some seven chapters were considered to be particularly efficacious as protection against disease, the evil eye and sorcery.[39] Individual verses from the Qur'an also had talismanic significance; these allude to the qualities of Allah as preserver, for example:

> His eternal power overspreads the heavens and the earth and their upholding wearies Him not.
> [Nay] God's guardianship is better, for He is the most merciful of the merciful.
> And have made them secure against every rebellious force.[40]

Interestingly, Lane reported that in Egypt verses containing the names of the Seven Sleepers of Ephesus, as well as that of their dog Qitmir, were sometimes engraved in a cup.[41] The Seven Sleepers, of course, were not Muslims, but they were nevertheless preserved by God, and we see a reversal here from the adoption of Muslim symbols such as the hand of Fatima by non-Muslims at the folk level. Is it not rather strange that the dog is mentioned, when many Muslims view it as an unclean animal? Jewish and Muslim physicians despised the sacred relics and amulets of Christians. Ibn Taymiyya used to write the following on the forehead as a talisman for nosebleed:

It was said: O earth! Swallow up thy water; and O sky! Withhold thy rain, and the water abated, and the matter was ended.[42]

However, Ibn Taymiyya was adamant that this should never be written in the patient's own blood 'as the ignorant do', because blood was ritually impure and ineligible in connection with God's Word. In such cases women visited a specialist. Colour also played a part; blue was considered 'lucky' and averted the evil eye and women pinned blue beads to clothing.

Therapeutics and folk medicine

What could the ordinary woman, concerned for her own health and that of her children, do in case of illness? In the short term, she might turn to tried and trusted remedies handed down within the family or community or buy a remedy in the *suq*. If the illness was serious, just what medical care was available, and to whom? A prime concern of women must have been how their children would fare if they themselves became ill, or even died. Would this have contributed to any preoccupation with personal good health among knowledgable women?

The Banu Muhallab tribe were famed for their medical knowledge. This may in part have stemmed from the necessity to treat the wounds of warfare, and endemic eye diseases.[43] Early historians of Islam mentioned women engaged in nursing; Umm 'Umara, for example, appeared on the battlefields, caring for casualties. This suggests that there were always skilful women around with an expertise in folk remedies.

Arab physicians had long recognised the beneficial effect of plants. Astrology also played its part, and great care was taken to collect material according to the Zodiacal signs. Women probably collected and prepared plants and herbs for therapeutic purposes. Since there were so many superstitions surrounding women's ailments, and childbirth in particular, at least some of this knowledge must have been passed on orally and been current among ordinary women.

Very little therapeutic knowledge from the Bedouins has been noted in official medical works, although al-Qurtubi occasionally mentioned the process of birth in that context. Inevitably, much folk medicine was in time incorporated into the Prophet's personal teachings as 'Prophetic Medicine' (al-tibb al-nabawi), to counter the introduction of Greek medicine, which the theologians saw as suspect and the science of infidels, so it must in any case have reflected practices current among the Arabs in the Prophet's own time. Prophetic Medicine apparently 'met with strong response from the people'.[44] This naturally would be on account of the great esteem in which the Prophet was held, a desire to follow his personal example, and in recognition of his testimony to the validity of their own practices. The Medicine of the Prophet expanded to include formulae for taking refuge in God, and pious supplications.

Itinerant practitioners of traditional medicine did exist. Hunayn was of the opinion that 'itinerant doctors have killed many people' with milk of euphorbia.[45] Elsewhere Ibn Qayyim al-Jawziyya referred to 'the medicine of the itinerants and old women'. They peddled their remedies from house to house in town and village, as well as the market-places. Women would turn more readily towards other women, especially in very personal circumstances, and those going around the doors selling women's remedies, with access to the harim, must have been female. There were doubtless some quasi-medical practitioners. The old name for an oculist, kahhal, derives from the same verbal root as kohl. Kahhal is the so-called 'professional form' in Arabic, which suggests at least some publicly-acknowledged status. An archive from a Muslim court in Jerusalem in 1551 named a Jewish woman occulist, Lifa, 'whose business is curing eyes', who sold a house to the son of a judge.[46] This was evidently a substantial property and, even if she had inherited it, her own employment must have been fairly lucrative. One Bedouin woman, Zaynab, was recorded as treating cases of ophthalmia, inflammation of the eye. Given the prevalence of eye disease, at grass roots level there were various popular treatments. Undoubtedly, as elsewhere, medical tradition, common sense and, at the popular level, folk wisdom, all played their part, and it was perhaps a matter of achieving an equilibrium. 'Old wives' tales' must also have played their part, such as that snakes were believed to induce abortion, affect sight and had to be killed. Was this the snake itself, or the resulting shock of seeing one which, it is agreed, might cause one to abort? The hadith are valuable sources for public health issues on clean water and food, clothing and the home. However, some of these presupposed a fairly good standard of living and pious observers of the faith, and there were many women who fell outside that category.

Numerous drugs from vegetable bases were listed in official manuals for doctors and druggists and, since many of the plants and herbs mentioned in connection with contraception and abortion discussed in the following Chapter were literally of the 'common or garden' variety and readily to hand, it is further suggested that women in general knew of their alleged beneficial properties for other ailments. One cure for scorpion bites was to eat roasted locust of the wingless variety.

The fourteenth-century *Qamus* dictionary ascribed several medicinal properties to *khatmi,* a preparation derived from the mallow, for example as an antiseptic for ulcers and burns. It was a multi-purpose remedy, and also good for gargling, treating stings and suppuration. It was mixed with vinegar for the treatment of leprosy. Citrus peel was useful for alleviating the pain of snake-bites; snakes would be a childhood hazard in some areas. Interestingly, the juice from the pulp of the citrus fruit known as *utrujj* was said to quieten 'sensuousness in women'.[47] One can only speculate at whose instigation it was taken, wives or husbands, and for what reason? There were many other therapeutic ingredients in and around the home.

It is unlikely that many mothers personally consulted medical tomes, such as Avicenna's *Care of the New Born,* which advised rubbing a teething baby's gums with hen's fat and a rabbit's head. Alternatively, the child could be given liquorice root to chew on, which would prevent ulceration and alleviate the pain of sore gums. This particular advice, using ingredients which were ready-to-hand, sounds of the type that would be in any case be in wide circulation among women, from whatever source. Among its special usages, henna was recommended to be applied to children's feet during the early stage of smallpox, to prevent it spreading as far as the eyes.[48] It was also helpful in clearing up ulcers and blisters in the mouth, and good for children's mouths infected with thrush. Mothers would find sandalwood paste useful as a cooling agent for inflamed skin and skin eruptions.[49] Insect-borne infections were common, especially where there were lots of animals, and citronella oil was an effective if pungent insect repellent.

Salt and honey were also useful in avoiding mouth ulcers. Mint was beneficial for stomach ailments. The eleventh-century *al-Muhkam* dictionary referred to the 'blackness of gum' caused by *safuf* which was made from ground-up aniseed, black caraway, cumin and poppy.[50] This suggests a preparation which was sucked or chewed. A stem of celery of the 'garden variety' worn around the neck was said to relieve toothache, and clove oil was applied to the site of painful toothache. While some of these remedies appeared in official medical manuals, they were nevertheless widely known.

Vinegar had many uses, for example for alleviating the bites or stings of insects and snakes, as well as itching and healing of sores. It strengthened the gums and its antiseptic qualities rendered it an effective mouthwash[51] and it was also used for 'ringing in the ears'. Vinegar was additionally a stimulant to digestion, when taken in moderation, as Muslim physicians were aware. Its use in food preparation would therefore be almost a prerequisite in days before refrigeration, especially when fowl were slaughtered. Salt, too, had antiseptic properties.

In the kitchen, women's preparation and handling of food benefitted from the proscription of the use of the 'impure' left hand, which was reserved for unclean personal tasks; this would also decrease the hazards of the common meal eaten with the hand. However, an over-emphasis on health issues could have had a detrimental effect, for a lesser attention to hygiene might ensure that children built up some degree of immunity. Immunity would be assisted by the presence of siblings and cousins in the extended family and their exposure to childhood diseases, but it was also a two-edged sword in respect of serious ailments. It is unlikely that the majority of mothers in any culture were deliberately negligent over their children's welfare, but superstition and ignorance would exact their toll.

Public health

Late in the tenth century al-Muqaddasi (who was not a doctor) offered graphic insight into the hazards of urban life, saying:

> If you want to know the quality of the water in a town, go to the dealers in cambric and spices, and examine their countenances. The more lively these are, the better is the drinking. If you see cadaverous faces and hanging heads, leave the place as quickly as you can.[52]

These particular traders dealt in the goods with the highest profit margins, and their wives and children would have enjoyed a safe water supply. Other women would have made sure that their young children did not drink poor water.

Members of the upper classes were evidently very careful about their health and would not patronise certain shops. They refused to drink 'of the water in the shops of the water-sellers, nor of the water of the mosques and public fountains'. Storing drinking water in large jars could lead to pollution.

For example in ninth-century Qayrawan, Ibn Sahnun was asked to pronounce judgment on:

> A certain man who brought flour to another to knead it and bake thereof. He brought the flour, poured out water from the great jar unto him who kneaded the flour. And when he emptied the vessel he found therein a dead mouse.[53]

People used 'dribbling jars and trickling jugs' – these were earthenware and 'wept', through evaporation, which ensured a refreshingly cool drink. Because of their size, the water had to be regularly used and replenished. Water sellers went around town every morning with their water skins which they refilled from rivers and canals upstream from the towns. Al-Jahiz's unscrupulous miser waited for a heavy rainfall before hiring a man to clean his cesspit 'to scoop out the matter into the street, that the flow might carry it and convey it into the canal'.[54] Water from the Tigris was 'sweet and agreeable' and the Arabic name for the Euphrates, *furat*, indicates 'pureness'. Nevertheless, one must ask how pure the water was in wells in private courtyards in a highly populous city along the riverbanks.

Other citizens prudently shunned 'the shop of a mincer of meats and pies' or other market stalls; minced meat became contaminated very quickly indeed, especially in hot weather. The same fastidious people undoubtedly avoided having 'their hair trimmed by a public barber in his shop', and did not enter the baths 'without their own towel-wrap'.[55] Al-Jahiz's *Book of Misers* mentioned the wealthy who 'take unto them baths in their own homes'. Unfortunately, not everyone was or could be so particular and poorer women who had no kitchens would have no choice but to buy ready-prepared meals from the market-place and use a public bath.

Physicians and charlatans

Medicines in the forms of herbs, spices and chemicals were traded on a large, international scale and at the local level merchants specialised in one particular produce, such as antimony, saffron and so forth.[56] If women did not have a doctor they could go to the *suq* and obtain preparations from the pharmacopoeia manuals of druggists; by their very nature, these manuals suggest an 'approved' list of drugs by a professional body.

Druggists made up compounds and other preparations and provided narcotics such as opium and hashish. Their wares were sold pre-packed in ceramic pots, glass bottles and paper packets. The drug manuals were often set out to list diseases and ailments, then the appropriate medicines as remedies, and it is likely that women in urban areas who could afford to pay went along to a druggist, detailed their symptoms, and received a prescription. Anyone in the *suq* selling other preparations was probably considered a charlatan, and with good reason. A twelfth-century report by Ibn 'Abdun on the ordinances of the Seville market recommended that:

> Only a skilled physician should sell potions and electuaries and mix drugs. These things should not be bought from the grocer, or the apothecary, whose only concern is to take money without knowledge. They spoil the prescriptions and kill the sick, for they mix medicines which are unknown and of contrary effect.[57]

In one of three surviving shadow plays by Ibn Daniyal, the underworld 'hero' Gharib ('stranger') practised magic and boasted:

> I have treated people, and how many of them have I killed with my astringents and purges! And I have given treatment for their eyes, and how many eyelids will never sleep any more after my application of *kohl*![58]

His name confirms that Gharib was one of Ibn Qayyim al-Jawziyya's 'itinerants'.

The great natural scientist al-Biruni, among others, wrote treatises on weights and measures, the importance of which cannot be overstated in the preparation of medicines. This confirms that there was official unease about the quality of so-called medicines available to the general public. The appearance in different genres of widely-read Arabic literary works of quack medical practitioners confirmed that they were a reality, characters with whom society at all levels could identify. Why would women have consulted them instead of qualified pharmacists? Were their remedies cheaper, and were their mixtures as efficient as those from druggists and doctors? As for everyday ailments, doctors, whatever their sex, had a limited knowledge of drugs and spices and preparations for the more common sorts of illness. Many women must have relied on 'over the counter' preparations or home-made recipes.

It is sad that the people who relished the popular entertainment in the streets were the most likely gullible purchasers of magical charms and 'cures' from quacks. An old woman in Cairo had an apparently miraculous well, known as 'the well of jaundice', (*bir al-yaraqan*). This well had two mouths. Under one was a dry container and people were invited to throw food items such as sugar, coffee and the like. One wonders about the success rates of her 'cures'.[59] Resort to such practices could only have been downright dangerous, and such charlatans were a reality acknowledged by physicians. Al-Razi produced a treatise on *Why people prefer quacks and charlatans to skilled physicians.* Some doctors admitted that they could not always effect a cure and conceded that some alternative medicine was successful, hence al-Razi's other treatises *On the fact that even skilful physicians cannot heal all diseases* and another, *Why ignorant physicians, laymen, and women have more success than learned medical men.*[60]

Even for those children who managed to survive a highly dangerous infancy there was ever the prospect of a relatively short life. The lot of many women with large families, additionally burdened with the care of the elderly extended family, could not have been easy, and was fraught with anxiety.

The rearing of children

Turning now to the upbringing of children, al-Ghazali set out some very sensible precepts for 'all sorts and conditions of men' in a minor treatise, *Fitting Conduct in Religion, (Al-Adab fi Din).* A parent should not always 'be reminding his child of his responsibilities towards his parents and the necessity of accepting their directions'.[61] Due attention was to be paid to religious observation and practice, and parents should not demand from the child 'an obedience beyond his ability'. Ibn Qayyim al-Jawziyya's *Prescriptions Concerning the Newborn Child (Tuhfat al-mawdud bi-ahkam al-mawlud)*, cited the *hadith*: 'One of the child's rights in respect of the father is to be treated on an equal footing with his or her brothers and sisters.'[62]

He also dealt with the moral education of children and stressed character formation. Fathers played an important role in imparting the rules of religion to sons, including the Qur'an and *Traditions,* ritual purity and the use of the right hand when eating, and, from the age of seven, prayer. They could be chastised from aged ten upwards. Children's wishes were to be indulged, and strong anger and frightening behaviour were to be avoided.

Everyday mishaps were often serious, particularly so when children were working with animals. It is arguable that the greater freedom allowed boys, allied to an innate sense of adventure, frequently resulted in accident and death. In the countryside drowning and falls from roofs were common-place,[63] and venomous bites from snakes and scorpions were common hazards. Little girls did what small girls have always done, namely helped their mothers with household chores, looked after smaller siblings, and learned handicrafts such as sewing.

Many households employed nursemaids, or had slaves to look after their children. Nubian women, who were regarded as being of affable temperament and kindly towards children, were especial favourites. An eleventh-century guide to purchasing slaves drawn up by the Christian doctor Ibn Butlan listed the qualities of slaves from various regions, and confirmed that, 'black slaves are calm and the best nurses', adding also that 'Persian women are kindly towards children'.[64]

A male child was circumcised as a religious requirement generally around the age of five or six years, but certainly before he attended school. This was an important rite of passage accompanied by feasting and the giving of presents. At the circumcision of five of the sons of the Caliph al-Muqtadir (908-32) some six hundred gold pieces were disbursed as gifts, and many orphans were also circumcised and given gold and sets of clothing.[65] While this was an important time of rejoicing, there must nevertheless have been an element of thanksgiving, given the dangers of haemmorhage and unhygienic practice. At the end of the fifteenth century the Christian pilgrim Felix Fabri saw Muslim schoolboys in Jerusalem 'Sitting in rows upon the ground, and all of them were repeating the same words in unison in a shrill voice, even as the Jews are wont to do when saying their prayers.'[66] He recorded both their words and the musical notes of their chant.

In the event of divorce, boys returned to their fathers about six or seven years of age, but girls could remain with their mothers until they were of marriageable age. In practice, there was little advantage or comfort for the mother if they were married off by their fathers while very young and below the age of consent. This factor might have been highly relevant in cases where he was supporting a new family, for financial reasons, and possibly at the instigation of a new wife. So divorced women, bereft even of their children from an early age, paid a very high price for marital breakdown.

Lane was extremely impressed with the 'sense of propriety' he observed in relationships between parents and children in nineteenth-century Egypt, and commented:

However much the children are caressed and fondled, in general they feel and manifest a most profound and praiseworthy respect for their parents. Disobedience to parents is considered . . . as one of the greatest of sins.[67]

Children's games

Turning now to childhood recreation, a visitor to the court of the Caliph al-Walid II left a charming account by a handsome young poet 'with the loveliest face' who described an incident in his childhood. He sang the song *And she was wearing at that time a veil* and described how, as:

A boy of boys, my waist-band hanging loose,
Just ten, a little gold ring in my ear.
And she was wearing at that time a veil,
And had a family of slave-girl toys.[68]

The girl of the poem must have been from a noble family – the poet sang at court – where girls tended to wear face-veils from around eight or nine years of age. Gold coins (*nukut*) presented to infant girls on the seventh day after their birth were frequently kept and used to decorate headdresses. These coins demonstrated both the family's wealth and the esteem in which they were held.

Several contemporary dictionaries described *dumya* as 'an image of ivory or the like . . . variegated, decorated, embellished or coloured', or simply a doll 'made of bone, the length of a hand with a face fashioned thereupon'. Dolls were obviously prettified – 'any beautiful female is likened thereto, because adorned'. *Dumya* carries the additional meaning of 'in which there is redness like blood'.[69] Presumably the doll had rouged cheeks and conformed to women's fashion. In the eighth century dolls of 'fired clay and cane' became very popular. They were 'models of girls with which maidens are wont to play' and would have cost less than the ivory models of the courts, although it is probable that even the children of the poorest mothers had home-made dolls.

The appearance of dolls in several dictionaries from the eleventh to the fourteenth centuries confirms that they were by no means a novelty among small girls, but a reality. On the eve of the eleventh of June, at the end of the ninth century, 'Caliph al-Mu'tadid's New Year's Day', little girls played *dubarak*, a Persian word meaning 'bride'. (The caliph had changed the tax year because the holy month of Muharram had fallen at the same time.) A large girl-sized doll was made and dressed up as a bride. She was then displayed on a rooftop and everyone celebrated her 'wedding'. Bonfires were lit, accompanied by all the paraphernalia of a real wedding, musical instruments and the like.[70] In Baghdad at Nawruz, the Persian new year, it was customary for people to dress a doll in bridal clothes and place it on the roof of the home. Did this in any way signify a rite of passage for all, a 'new start' for a new year? One sees once more the pervasive influence of the Persian court.

Children also received presents of animal figures, including giraffes, on Nawruz, and this illustrated the difficulty of adhering strictly to religious principles at the personal, popular level. Surprisingly, dolls and other figurative toys were also given to children at the great feasts at the end of Ramadan and the *hajj*. These were religious festivals, but even then the strictures of the theologians were in vain. Figural representation 'in the round' was especially reprehensible, and technically impinged on Allah's role as the only Creator, but how this could possibly have been enforced in the area of innocent children and their playthings? Indeed demand was so great at those periods in the calendar that the market superintendent (*muhtasib*) Abu Sa'id al-Istakhri had to create a special toy market (*suq al-lu'ab*) in the mid-tenth century. Another source mentioned spinning tops, equally popular with girls and boys. Al-Ghazali reported that the Prophet reportedly said:

He who goes to a fair organised by Muslims and there acquires something which he takes home and sets aside for the girls and women to the exclusion of males, God sets on him His gaze.[71]

Could the 'something' for girls have been toys, even dolls? That may have been a reproof to those in society those who set more store on their sons than their daughters.

Another toy, the hobby-horse (*kurraj*) was particularly popular with little girls at weddings. It was draped with colourful material, and a rope put around its neck, and there was much singing and screaming by the children. Even adults enjoyed games with hobby-horses. In the early ninth century the Caliph al-Amin arranged an entertainment, when:

Behold, the mansion was filled with handmaidens and pages, and all did sport and play, and Muhammad (al-Amin) in the midst of them riding the hobby horse did dance thereby.[72]

Ibn Khaldun's later and fuller account of adult wedding festivities confirmed that the game was still popular in the fourteenth century, saying, 'Other dancing equipment, called *kurraj*, was also used'. He described the *kurraj* as 'a wooden figure resembling a saddled horse',

> Attached to robes such as women wear. (The dancers) thus give the appearance of having mounted horses. They attack and withdraw and compete in skill (with weapons) . . . There is much of that sort in Baghdad and the cities of Iraq. It spread from there to other regions.[73]

The children's version probably did not include 'weapons', other than their hands. The *kurraj* was evidently another Persian innovation. One authority mentioned its little round bells (*khalajil*).[74]

Boys played a game called *zadw* or 'nuts'; unsurprisingly, in the context of children, this seems to be a colloquial name. The ninth-century philosopher al-Kindi, like many landlords, strongly disapproved of this game which caused great damage to their courtyards. His contemporary al-Jahiz provided a full account. Boys excavated,

> True wells for their *zadw*, and each one of these holes was called the *muzdat* (nut holder), wherein were stored the nuts with which the boys did sport. And the purpose of the sport was to hide therein the nuts or pebbles if nuts might not be easily had – that the questioner thereto might ask by these two words as expressed in the speech of the children, to wit: '*Khasa aw zaka?*' That is, 'Even or odd?[75]

Buqayra was a game where a child concealed something in its hand, while pushing it into a heap of sand or earth, asking 'Which hand is the thing hidden in?' sounds similar.

At night two teams played '*uzaym waddah* ('shiny knucklebone'). A white bone was thrown into the air and the children scrambled about. The finders shouted, 'Shiny knucklebone shined tonight? Will never shine another night!' They then jumped piggy-back on the losing team back to the start. '*Uzaym* seems to suggest the rough-and-tumble sort of game which boys enjoy. One wonders if it was considered suitable for younger girls as well, but it would certainly preclude older boys and girls from playing together.

Two teams were also involved in *al-khatra* (the 'brandishing') in a struggle over a whip made of plaited rags. Whichever person yielded the whip was beaten by it, and his team lost. Losers again had to carry the winners piggy-back.[76]

Another popular group game was *al-dara*, 'running about'. Children formed a circle, as the name suggests, around two sitting back-to-back in the centre. The object was for those in the outer circle to hit the ones in the centre, who tried to capture them. Whoever was caught went into the middle.

Lu'bat al-dabb or 'game of the lizard' sounds rather like the party-game of being blindfolded and having to pin the tail on a donkey. Here a picture of a lizard was hung up, and one child stood with his back to it. Parts of the lizard were called out, and the child had to touch the part over his shoulder. The punishment for failure was again to give the other children a piggy-back ride.[77] These games are typical of universal children's pastimes, in all eras. The extended family provided a ready source of playmates, boys and girls. Many of them would take place under the watchful eye of the womenfolk of the household. Such youthful mixed games, especially with rough and tumble, came to an abrupt end at puberty.

Puberty signalled the time when restrictions were imposed on girls, and many had to wear a veil from about nine or ten years of age. Gone were the carefree days of childhood mixing, and from then on girls could only play with their brothers and the boys of other close blood relatives. In time, many of these playmates, known intimately all their lives, would marry, with the advantages of long acquaintance, tolerance and mutual respect.

The extended family, consciously or unconsciously, presented female role models across the generations for small girls as mothers and nurturers, guides and friends. Ibn Hazm was brought up and educated by the women of his father's large *harim* in Cordova. This seems to have given him great insight into and affection for women, and he wrote nostalgically and with feeling of:

> The cord of loyalty, respecting those ancient dues and strongly-rooted affections, the rights of childish fondness and the comradeship of youth.[78]

But one sad, modern first-hand account of a young Egyptian girl illustrates vividly the personal feelings of separation and isolation of the sexes from an early age which many a young girl also experienced:

> Suddenly I was required to restrict myself to the company of girls and women. l felt a stranger in their world – their habits and notions startled me. Being separated from the companions of my childhood was a painful experience.[79]

CHAPTER 3

Contraception and Abortion

Birth control and contraception have ever been prime considerations for women, and Arab women did not need physicians and jurists to advise them about personal health and the dangers of pregnancy, far less multiple pregnancies. The evidence was around for all to see of how quickly the bloom of youth faded after marriage, and how many children were orphaned by their mother's death in childbirth. Since marriage partners were subject to strict social selection, it is likely that the good health of tribe and family was also taken into account. Regardless of men's views and religious stricture, many women undoubtedly resorted to their own remedies to try to control the size of their families.

In the early days, the general level of women's health must have been poor, and it would certainly be that only the fittest survived. There was not solely concern for the child about to be born, and the trauma of an infant's death, but the reality for many mothers and fathers was the dilemma of how an extra mouth could be fed. Further, in order to survive, tribes relied on the raid, and many men were killed, leaving wives and children as a burden on the extended family. An additional factor was the fear of producing a daughter, who would be lost to the parents on marriage and unable to support them in old age and infirmity. One other pertinent consideration was that a daughter might be carried off in warfare, as a trophy, to a fate unknown.

The ancient Arabs were utterly dependent on their camels and highly-skilled in all aspects of their rearing. Indeed, the physician al-Qurtubi commented on several occasions on the expertise of the Bedouin in the context of births, and thus they were likely acquainted also with conception – and its prevention – among humans. So what options were open to women? Our written sources of information are legal pronouncements based on the Qur'an and tradition, medical works, pharmaceutical lists, manuals of druggists and erotic literature, a sub-section of *belles-lettres*. As in any society, there was undoubtedly a body of information circulated orally by women and, at the popular level, by entertainments such as the shadow play and tales in the manner of *The Thousand and One Nights*. It should be noted that the source material was formulated in the urban world of religious and medical specialists and *littérateurs*. Recommended contraceptive practices in towns would not necessarily apply in the countryside and in the desert environment, where folkloric and magical remedies handed down through the ages were the norm.

Jurisprudence and breast-feeding

There was a rich Arabic literary vein of sources of contraception in the Middle Ages, each in its way reflecting particular religious, medical or social preoccupations. The ethical and social contexts of birth control were the subject of much debate in Islamic jurisprudence, and apparently offered wider scope for interpretation than the predictably clinical prescriptions of physicians.

The right of the free woman to children and sexual fulfilment was upheld by Islamic law (*shari'a*) and there were arguments both for and against large families, and contraception. The Qur'an was unequivocal that procreation was the purpose of marriage and, as in the Bible, mankind was ordained to multiply:

> God has given you mates of your own kind and has given you, through your mates, children and children's children, and has provided for you sustenance out of the good things of life.[1]

Some jurists read this to imply Qur'anic disapprobation of contraceptive practices. Natural methods of birth control, however, had theological approval. A verse in *Sura* 2 justified spacing the family, prescribing: 'And mothers shall suckle their children two full years for whose who wish to complete breast-feeding', and Sura 31 confirmed this, 'And his weaning is in two years.'[2] In his *Care of the New Born*, Ibn Sina (known in the west as Avicenna) followed Qur'anic prescription and recommended a period of twenty-one to twenty-four lunar months. This, combined with any religious sensibility concerning sexual relations with a nursing mother, could arguably minimise to an extent the risk of a further pregnancy.

Some authorities did not recommend intercourse with a nursing mother (*al-ghayla*) and, given the taboos surrounding menstruation and birth, one wonders whether there was any notion of danger to men from the ritual impurity of women, or that the blessing of the mother's milk was somehow nullified? Or was it simply accepted that breast-feeding was not a guaranteed method of contraception? Medieval dictionaries cited a *Tradition* of al-Muslim that the Prophet had intended to forbid *al-ghayla*, until he 'remembered that the Persians and Greeks practise it and it does not injure their children'.[3] However, it may be that the social circumstances of women from these civilizations were much better than those of women at the advent of Islam and that a good standard of personal nutrition was taken for granted. Early Islamic legal texts also considered health issues. The risks of multiple pregnancies for both mother and child, including the danger to the health of the breast-fed child, and the undesirability of repeated pregnancy for a woman in poor health were all recognised. Apart from their concern for the life of the mother, there would also be that of the effect of her death and the burden on the existing family. These matters were not the prerogative of the jurists, but posed very real anxieties for women every-where.

Economic circumstances for many women therefore dictated family size, taking into account the relative fragility of life, the number of existing children and the father's occupation. Most parents would have agreed with the *Tradition* that 'the most gruelling trial is to have plenty of children with no adequate means',[4] and 'Abdullah ibn 'Abbas, a Companion of the Prophet, pithily remarked that, 'a multitude of children is one of two cases of poverty, while a few children is one of the two cases of ease'.[5] Al-Ghazali acknowledged as legitimate concerns 'fear of excessive hardship on account of numerous offspring and against the need for resorting to evil means' (presumably abortion) and 'the difficulties of providing for the family's legitimate keep in these times of disturbances of living'.[6] In periods of stability and rising aspirations for one's family, there would be a natural desire to maintain standards; this view is confirmed by the reduction in family size in prosperous modern societies.

There were other pertinent factors from a woman's perspective. Slaves were plentiful and cheap and even a fairly modest household could afford them. But the child of a slave by her master was considered free-born and could therefore share in the family's inheritance, like his children by his wife or wives. Further, slave women, who were otherwise commodities, could not be sold after bearing their masters' children, with the implication that both became the master's responsibility. In such circumstances, social and financial considerations were also prominent, especially so for the principal wife. Economic responsibility rested solely with the male head of the household, and the viability of his immediate and extended family would be affected by the outcome of such a liaison. Many men likely attempted to pressurize their sexual partners to take precautions to avoid pregnancy. It is tempting to think that some slave women tried to circumvent this, in their own interests and concerning the upward social mobility of any children they produced. On the other hand, some lawful wives possibly sought to minimise the risk of divorce or abandonment by disregarding contraception and producing a large number of children as a financial deterrent to straying husbands.

Coitus interruptus (al-'azl)

Coitus interruptus or withdrawal was practised in the early Islamic period, and it was likely so beforehand. The Jews in Arabia, who were numerous in Medina, equated withdrawal with infanticide. The Prophet was aware of *al-'azl* and apparently did not condemn it. As one authenticated authority said:

> We used to practise *al-'azl* during the time of the Prophet. The Prophet came to know about it, but did not forbid us.[7]

However, not all of the Companions of the Prophet necessarily approved of this natural method of birth control and opinion in religious circles was divided. Some authorities regarded it as permissible in every case, some not at all, and others recognised it subject to qualification. Some believed that the necessary legally-enshrined rights and consent of a free woman, supported by Abu Hurayra who cited a *Tradition*,[8] were invalidated by practising *coitus interruptus*.

Other commentators took the view that withdrawal was permitted without the consent of a free woman 'because the times are bad'[9] which is fair comment, since the financial burden ultimately lay with the man. Although withdrawal was obviously initiated by the man, it appears that women, in theory at least, had some say at some times in the manner of contraception practised by the couple. Arabic sources reveal that women were frequently instrumental in asking men to practise withdrawal, and demonstrated ample evidence of fear of pregnancy.

Due to the checks and balances provided by the vast quantity of *Traditions*, opinions and teachings concerning sexuality and *coitus interruptus* varied, and proponents and opponents alike were able to quote selectively to justify their particular viewpoints. Al-Ghazali's *Book on the Etiquette of Marriage* posited *coitus interruptus* in terms of a legal contract preceding the acceptance of a contract between the parties, and he stressed their right to sexual fulfilment. Religious authorities did approve of the use of female contraceptive suppositories, which were also foremost in the recommendations of physicians.

The philosopher al-Ghazali, who was a man of his time in the eleventh and early twelfth centuries, sanctioned five reasons for using withdrawal, including 'Preserving the beauty of the woman and her portliness in order to maintain enjoyment, and protect her life against the danger of childbirth; and this, too, is not prohibited.'[10]

In this context, the preservation of a woman's physical charms appeared to be for her husband's pleasure. Privately, many women might have thought in similar terms, or at least viewed limitations in family size as a means of keeping their looks and reducing the husbands' temptation to stray. Yet al-Ghazali apparently saw no irony in castigating women who wished to avoid pregnancy for other personal reasons.

In Damascus in the the late thirteenth century Ibn al-Quff, who was both 'a man of the pen', (a theologian) and a physician, recommended pregnancy tests. One wonders if he was also engaged in legal disputes over paternity and inheritance, and sought to use his medical expertise in solving these? They posed a thorny problem for the jurists, since many men seemed to set such great store by the effectiveness of *coitus interruptus* that they could deny paternity with impunity.

Ultimately, withdrawal was dependent on the volition of men but it arguably also had some bearing on the rights of free women to sexual fulfilment and control of their own reproduction. It is more than likely that many women went ahead and took their own precautions, regardless of their husband's wishes – or even of his knowledge – to avoid both withdrawal and conception.

Medical sources

It is unsurprising that the health, even the life, of the woman were the primary concerns of medieval Muslim doctors, and contraception and abortion alike were considered permissible. Ibn Sina's chapter on contraception reiterated that 'the physician may be obliged to prevent pregnancy in a young woman in fear of her death in childbirth'.[11] This referred to very young girls in early marriages, who al-Razi reported were 'prematurely deflowered and became pregnant at a tender age'. The writings of these doctors reflected both their social status and that of their patients. First cousin marriage was preferred in the highest social groups for a variety of reasons expounded elsewhere here. This was frequently agreed when a girl – indeed child – was around ten years of age and thus unable to give her consent. and doctors must have examined many very young patients with gynaecological disorders.

Early medical works, such as al-Tabari's *Paradise of Wisdom* and the encyclopaedic *Kitab al-Hawi* of al-Razi of the ninth and tenth centuries respectively[12] or Ibn Sina's eleventh-century *Canon* (*Kitab al-qanun fi al-tibb*) contained chapters on contraception and abortion. Ibn Sina's *Canon* was highly influential in the Middle East until last century, and indeed remained an important source for western physicians until the seventeenth century.[13]

Physicians were apparently less concerned with al-Ghazali's observations on the cosmetic benefits in the woman from well-planned families, but of course al-Ghazali was not a doctor. Their interests naturally lay primarily in the physical and mental well-being of the mother, yet strangely, they seemingly perceived no danger to a child being breast fed by its mother's new pregnancy. It should be noted, however, doctors did not deal with the commonality of society. Given the prestige of medicine and learning and the large fees physicians could command, their patients in all likelihood enjoyed a comfortable lifestyle and a relatively enviable level of nutrition. Physicians rarely mentioned *coitus interruptus*. Was this because they did not recognize it as medically sound? If so, were not women's fears of pregnancy and resort to other practices therefore fully justified? Or was the scope of the jurists so wide-ranging and authoritative that doctors were 'free to mention only the reasons proper to their profession'?[14]

The birth control techniques recommended for women in medical literature, for example those in the *Kitab al-Hawi*, include potions to be taken orally, vaginal suppositories containing a variety of ingredients derived from plants, and 'miscellaneous techniques' which involved movements, such as the woman jumping backwards after *coitus*, sneezing, and fumigation of the private parts with herbs or spices. Fumigation was also used after parturition, possibly as an antiseptic. An analysis of recommendations from several famous physicians confirmed the overwhelming preference for female suppositories.[15] One is struck by the recurrence of components of preparations to be taken orally which were also included in the list of suppositories, for example cyclamen in different forms, cinnamon with myrrh and weeping-willow leaves.

Suppositories contained diverse materials, such as oil of flower of cabbage, peppermint juice and rock salt. 'Weeping willow in wool' was also noted. This suggests that a woman soaked a wad of wool in a solution and then inserted it; it would be easily removed if an end was left trailing. Leaves of bindweed and rue played their part, as well as 'seeds of cabbage in a pipe', which presumably resembled the modern sanitary cardboard tampon container, through which the seeds were fed.[16] The practicalities of some of these methods are not always clear, but it must have been necessary to remove the insertions, which enclosed and absorbed the properties of the ingredients. Since disease of the womb was a prime medical indication calling for medical intervention, one must ask to what extent the insertion of a large number of foreign matters into a woman's body affected her health or indeed reduced her immunity to disease?[17] Were physicians concerned only with medical indications because if, as Musallam suggests, al-'azl 'did not present a medical problem'[18] that is, it caused no contra-indications

Ibn al-Jawzia, a notable twelfth-century adherent of the strict Hanbali school of law produced a brief general work, The Gleaning of Benefits (Kitab iltiqat al-manafi') with a short section on the prevention of pregnancy, where three different prescriptions for women appeared for contraceptive or abortive purposes.[19] One included a vaginal suppository containing tar.

Ibn al-Jawzi included yet another strange-sounding miscellaneous technique, that of fumigation with the hoof of a horse, mule or donkey. This probably referred to the fumigation of the woman's genital area, which was certainly the case after parturition, using henna, sulphur and bitumen.[20] (One wonders if there was any inherent notion of the ritual pollution of the mother, particularly from a jurist?) While Ibn al-Jawzi included medical information, his short list naturally differed in some respects from the recommendations of physicians.

Although doctors possibly sought to exert their (male) authority over women, it is undeniable that women had to be pro-active in employing contraceptive preparations. This was a highly personal matter and afforded a woman an element of control and manipulation of her own fertility, provided that they were effective. The Gleaning of Benefits prescribed two male contraceptive methods. In medical prescriptions potions to be taken by mouth outnumbered male techniques such as smearing the penis with a substance and, predictably, magical methods rarely figured.[21]

Pharmaceutics and druggists' manuals

The wide Arabic pharmaceutical literature (*de materia medica* manuscripts) are mainly compilations drawing on over one hundred sources. This genre, which drew heavily on ancient folkloric material, was quite distinct from medical writing. Medieval pharmacopoeia lists contain some one hundred contraceptive and abortifacient preparations, representing some ten per cent of the simple drugs in the section on *materia medica*. Books such as the thirteenth-century *Manual for the (Drug) Store*[22] detailed simples and compounds and were compiled in the form of a dictionary. Full descriptions and properties of the material in both the herbalistic and medical contexts were given and, with one exception (tar for use as a male contraceptive), were prescribed for women. Doctors also referred to these manuscripts. It is noticeable that popular writings, where the majority of preparations were for male use, diverged from medical prescriptions, and each genre set its own agenda.

Druggists' manuals were sometimes organised from the therapeutic standpoint from the *materia medica* lists. First of all they detailed the diseases and complaints, then the remedies.[23] This implies that customers were able to consult the druggists in their stores in the market-place, outlined their symptoms or requirements, and then purchased the requisite prescription of drugs, herbs, spices or chemicals. One can see the advantages for women; there was no embarrassing consultation with a male doctor which would have been instigated in any case by husbands, and they could obtain a prescription without the permission or knowledge of their husbands or lovers. Anonymity, aided and abetted by the veil, was assured.

Al-Suwaydi's huge thirteenth-century treatise was abbreviated in sixteenth-century Cairo by al-Sha'rani and became very popular. It contained preparations to encourage and prevent conception, to prevent and procure abortions, and aids for women in labour and the like. One prescription called for 'blood of menses'. Of the thirty or so purely contraceptive prescriptions, only one was a technique to be used by the man. In that case preparations, including tar, were used to rub on the penis. The others were prescribed for women and included some twelve recommendations making their first appearance in the lists.[24] The usual suppository ingredients of cucumber, cabbage and a form of iron reappeared, and stems of indigo in the 'flock of cotton' mentioned elsewhere were noted; Nafzawi also mentioned a female suppository of a 'flock' of wool with myrrh and cinnamon. He may have written for well-to-do women, but the instrument was the same. His fourteenth-century *Perfumed Garden*[25] was possibly the only manual on sensual love known to non-specialists.

We see once again that it was the woman who was ultimately responsible for using these particular remedies. Druggists were able to supply both the material recommended by physicians and that widely known to the general public via popular knowledge, and it seems that their lists were more widely socially applicable than the pharmacopeia. So far as contraception is concerned, it is safe to assert that their customers were predominantly female.

Belles-lettres (*al-adab*)

Refined literature also expressed similar concerns to those of the legal and medical professions over unwanted or undesirable pregnancy and social responsibility. There was an implicit notion that women used fear of pregnancy and social scandal as an excuse to avoid their lovers and believed that pregnancy always resulted from sexual relations. It is not possible to say if these attitudes reflected any general lack of faith by women in the many current contraceptives, but it is they who were most personally affected by unwanted pregnancy. *Belles-lettres* (*al-adab*) and its subsection on sexuality, erotica, had great popular appeal. They were mainly preoccupied with male potency and male contraceptive methods and the very titles confirm the audience, for example the tenth-century *Encyclopedia of Pleasure* (*Jawami' al-ladhdha*) and the thirteenth-century *Rejuvenation of the Old* Man (*Ruju' al-shaykh ila sibah fi al-quwwa 'ala al-bah*).[26] Such works by men for men (perhaps containing an element of wishful thinking) were readily available in public bookshops, and as literature formed the subject of discussion in literary salons. This genre also disregarded the medical indications pertaining to women. It was frequently scabrous in content, so it is debatable whether many wives had direct access to it. Enlightened husbands possibly discussed the contents with their wives. If so, they would circulate orally in some form among women, and in time percolate down to less 'refined' society. Perhaps it is being fanciful to suggest that male contraceptive information from erotica was the equivalent of what the readers would otherwise condemn as 'old wives tales' in the female context, but rendered authoritative by writing.

However, tested female contraceptive practices were reported in *belles-lettres*; as early as the ninth century al-Jahiz identified contraception as a basic human trait which distinguished humans from animals. He noted that 'Some women today use a measure of antimony, after purity (that is, after the ritual washing and before intercourse), because they believe that it will prevent births.'[27]

Antimony, as a constituent of *kohl*, would be readily to hand, but it was evidently not invariably effective, for he cautioned, 'But I have seen a woman use it and (nevertheless) give birth to a child'.

Al-Jahiz also reported that prostitutes in India used a suppository of elephant dung, mixed with honey, 'in order to keep their customers';[28] this probably also reflected the concerns of their male clients who feared being responsible for a child, but in many cases women's anxieties about their own health and ability to work, as well as economic necessity, would have been the spur. An eleventh-century literary anecdote quoted a man who counselled marriage to a prostitute. Among his reasons was that she knew how to please men and that 'she takes precautions so as not to bear you children'.[29]

Asceticism, including sexual abstinence, was not a feature of Islam. Post-menopausal women perhaps held their own attraction for older men who did not wish more children. Relatively few women in society could have been among those of whom al-Jahiz speculated, 'a woman can be with (a eunuch) and be safe from the greatest shame, something which will heighten her pleasure and passion'.[30] The 'shame' here, of course was pregnancy, although the perils, pain and penalties of conducting such an affair in their own homes surely deterred many women. That apart, castration was not invariably successful.

Magic and amulets

Ibn al-Baytar al-Maliki's thirteenth-century *Treatise on Simples* (*Al-jami' li-mufradat al-adwiya wa al-aghdhiya*) is evidence of a divergence from the female suppositories of the medical writings towards a reliance on magic and potions, including an amulet of seed of patience wrapped in linen, and urinating on the urine of a wolf, which must have been something of a last resort. One reads too of the late sixteenth-century work of Dawud al-Antaki who seems to have substituted magic in the form of writing and numbers for female suppositories. Predictably, there was no mention of magic by the zealous Ibn al-Jawzi, but he recommended one potion, rather verging on the incredible, of the 'foam' from the mouth of a male camel in the rutting season; men may have considered this the ultimate symbol of male virility.

He had also mentioned tar in this context.[31] Magical methods were also noted elsewhere in erotica, such as the early fourteenth-century *Nihayat al-arab fi funun al-adab* of al-Nuwayri.

Folk medicine

Finally, we turn to folk medicine and old wives' tales. Al-Suwaydi's thirteenth-century compendium evidently drew not only on requisite medical sources, but also the more popular folklore tradition, detailing for example 'blood of work horse' and 'urine of ram' as potions, and four remedies relating to magical practices. These included 'skeleton of frog' and 'ankle of weasel' as charms to be worn, and smearing the woman with parturition blood from a first-born child. Blood and the taboos surrounding it are discussed in Chapter 8. Such works represented the dispensing of esoteric knowledge by a male specialist, although one suspects that many women continued regardless with their own tried and tested folk remedies. While wealthy women within the confines of the *harim* were well able to afford physicians' fees and private consultations, it is likely that their many outside contacts through women brokers, hairdressers and so on ensured that they had the option of procuring popular remedies. For one thing, they could presumably only consult a physician with their husbands' knowledge and permission and, for whatever reason, it is likely that many women preferred to keep such matters intensely private and personal.

But what about the mass of the population? Many of the suppository ingredients listed by al-Razi and others were literally 'common or garden'. Onion, cyclamen, aloe, colocynth (a type of cucumber), pepper, leek seeds, wild carrot roots, headed thyme, water mint, dill and cardamom all appeared in source material, and some of these at least must have been known in connection with birth-control and widely available to ordinary women and especially so in the extended Muslim family, from their gardens or the market-place. Knowledge of these plants and their alleged properties would be disseminated through the network of mothers, sisters and friends which have always existed among women.

Abortion

There is, of course, one other method of birth control, and that is abortion.

This is a complex and emotive subject in any culture, and the Muslim jurists'
position was unequivocal; life must be respected and preserved from the
moment of gestation. Abortion was regarded as akin to infanticide in severity
and punishable accordingly;[32] this was particularly so when it occurred after
the fourth month. As al-Ghazali said in his *Ihya*:

> If the spirit is breathed into it and the created being takes form, then the
> crime (of abortion) becomes more serious still.[33]

After this four month period, abortion was regarded as homicide, when
the principle of 'an eye for an eye' (*lex talionis*) came into force.

However, the standard medical view of abortion was that it was
permissible where there was concern for the mother's health on various
grounds, for example 'in the cases of women who are weak of power and
sickly of body'[34] and where the life of a very young girl was endangered
should the pregnancy go to full term. Medical criteria which justified
contraception were similar to those applied to abortion; both came under the
heading of 'birth control'.

Ibn Sina recommended aborting a foetus by inserting in the uterus a
rolled piece of paper, a feather or a stick cut to the size of a feather made of
saltwort, rue, cyclamen, or male fern. 'This will definitely work, especially
if it is smeared with an abortifacient medicine such as tar, the water of
colocynth pulp, or some other abortifacient medicine.'[35]

Several of these ingredients have already been noted as contraceptives.
The damage caused by the insertion of sharp and unhygienic foreign matter
into the body must be a matter of speculation. Ibn Sina also mentioned
strenuous exercise, the carrying of heavy loads, sneezing, jumping and the
inducement of vomiting as effective means of procuring abortion. It is
impossible to say if Ibn Sina's personal prescriptions were well known by
women, even if the ingredients were common abortifacients, but women in
general are well aware that violent and strenuous movements can induce
miscarriage and abortion.

Abu al-Hasan al-Tabib's work *Book of the Creation of Man (Kitab khalq al-
insan)* included a chapter 'On Medicines Which Abort the Foetus'.[36] Several
materials found in other sources such as myrrh, wild carrot and cyclamen
recurred. However, he recommended many more potions and mixtures
taken orally than other authorities, and two types of fumigation, with herbs
and sulphur. Other doctors were more conservative.

Ibn al-Jawzi reported that a Bedouin was overheard at the entrance to the city of Basra saying, 'Love is kissing and the touching of hands. Going beyond that is asking for a child',[37] and a passage from *The Thousand and One Nights*,

Three things alone
Prevent her black eyes saying 'yes';
Fear of the unknown, and horror of the known,
And her own loveliness,[38]

is a grim reminder and dire warning to women in forbidden relationships who might be tempted to say 'yes'. For them, abortion was an imperative, given the notions of honour and shame prevalent in society, the retribution taken by her own family, and the severe punishments meted out for adultery. They themselves induced an abortion or had someone else do so. There must have been female collusion and conspiracies of silence to keep this from the men in their lives and unfortunately this truth lends substance to the prevalent male opinion of women as 'scheming'. This is borne out by the fact that a twelfth-century doctor, 'Ali ibn 'Abbas, was against even mentioning abortive agents, 'to prevent their use by women in whom there is no good'. He presumably referred to sexually loose women, yet he conspired with women without any sense of irony in his prescription 'to women he can trust' of 'medicines which cause the menses to flow, (presumably on sound medical grounds) or medicines which expel the dead foetus'.[39]

But how great was the general knowledge of women of abortion practices? The many remedies available to encourage abortion (or conception), either from peddlers and quacks in the market-place or women in the community have demonstrably been of particular interest to women. The properties of plants were widely recognised in society at large. A ninth-century poem by Ibn Qutayba praised rue, which was both popular and perceived to be efficient. 'Let us praise God and thank Him. Were it not for the uses of rue, the children of the singer-prostitutes would have covered the earth.'[40] A woman could procure an abortion by mixing rue in hot water and taking it for three or four weeks. It is surely significant that the name 'rue' was derived from the Greek *ruta*, 'to set free', but also has connotations of sorrow and repentance.[41]

There was evidently a great mass of general information on birth control in the Muslim world of the Middle Ages which filtered down to society at large through the medium of popular literature and lore. Source material has revealed that the parameters of religious and social sources such as *belles-lettres* and erotica ranged much further than the apparently purely medical reasons for contraception and abortion posited by physicians. It might be that writers were responding to a very human need which created the demand, or that they recognized demographic trends and the deleterious effect of multiple pregnancies on women. Women themselves were no less concerned, whatever their motives, and were very active participants in, if not instigators of, the control and manipulation of their own fertility.

CHAPTER 4

Food, Etiquette and Hospitality

Literary sources and the court

Al-Mas'udi's *Meadows of Gold and Mines of Gems* (*Muruj al-dhahab wa ma'adin al-jawhar*) offered the discerning tenth-century reader:

> A glimpse of the culinary art, some knowledge of which is essential to the subordinate and, indeed, which no cultivated person should be without, and some indications of the new fashions in dishes and of the skilful combination of spices and aromatics in seasonings.[1]

Our knowledge of *haute cuisine* in the medieval Arab world came from the extensive humanistic literature emanating from the highest male social circles, and encompassed the diet and etiquette of refined society. These were no mere cookery books; they reflected personal, social or cultural preferences. Al-Baghdadi was not alone in subscribing to the 'doctrine of the pre-excellence of the pleasure of eating above all other pleasures', which included drinking, sex, clothing and the ambience of colours, scents and sounds.[2] He might have mentioned the accompanying music, poetry and lively literary and political discussion.

The doyen and inspiration of Arab food writers was Abu Ishaq Ibrahim, the son of the Caliph al-Mahdi and his concubine Shikla, born in Baghdad in 779. From his youngest days Ibrahim was something of a gourmet. He was actively encouraged by his brother and guardian Harun al-Rashid with the gift of a slave-girl, Badi'a. Ibrahim instigated a new style of cooking in the 'Abbasid era and had the means to pursue exotic ingredients, attend many banquets, experiment and create his own recipes. His lamb dish *ibrahimiyya* set out in al-Baghdadi's work stands as an appreciation by thirteenth-century bourgeois society of Ibrahim's great contribution to the culinary arts.[3]

Al-Warraq produced the earliest compilation of cookery books in Baghdad in the late tenth century. His surname is in the 'professional form' of Arabic, and indicates that he was both scribe and bookseller. Was he motivated principally by culinary or financial interests? The ready availability of paper and the ease of manuscript copying ensured that books in general were widely available in the Near East, and the evidence is that al-Warraq tapped into a large, popular market for markers of refined living. In Baghdad alone there were some one hundred booksellers in the *suq al-warraqin*, occupying both sides of the roadway from the Harrani archway to the New Bridge over the Sarat canal.[4] Ibn Khallikan mentioned an Egyptian bookseller in the early thirteenth century who:

> Used to sit in the vestibule of his house for the purpose of exercising his profession, offering books for sale to men of rank and learning. They were accustomed to assemble there every Sunday and Wednesday, and remain till the hours of sale were over.[5]

Were women at home among the readers, or was their knowledge second-hand, from their husbands? Indeed, what was the level of literacy among women, even among the bourgeoisie?

Al-Warraq sometimes added a final touch to his recipes with 'zayn!', 'beautiful!', from the verb meaning 'to adorn'; this is particularly evocative of a well-pleased cook standing back to admire her handiwork, or someone who keenly appreciated good food.

Muhammad ibn al-Hasan ibn Muhammad ibn Karim al-Katib al-Baghdadi updated his early thirteenth-century *Book of Cookery* (*Kitab al-tabikh*) to include new ingredients, and it has come down to us in fragmented form. Yet another cookbook, *Wusla ila al-habib*, was compiled by an Ayyubid prince, a nephew of Saladin. Such works were primarily concerned with large-scale banqueting. The *Kanz al-fawa'id fi tanwi' al-fawa'id*, but from Egypt, was roughly contemporary in period and contained some eight hundred similar recipes. Nevertheless *haute cuisine* was based ultimately on the local regional dishes traditionally prepared by women. Recipes were adapted and the names themselves showed slight variations.

Good food, in like company, was much relished by the Arabs and frequently appreciatively spoken of in literature. In theory it should have been a great personal advertisement for the person who created the recipes, if not actually cooked them; unfortunately, little is known about these early, largely anonymous, cooks, or even whether they were female or male. Where they are named, it was in the context of the court. The patronage and influence of the courts cannot be overstated, since rulers could ship vast quantities of specialities from their far-flung borders for their own use with scant regard for cost, and it remains questionable to what extent ordinary housewives could afford exotic ingredients.

In a sense, the court and the merchant class were in a reciprocal relationship. Merchants in turn influenced tastes beyond their own circles, and poets at social gatherings and writers and commentators on refined society created a wider market. The audience for these works was evidently highly literate, and they had the time to give themselves over to feasting and merrymaking, and dressing appropriately and expensively. It included *littérateurs*, scholars and the professional and ruling classes, but their wives must have been influenced by the tastes of their cosmopolitan husbands, and had a role in the experimentation and adaptation of fairly basic traditional cookery. These women were able to try out new dishes and ingredients, or to adapt old favourites, whether or not they personally did the cooking.

Although non-Muslim women followed local and regional culinary traditions – albeit with specific religious variations or proscriptions – one should bear in mind the culinary influence of immigrant communities of Armenians, Sephardi Jews from Persia, and Iraqi Christians originally from Mosul and Kurdistan. The ingredients and methods of cooking of certain named dishes could and did vary from region to region.

Nor should the efforts and influence of the not-so-humble, talented foreign slave-girls be disregarded. Ibrahim's Badi'a was a renowned cook whose speciality was desserts, and her cold dishes (*bawarid*) were especially relished at *al-fresco* parties.[6] Bad'ia extended her wide range of accomplishments by preparing elaborate dishes of food for her master, a shrewd move on her part, since feasting formed such a large part of court activity. The Caliph Mu'tamid reputedly only ate food prepared by the accomplished cook and singer Shariyya.

'Arib, a very famous musician at the 'Abbasid court in the mid-ninth century, wrote in outrage to the governor of Mosul who had sent her food in response to her request:

In the name of Allah, the Merciful, the Compassionate! O you stupid barbarian! Did you think that I belong to the Turks or wild soldiers that you have sent me bread, meat and confectionery? May Allah protect me from you!

With this missive she sent him personal examples of *haute cuisine* – her definition of 'food' – from her own kitchen.[7] These included palm blossom and a type of bread, (undoubtedly fine), stuffed with fried breast of partridge and vegetables. To add insult to injury, her offering was covered with gold brocade. She incidentally insinuated by her disdainful tone and action that she was socially superior to any mere official appointee of the ruler. On another occasion 'Arib begged an admirer to tarry awhile and sample a pudding with fresh almonds which Bid'a, her pupil, had prepared. Even fairly modest households had foreign slave-girls, and they too must have influenced ordinary everyday Arab cookery through their personal recipes.

The widely-travelled Mas'udi reported that *harisa* had been a favourite dish of Sasanid emperors, and quoted a guest at a royal banquet who gave as his preference *harisa* made by a skilful woman because 'Women's hands are resolute and pure, They have a lightness and a vigour sure.'[8]

Harisa was made from a paste of meat, wheat and spices and known colloquially as '*Umm Jabr*', or 'Mother of Strengthening', with the emphasis on bone structure; this seems to imply that it was a very popular meal. Ideally, *harisa* required well marbled meat on the bone, ground wheat, chicken joints, cummin, cinnamon bark 'of condiments the king', and powdered cinnamon. The wheat thickened the juices and added body, and when cooked thus it was a great delicacy. It was served with lemon juice, and it was reputedly tastier when cooked in the oven than over an open fire. Al-Baghdadi's version substituted coarsely ground rice for the wheat, with a final sprinkling of sugar. *Harisa* does not seem a particularly gourmet dish (by today's standards) in terms of ingredients, or a difficult dish to cook, but it sounds delicious. However, few housewives working with a modest budget could have produced *harisa* to these recipes.

A poet eulogised aubergine with *buran*, a sweet fruity date sauce, and the influence of Persia is evident in the name. For those who could afford meat, mutton was also eaten, and beef from Wasit (between Basra and Baghdad) was reported by chroniclers. At one time in Mosul beef was reported in short supply and as in all cases of supply and demand of whatever commodity, prices were higher in times of shortage. Officials in the Mustansiriyya college received in kind remuneration of quantities of meat and vegetables according to qualifications and seniority. For example, a lecturer was allocated twelve dinars a month plus allowances in kind, while a librarian's salary was ten dinars, with a proportionately smaller amount of meat, and apparently no bread.[9] These people were well educated and enjoyed a better than average diet. Ashtor calculated that when considering these in kind payments, the lecturer's monthly salary was in effect worth a handsome twenty dinars.

It should be borne in mind that as the Mustansiriyya was exceedingly well endowed, it could have employed the best-qualified officials, and functionaries in similar establishments elsewhere were not necessarily paid the same. However, is it not surprising that these good salaries were supplemented in this way? Since the Mustansiriyya was a religious foundation, was there an implicit recognition of the obligations to one's extended family? If nothing else, it guaranteed that the wives of officials had food and fuel for their families, but one can only speculate on the plight of the less fortunate. An eleventh-century historian of Baghdad unearthed a household bill amounting to thirty dinars, 'For Abu . . . the butcher'. This covered one hundred *artal* of meat and a dinar's worth of suet. It is not clear whether this was weekly, or monthly, but it certainly referred to an extensive and very well-off family.[10]

Women cooks also had a choice of lamb, which was preferred to beef, and it was served stuffed with almonds, raisins and rice, coconut or spices and cloves from India. Roast kid (*jady*) was a delicacy. At a banquet given by the 'Abbasid Caliph al-Mustaqfi, a poet rhapsodized over a yearling kid roasted with tarragon and mint. An acquaintance of al-Tanukhi told him how, at the table of al-Nu'man, 'a fatted kid was served . . . and a dish of almonds made up with pistachio nuts'.[11]

The dish known as *sikbaj*, from the Persian meaning vinegar, referred to the cooking of lamb with a variety of ingredients. One medieval dictionary definition read:

> A sort of food composed of flesh meat cut in pieces to which are afterwards added raisins, a few figs and some vetches, with vinegar or honey and acid syrup.[12]

The Persian source indicated that it was 'spoon' food. It was obviously highly appreciated since, in the jargon of the much-despised professional gatecrashers of social gatherings who sought to justify their presence by 'singing for their supper' in elaborate praise of food, it was the 'Mother of Hospitality'. Fowl and partridges were roasted, and game was widely available. When Nasir al-Dawla in Baghdad ordered food to be brought quickly, he was served with a roast fowl, a loaf of bread, sugar, salt, vinegar, and a little in the way of vegetables.

Grazing for sheep and goats was found only nearer the settled lands and although the Qur'an did not proscribe camel-meat, very few Arabs ate it. Apart from being sentimentally attached to their camels, the Bedouin were absolutely dependent on them for life, and they represented a considerable portion of their wealth and prestige. However, one passage from the *Muʿallaqa* of ʿUmr al-Qays reads:

> On that day I killed my camel to feast the maidens,
> (And how strange it was to see them carrying the saddle and trappings),
> They continued helping each other to the roasted flesh,
> And the delicate fat like the fringe of finely woven white silk.[13]

One notes the pleasure derived from the poet's highlighting of colour and contrast. These maidens were indeed honoured.

There were relatively few rice dishes recorded in contemporary Arabic culinary literature, since it was considered by some in areas where it was locally grown as a poor man's meal. This was not necessarily so where it had to be imported, and possibly prized. Rice was introduced from India and only became known to the Arab conquerors of Iraq in the seventh century. Ibn al-Faqih told how a commander in the vicinity of Basra counselled his soldiers: 'Eat the dates, but leave this other thing, for it must be poison which the enemy has prepared for you.'[14]

In time the cultivation of rice moved westwards and women and children in humid regions worked alongside the men in the rice fields. Al-Tanukhi repeated the following verse by the prince ʿAdud al-Dawla Abu Shujaʾa as a riposte to a guest who had praised in poetry all the other dishes offered at a banquet:

> Buttered rice in crystal brimming
> Looks like pearls in camphor swimming.

This may be sarcasm, and confirmation that in his opinion rice was humble fare indeed and unworthy of a poem. However, at another court banquet a dish of rice pudding elicited the following:

> *Judhaba* made of choicest rice
> As shining as a lover's eyes:
> How marvellous in hue it stands
> Beneath the cook's accomplished hands![15]

Unfortunately, the cook remained anonymous.

Ibn Taghribirdi's *Chronicles of Egypt* mentioned a rice caravanserai (*funduq al-aruzz*) on the Nile shore, where the product was unloaded from ships. Al-Baghdadi's recipes occasionally included rice, for example *aruzz mufalfal*, a dish with pepper (*fulful*), with connotations of 'burning the tongue',[16] and rice was very useful for thickening gravies and sauces. Women often cooked rice in milk in meat dishes such as *rukhamiyya*, which name evokes its 'marbled' appearance stemming from the contrast between the fried minced lamb and the creamy rice. Again, one sees the preoccupation with the presentation of culinary delights. This is one traditional dish Jewish women would not cook, since the mixing of milk and meat products – even cooking utensils – was proscribed. An old Arab saying, 'What do the people of Paradise eat? Rice in butter.' suggests that rice was beyond the purses of many women.

Unfortunately, al-Baghdadi's work, like others in the *genre*, rarely gave precise measurements of ingredients, nor cooking times. In theory, this offered much scope to the imagination and inventiveness of the cook, but one imagines that the ordinary housewife was on more sure ground than those who produced food for royal banquets. Rulers were notoriously difficult to please, with dire consequences for some, although they could reward generously.

There is some ambiguity in the terms for weights, as well as indications of cost. Al-Baghdadi's recipe for *rutabiyya* (indicating that it included fresh dates, *rutab*) curiously mentioned 'about two dirhams' of dry coriander, cummin, pepper, mastic and cinnamon. It also called for 'ten dirhams of scented sugar'.[17] A dirham was a silver coin, and one wonders if spices were bought in a standard measure, perhaps a twist of paper, which cost one dirham? If this was the case then these seasonings were extremely expensive and his compilation could only have been used by palace cooks and better-off women. However, prices were not stable, so did he refer to a quantity covering a dirham piece? Another recipe for *rutabiyya*, specified 'a *danaq* of camphor'. The *danaq* was a small silver coin, about one sixth of a dirham and therefore a much smaller measure. Alternatively, was a coin itself used as a weight? Pharmacists sold prescriptions in small paper bags (*qaratat*) and the name possibly implied that their ingredients were of a specified weight.[18] A slave-girl of Ibrahim al-Mahdi prepared *sikbaj* (a stew) for the Caliph al-Amin and added a *mithqal* of amber and two *mathaqal* of Indian aloes. A *mithqal* represented 'a dirham and three sevenths of a dirham', so these additives were costly.

Nothing was too much bother in the presentation of a meal, for example even the inside of the garnish was lovingly prepared. A recipe for *rutabiyya*, a meat dish, read:

Take sugarcandy dates, or Medina dates, as required: extract the stone from the bottom with a needle, and put in its place a peeled, sweet almond.[19]

The upper classes enjoyed a varied diet, with a wide assortment of citrus and other fruits. An early poet mentioned lemons sprinkled with *nadd*. This was a special type of perfume or a compound of aloes-wood aromatised with ambergris and musk, and thus obviously confined to the highest social circles. It is possible that such dishes were served to cleanse the palate between courses. An Arabic proverb ran, 'A table without vegetables is like an old man without wisdom'.[20] Although one tenth-century poet, Kushajim al-Sindi, wrote a verse in praise of asparagus, 'They might be bezels set in rings of pearl. Thereon a most delicious sauce doth swirl', source materials scarcely mentioned vegetables. Was this because they were cheap and readily available in the market?

Saffron from Egypt and the shores of the Gulf was frequently called for in recipes. It was simply sprinkled on dishes, or dissolved in rosewater or honey according to taste and aesthetic presentation; like honey, saffron was expensive. Turmeric was a cheaper alternative, but was useful only as a colourant and lacked the delicacy and perfume of saffron. Unscrupulous shopkeepers sought to deceive by substituting turmeric for saffron.

These are fascinating literary accounts, all the more so that they were written by men, who were, presumably, not doing the cooking, and they confirm the great appreciation of food and the importance of hospitality in the Arab world.

Medicine, dietetics and tradition

Medical writings are a valuable source of information on dietetics. The earliest scientific work in Arabic on diet and nutrition, the respected physician Abu Marwan ibn Zuhr's *Kitab al-aghdiya*, appeared in twelfth-century Spain.

Medical tomes were written by and for the highest in society but many remedies were based on the Medicine of the Prophet, which had absorbed remedies long in use among the Arabs. The Prophet recognised the advantages of a balanced diet. He suggested supplementing barley-bread with dates, as the people of Medina did. A *Tradition* passed down from the two sons of Busr told how, 'The Messenger of God came to visit us, and we set before him butter and dates. For he used to like butter and dates'.[21] The Prophet also relished the traditional dish *tharid,* and considered that 'The superiority of 'A'isha over other women is like the superiority of *tharid* over all other food.' *Tharid* was defined by the *Sihah* and other dictionaries as 'Bread crumbled or broken into small pieces with the fingers, then moistened with broth, and then piled up in the middle of a bowl'.

It generally contained some meat, for example kid or lamb, chicken or beef, and a poet enthused, 'When you season bread with meat, that – God be my witness – is *tharid*'.[22] Ibn Qayyim al-Jawziyya declared that *talbina,* a broth from ground barley, was 'more beneficial to the people of Hijaz than the broth of whole barley'.

Physicians prescribed particular foods: for example rice was 'the most nourishing of grains after the wheat'. Ibn Qayyim al-Jawziyya reported that the Prophet recommended rice, for 'it contains healing and no illness'.[23] One medical volume even gave a recipe for *sakbaj,* prepared as follows. Small pieces of meat were boiled then laid aside to dry out. Carrots, onions and other vegetables were boiled with spices, then the meat, sugar and honey, or both, were added, and the whole cooked over a moderate heat. Al-Majusi classed onions, garlic and lettuce as having remedial properties. These were common produce, and it is likely that their qualities – and those of other foods – were well known to women in general.

Ibn Qayyim al-Jawziyya held that 'Water is the substance of life, the chief of drinks, one of the four elements of the world, indeed its chief element', and prescribed 'Water that is kept in various water-skins (*qirab* and *shinan*) . . . is sweeter to taste than that which is kept in a vessel of earthenware, stone or other such materials, especially good quality skins of hide (*adam*).'[24]

He described quail as 'hot, dry and beneficial for the joints', and any damage to the liver could be counteracted by vinegar and coriander. Although beneficial for dropsy, the sandgrouse was 'one of the worst foods'.

A glance at contemporary recipes revealed much use of vinegar, and it is easy to establish the connection between health concerns and usefulness in cooking. Cold dishes (*bawaridiyya*) using vinegar or tart fruit juices were regarded by the medical profession as useful in 'cooling the temperament'. Vinegar had other uses, for example it relieved toothache – 'it calms the pain', and 'strengthens the gums'; further, 'it dislodges the leech which has attached itself to the roof of the palate'.[25] Condiments included cooked green vegetables in vinegar, sour grape juice, *sumac* juice, apple juice, rhubarb juice and curdled or clotted milk.[26] Women used these as preservatives in extremes of climate and as a stand-by according to seasonal and other factors.

Dietary rules formulated in Islam and Judaism generally reflected custom and good practice, taking into account climate and ecology, and in *Sura* 2 'carrion, blood and the flesh of swine' were expressly proscribed. It was known that improperly cooked pork presented a health hazard, but its prohibition may have reflected some prejudice on the part of an early pastoral society against the inhabitants of the settled lands and their eating habits. Pork was not eaten by the Christian Copts of Egypt. Women used citrus fruits extensively for seasoning and they were particularly useful in washing poultry to reduce infection.

Ibn Qayyim al-Jawziyya threw an interesting light on the makeup of al-Mas'udi's 'cultivated' persons, and decreed that:

> Scent is the nourishment of the spirit, which is the instrument of the faculties. The faculties are doubled and increase with scent, just as they increase with food and drink, quietness and happiness, the company of those loved . . . and the occurrence of pleasant matters.[27]

Staples

Despite the epithet 'Fertile Crescent', it should be noted that food was not plentiful at all times. Thousands in Baghdad in the mid-tenth century died in a famine, and Miskawayh reported, 'so many were the corpses that they could not be buried in time (and the dogs devoured their flesh).'[28] At times like these, women used their ingenuity to the full to provide food for their families.

There were frequent outcries for the government to impose fixed prices 'upon butchers, bakers and such other merchants whom all the people need', otherwise the populace 'would perish'.[29] The authorities had to acknowledge bread's importance as a staple – indeed the staff of life – for the masses, and the state sought to guarantee the grain supply to the cities, since shortages and price escalation frequently led to outbreaks of civil unrest; this still happens in the Middle East when the price of bread and cooking oil are raised. By 1208 Ibn al-Sa'i wrote that bread had never been so cheap; and in Wasit, Iraq, it was also available at reasonable prices. This begs the question of how many urban women baked their own bread, since it was widely available in the market-place? Salaries and wages in urban areas were frequently augmented by 'in kind' payments of bread and the inference is that bread featured largely in the diet. If this subsidy was necessary for the educated classes, what hope had a woman of limited means of providing a nutritious diet for her family?

Home-made bread, baked in the stove (*tannur*), was much preferred to that from the neighbourhood oven (*furn*) of the baker. There is something immensely satisfying about baking one's own bread, and the women and girls of the household likely all took part, because it was hard and sometimes painful work. This was a lengthy process, especially if the grain had to be pounded and a leavening agent added. For country women, bread-baking was likely to be one of their many chores. Others must have made do with a dough of any quality, cooked on the ashes of a rudimentary fire or a clay griddle.

The ingredients and type of oven differed according to location. The domestic *tannur* was a beehive-shaped stove fuelled preferably by good charcoal, with the heat controlled by vents; it was apparently of ancient Mesopotamian origin Ibn Durayd suggested that *furn* was not an Arabic word, but 'a word of the dialect of Syria'. Bread baked in the *furn* had 'a raised and pointed, or hollowed, head' and sounds as if it was plaited. Bread was fried or roasted, 'then well moistened with milk and clarified butter and sugar'.[30] In short, it had a sweet glaze and was filling, if much less adaptable than plain bread. A Bedouin woman provided a quick meal for people constantly on the move from flour, water and salt. Women's own loaves were likely more irregular in shape and size than bought bread, with a distinctly 'home-made' look, tailored to their individual household requirements and preferences, and dictated by the size of their utensils. Particular types of loaves were produced at various dates in the religious calendars.

There were several types of bread. *Qurs* was a round, flat disc[31] sometimes unleavened. It was about a handspan wide, and one finger thick, and therefore useful in picking up other ingredients of the meal. *Khubzidhan* was classified as 'fine' bread. It was also the most nutritious loaf, and likely the preserve of the better-off. One synonym for white bread, *khubz hawwari*, was *Abu nu'im*, 'Father of Pleasantness'. *Hawwari* emphasised its whiteness with connotations of extra refining and superior quality. Such epithets were coined by the gatecrashers of banquets.

Other fine bread was mostly made from wheat, but chroniclers also mentioned rice-bread and barley-bread. The latter was dark, heavy, of poor quality and prone to crumbling; as such, it would have been difficult to to pick up morsels of meat and other food, and the implication is that barley-bread was the staple fare of poor families and a metaphor for poverty. Ibn Battuta, visiting Latakia in Syria, was appreciative of gifts of warm bread which 'the women have sent to you . . . and beg your prayers'. Was this the sweet *furn*-baked variety, or another Syrian speciality, *rikabi*, an olive-oil bread, which al-Tha'alibi considered excellent? *Rikabi* indicated that it (or perhaps the olives) was transported on the backs of camels or other literal 'riding beasts'. Olive oil made it particularly tasty and wholesome and it accorded well with pious tradition, 'Eat olive oil with your bread, and oil yourselves with it, for it is from a blessed tree.'[32] Women from the poorer classes fed their families bread seasoned with thyme, 'the father of ninety nine remedies', or bread and onions.[33]

Ibn 'Abdun reported that bread in twelfth-century Seville was sold by weight. Sometimes pebbles were added to underweight loaves. Bakers were not above adding inferior dough to an outer layer of better ingredients for the crust, so the baking and crumbs were also subject to inspection by the authorities. These practices persisted in spite of strict regulation in the marketplace, and the thrifty housewife who was forced to buy her bread would have had to be on her mettle when shopping.

Dates formed the basic nourishment of the Bedouin, as well as much of the rural population in the Middle East. Tradition described the date as 'the chief of the fruits of this world' and one of the things brought to earth from Paradise by Adam, and the Prophet regarded them useful in keeping evil spirits at bay. Medina was rightly celebrated for its dates. The famous early eighth-century saintly Sufi ascetic and teacher, Rabi'a al-'Adawiyya of Basra, resigned herself to the will of God and celebrated her extreme poverty as a means of inward purification. When her friend Sufyan Thawri visited her when she was ill and anxiously asked her, 'O Rabi'a, what is your desire?' she replied:

> I swear by the glory of God that for twelve years I have desired fresh dates, and you know that in Basra dates are plentiful, and I have not yet tasted them.[34]

This touchingly revealed the depth of Rabi'a's devotion and indigence, since the small hollow at the centre of the date stone was used as a metaphor for extreme poverty. One poor man possessed 'neither a thread of a date-stone, nor the cavity that contains it'.[35]

Honest fare was relished in the highest social circles. One poet delighted in a dish of 'little dates like pearls, that glisten on a necklace one by one'. and the versatile loaf of bread was eulogised. At a court banquet a poet quoted the famous ninth-century writer Ibn al-Rumi, who praised a dish of fowl which included among the ingredients 'a pair of loaves, of finest wheat, the like of which on earth was never seen'.[36] This meal was beautifully presented and reminded one of '*washi* cloth of Yemen', that is a type of shot silk, with different colours sometimes threaded with gold. The description of the visual effect referred to the layering, the *wast*, which simply means 'in the middle of'. Yet gourmet food palled for Maysun, a caliph's wife and a country girl at heart, who said wistfully, I'd rather have breadcrumbs in my own house than a whole loaf in a palace.[37] Maysun was not alone in her delight in plain fare; the *Na'ib* of Aleppo, Tashtimur al-Badri was nicknamed *Himmis Akhdar* because of his predilection for green chickpeas, a decidedly lower-class meal. After the publication of *Wusla al-habib*, mutton fat appeared in menus, and the elite in Mamluk times savoured fat sheep's tail. These were basic foods elevated to the realms of *haute cuisine* by skilful adaptation and the addition of expensive spices and flavourings.

The masses at the lower end of the social scale had no recourse to *haute cuisine*, but ate cheap and sustaining derivatives of cereals such as types of wheat, millet and barley, pulse vegetables, dates and dairy products, all of which formed the staples of a restricted and simple diet. Wheat was the basic crop in the Middle East, and a *hadith* described 'an ear of wheat, which is the chief food of the world' as one of the three things which Adam brought from Paradise. Women prepared *burghul* by boiling, then drying and cracking wheat grains. A Syrian folk saying runs, 'Good living is with rice, and let the *burghul* bury itself.'

Women preserved their clarified butter in earthenware jars suspended from the ceiling, and they concocted many basic dishes based on a stock or broth thickened with a variety of cereals. For example, flour was mixed with water or milk and corn was roasted. Contemporary dictionaries defined *harira* as 'a kind of soup of flour and grease or gravy, or flour cooked with milk; when this was of the thickest consistency it was known as '*asida*, then *najira*, then *harira*, then *hasw*'.[38] *Khatifa*, a dish made with milk, was heated; flour was then sprinkled on it and cooked. It was evidently of a thick consistency. The dictionaries suggest it was eaten with the fingers or a spoon, and there is also a notion of it being hastily 'snatched up'. Was this because it was relished, or was it a quick, filling meal for someone with little time to spare or with scant interest in a dish that was served with monotonous regularity? One surely added other ingredients for flavouring these very simple meals.

Women transformed parched barley meal (*sawiq*) another staple, by adding milk or water. *Sawiq* in its original form was a gruel made with clarified butter or the fat from a sheep's tail, but sugar and dates could be added. A variation of *sawiq* using the versatile chick pea was available in the market-place. Bread softened with mutton fat, which was perhaps cheaper than refined cooking oil and more filling, provided another simple nutritious meal. *Khazir* was a soup with seven ingredients, rather like *'asida*, but with the addition of meat. Salt was added and when it was thoroughly cooked some flour was sprinkled into it. According to the sources, 'it is stirred about with it, and seasoned with any seasoning that the maker pleases to add'.

However simple, these dishes were sustaining and required little in the way of fuel. They had the added advantage of no elaborate preparation, and suited women with limited time and resources who had to work outside their homes. Unfortunately, for many women and their families, there was little element of choice in their diets.

Nomads seldom ate meat, but captured game, including quail, partridge, hare and gazelle, from time to time. Meat was smoked over a domestic fire, and it was also sun-dried; preserves were stored in sheepskin pouches and could easily be reconstituted with liquid. Either method of preserving also made it ideal for the traveller or nomad. Truffles (*kama'*) were plentiful after storms, when the desert soil was washed away, and the Bedouin aptly called them 'thunder plants'.[39] They ranged in shade from dust-colour to red, and were eaten cooked or raw; one red type was deadly poisonous. Truffles added a touch of variety to a monotonous diet of bread, dates and other fruit, and would be eagerly sought by the women and children gathering firewood and forage. Were truffles the *manna* in the Bible which God sent for the children of Israel? In Arabian towns, meat dishes were sometimes served with black truffles which Bedouin women took into the markets to sell. They were possibly a luxury there and, as such, might command a good price and provide a fair, if irregular, source of income for the Bedouin women. Despite any presumed social cachet, the physician Ibn Qayyim al-Jawziyya professionally observed: 'They [truffles] are called the smallpox of the earth because they resemble the shape and substance of smallpox [*judari*].'[40] The Prophet prescribed their juice for the treatment of eye ailments.

Al-Yaqut the geographer observed that in thirteenth century Wasit, Iraq, dairy products were very reasonably priced; one could purchase a jar of fresh butter or twelve *artal* of salted or clarified butter for two dirhams, while one hundred and fifty *artal* of sour milk cost 'only' one dirham. However, al-Yaqut is not addressing the average housewife as consumer and one wonders what the poor made of these prices? Women took their home-produced dairy products into the market, and their wares reflected their social status. These were pastoralists with some animals and the use, at least, of a parcel of land, who nevertheless sold their butter to supplement the family income. Peasant women made cheese from their ewes' milk and pilgrims and travellers were fortified by a snack of cheese and almonds. Bedouin women used camel milk. The majority of people only ate meat literally on high days and holidays, such as the great religious feasts, the anniversary of a death and perhaps the celebration of other rites of passage.

Western travellers to Cairo around 1350 were amazed at the many

low buildings like ovens; in them are furnaces, wherein eggs are laid upon dung, and by this heat chickens are hatched. The master then takes them to an old woman, who nurses and cherishes the chicken in her bosom. There are numberless old women in those parts who have no means of livelihood save by nursing and taking care of chickens.[41]

This method of chicken rearing in the spring had persisted from ancient times and evidently played a prominent role in the Egyptian economy. Lane elaborated on the highly-technical practice last century. Each hatchery received 'about a hundred and fifty thousand eggs . . . one quarter or a third of which number' failed to hatch. Local peasants took their eggs to the superintendent and received one chicken in return for two of their eggs. Lane reported: 'I have not found that the fowls produced in this manner are inferior in point of flavour, or in other respects, to those produced from the egg by incubation,' adding that 'most of the superintendents, if not all, are Copts'.[42] Ordinary housewives cooked the rich giblets scorned by the affluent in sauces, aubergine stews and *harisa* with chick peas.

Ready-cooked food

At lunchtime many men engaged in trade and commerce frequently ate reasonably priced meals in shops and taverns. Ready-cooked food is not a modern phenomenon; it was available in the medieval market-place (*suq al-shawa'in*), and the name indicated that the shopkeepers or stall-holders offered a variety of broiled, fried or roasted meats. These establishments were patronised exclusively by men, like modern day coffee-shops, and it is unlikely that the cooks were women. A contemporary account of a cookshop meal detailed roast meat, fine wheaten bread and *sumac*. *Sumac* was a wild bush grown in rocky Mediterranean-climate areas and its bitter seeds were dried and ground, then mixed with thyme and used as seasoning. Too much *sumac* made the food unacceptably dark. The bread was toasted and topped with sliced roast meat and gravy. Despite tight restrictions on commercial activities in general, an eleventh-century source mentioned a greengrocer's in the exclusive quarter of Baghdad, *Bab al-maratib,* with a grill for roasting aubergines at the front of a shop.[43]

Ibn Battuta, on his travels in the 1320s in Damascus, reported that 'Most of the people there eat no food but what has been prepared in the market'. This was possibly due to fuel costs and severe weather. Tiles, stone or earth floors were the norm, and poor homes only had rudimentary matting. On the other hand, German pilgrims en route to the Holy Land in the late fifteenth century were surprised at the large numbers of vendors of hot food in Cairo. Breydenbach was informed that there were some twelve thousand in the streets.[44] Refined people, in the view of al-Washsha', did not deign to patronise the shop of 'a mincer of meats and pies'. Some might consider eating in public shameful, but it may have been less to do with social mores than public health concerns. Minced meat was notoriously prone to contamination, and one never knew what went into pies. The Prophet reportedly did not eat food kept overnight and reheated.

Even poor people ate ready-made food, and the inference must be that it was relatively cheap, that women in the lower classes did little cooking, and workers returning home in the evening perhaps carried it in. How much of this resulted from the fact that many women were forced to work outside the home? Others preferred their wives' home-cooking for, as al-Tawhidi said: 'The fraternity of the present time resembles the broth of the cook in the bazaar, fragrant, but tasteless.'[45]

Were there cooking facilities in modest living quarters? Large houses certainly had kitchens, perhaps even more than one. Sometimes there was a cistern with a tap and a kitchen sink, all on the ground floor. Kitchens were also, according to al-Jahiz often 'in the upper storeys, upon the surfaces of the terraces'. He may have referred to apartment-houses. The *tannur* was not used solely for baking bread, and a variety of meals was cooked in it. A well-equipped kitchen often had a brick-built hearth or fire-place (*mustawqid*) about three feet high, capable of taking several pots and pans. This could only have been the preserve of better-off women who had a large variety of cooking utensil, the means to buy the fuel, and large quantities of food. Al-Hamadhani's boastful merchant, who resided in a choice area of Baghdad, painted an amusing picture of his wife:

Thou shouldst see her in person strap on her apron, run through the mansion from oven to cauldron from cauldron to pot, puff up the fire good and hot. Grind in the spices piping hot; And see the smoke begrime her pretty face, on her polished cheek leave a long sooty trace.[46]

To the uxorious husband she was 'A sight simply to make one's eyes race!' Al-Hamadhani wrote for a bourgeois audience familiar with the locale of the tale, and confirmed that even well-to-do wives did the cooking themselves, doubtless with help in the kitchen from servants or household slaves. But his account was a literary device: the point of the tale was the title, *Al-Madira*, (*The Stew*), because the narrator had the effrontery to decline a portion of *madira*, a great delicacy, in order to to cut his boastful host down to size. *Madira* was prepared with cubed lamb and so named because it was cooked slowly in sour milk, which gave it a sharp taste and 'bit' the tongue. It was initially a traditional dish involving the use of left over milk which had turned sour. Ibrahim al-Mahdi adapted it at court by adding aubergines, and in time it too evolved into a classic Arab meal popular among the bourgeoisie. One poet rhapsodised:

Madira on the festive tray Is like the moon in full array:
Upon the board it gleams in light Like sunshine banishing the night.[47]

There was probably a rudimentary cooking space, at least, somewhere in or around even the poorest of homes, where a fire was lit and a cooking pot placed on stones. In al-Hariri's seventh tale Abu Zayd acknowledged the indispensability of his long-suffering wife by referring to her as 'the third prop of the trivet'; unfortunately this was not a compliment. The thrifty al-Kindi complained that despite a landlord placing in a corner 'a stone slab for them to grind upon', women ruined his floor, using their mortars and pestles wherever it took their fancy'.[48]

Fuel

The women of the household always attended to the fire. Flint was set to touchwood or iron sulphur. The alternative was to leave the fire dampened down at night, and rekindle the charcoal in the brazier in the morning. A character in al-Jahiz's *Kitab al-bukhala'* (*The Book of Misers*) revealed how this was done:

We strove with tinder and flint, but when the stone's edge flaked off and turned dull, the thing became worthless and would not strike its proper spark; only a barren clod that might not ignite.[49]

Dyed rags were no good for tinder, which was prepared from plain old linen or cotton clothing. Itinerant fan-makers peddled date-palm fronds and matches, little sticks of trimmed wood smeared with sulphur. These men were blind, and hence had free access to women at home (but how could their disability be any guarantee of their morals or those of the women?). Another method of kindling a fire was to insert a burning rag into small coals in the aptly-named *jawwala*, a tiny brass pierced basket on a chain which was 'whirled around' until it glowed. It is no surprise that 'fire' in Arabic is a metaphor for 'hospitality', implying as it does much effort and the prospect of a cooked meal for the unexpected guest.

Wood or charcoal was another basic commodity for the Arab housewife and prices were also a factor in determining whether she cooked at home or bought in food from the *suq*. Fuel also constituted an 'in kind' payment in the 'Abbasid period. For example, even a lecturer in the Mustansiriyya college in Baghdad in 1234 received 'firewood' as part of his salary. A *ratl* (pl. *artal*) of poor quality charcoal in 1246 in Damascus cost six dirhams so it is likely that women among the masses who provided meals other than bread for their families cooked stews or broths in one large pan, which they filled out with bread, as necessary, although it should be borne in mind that far less hot food was consumed generally than is the case in modern times. *Ratl* was used interchangeably for both dry and liquid measures with an approximation of one *ratl* equalling one pound or one pint.

In the home of a ninth-century physician, 'there were screened gratings of wood beyond screened gratings of iron, and braziers within which there burned embers from the wood of the *ghada'* tree.'[50]

Ghada', a particular type of wood of the euphorbia variety from Najd, produced a superior charcoal which retained its heat. It was slow-burning and as such, a fitting metaphor for 'lasting sorrow' in classical Arabic. *Ghada'* was undoubtedly expensive, but other woods were available. For the wedding feast of the Caliph al-Ma'mun, 'They cut palm wood that was still damp, and poured thereon grease and olive oil that it might ignite'.[51] A poet sang:

Lubayna, light the fire! He whom you love has gone astray. Many the fire I've watched by night that nibbled the aloe wood and laurel.[52]

In rural areas, and according to location, wood from palm and olive trees was used, and cow dung also served as fuel. Bedouin women gathered thorn bushes in the desert and *'ufar* and *markh* woods were popular, since they were easily set alight when rubbed. Nothing was – or indeed could be – wasted among the desert-dwellers, and the women also used dried dates as fuel.

Those women who either had no kitchens or perhaps could not afford fuel were able to use the additional service provided by the local baker, and delivered their earthenware dishes in the morning to be placed around the embers of his oven. There they would simmer slowly and be picked up in the evening, after work. A typical meal was cheaper cuts of meat such as mutton using onions, chick-peas or haricot beans in a sort of *pot au feu*. This obviated the need for a variety of cooking utensils. This is pertinent, since many of the lower classes rented property which was probably cramped and cheap. Al-Baghdadi set out a recipe for *tannuriya*, evidently an all-purpose stew of lamb or veal seasoned with salt, cinnamon bark, coriander and dill and 'put into the oven (*tannur*) until the following morning'. It was dressed with breadcrumbs and sprinkled with cinnamon and cummin.[53]

Cooking utensils

Few women possessed what al-Jahiz described as 'Fine, translucent pottery used for cooking purposes; a piece of this may be used equally for boiling things, for frying or simply as a dish for eating from.'[54]

According to al-Baghdadi, the best pots were made of 'stone', which conserved the heat. These were ideal for long slow and economic cooking of a tasty family meal, and tough old meat was rendered tender. Many cooking pots and pans came from Persia. Tus produced white stone pots and frying pans, as well as drinking and other vessels as a substitute for glass.[55] Stone pots were not available everywhere, and other types were made from baked clay or lead. Sughd was well known for its kitchen wares and fine copperware was manufactured in Herat and exported all over the Muslim world. Very large pots were manufactured in Merv, and the quality of Syrian pans was acknowledged. Around the year 1320 Ibn Battuta visited a man 'of humble station' in Syria whose daughter was about to be married. It was the custom there to give copper household utensils as wedding gifts; these must have been costly, since they were stipulated in marriage contracts, presumably to guarantee their return in the event of divorce.[56] Apart from being desirable items for any new bride's kitchen, they were an important economic marker. Copper pans heated up very quickly, a great advantage where fuel was relatively scarce or expensive. Since many of these items were specialities of various lands, they reflected the local and regional cuisine. They possibly also signalled the adoption and local adaptation of dishes from elsewhere.

Al-Baghdadi outlined the sizes of cooking pots. For example the *'ashar* was an enormous vessel, and the name suggests ten times the normal size. These came into their own at large family gatherings to celebrate marriages, and for the two great feasts at the end of Ramadhan and the *hajj*. Juha, an Arab folk-hero and trickster, borrowed a heavy cauldron of fine copper for a dinner of whole lamb stew with rice stuffing.[57]

There was a high level of material culture in al-Andalus, where women had a wide choice of kitchen utensils which included pressure cookers with safety valves. It is very noticeable that their kitchen wares, while similar in shape and form to metalwork from elsewhere in the Islamic world, were mostly in pottery, despite the fact that minerals were mined in the Iberian Peninsula. This must have had some bearing on local cuisine as well as the availability of fuel. Metal is a good conductor of heat and therefore useful for quick cooking where fuel was at a premium, whereas food in pottery dishes could cook over a long period. Climate also played its part; casserole-type meals were more sustaining during severe winters.

Regional variations

The *Kanz* (*Treasury*, suggesting a hoard of special recipes) demonstrated a keen interest in the use of spices. Here, in a compendium produced in Egypt, there were few of the elaborate eastern garnishes, and perfumes were extensively used. Although Ibn Razin al-Tujibi, writing in fourteenth-century al-Andalus, included some recipes from the eastern Islamic world, his dishes were for the most part based on the culinary traditions of the west, the Maghrib and al-Andalus.[58] The title of his work, *Fadalat al-khiwan fi tayyibat al-ta'am wa'l-alwan*, confirmed this, and is evocative of food spread on a table (*khiwan*) to delight the eye through colours (*alwan*). Elaborate platters were aptly compared to gardens, and the combination of perfume and colour recalled Paradise. Later cookbooks referred to food as 'green', 'black' or 'white'. *Tharid*, the meat broth eaten with bread, was classified as a 'white' dish and this undoubtedly referred to the bread.

Arabic is particularly rich in colour terminology with direct affiliations with the plants, for example saffron and yellow and pistachio and green.[59] Women coloured dishes with green obtained from cumin, yellow from turmeric and red from sumac. Even the sight of food cooking caused one guest in al-Andalus to enthuse:

> Watching the movement of the birds with their heads up and down, together with white and black chick peas and green fennel, is one of the most marvellous and good things (to be seen).[60]

Anticipation was all, especially for a carousing session in the middle of a cold southern European winter. In southern Spain, older influences from Arab cuisine persisted during the sixteenth century. Indeed, it may be that the name of the modern dish *paella* is a corruption of the Arabic *baqiya* meaning 'remainder', which was prepared by the servants from the leftover food of their masters.

There was a wide choice of fruit in the markets. Melons and pomegranates were sold in panniers, and one source mentioned melons imported from Persia in lead containers packed with snow. Pomegranates of the sort called 'smooth skinned', or 'fiery coloured' came from Rayy in Persia, and grapes were sent to markets in baskets. Did the women weave the baskets? Apparently arguments always broke out between the vendors and purchasers, who demanded to know the condition of the fruit underneath the outer display. Nothing changes. This would be one reason why women selling in the market-place had to present a tough face to customers. Figs and grapes were classified with dates as 'the chief of fruits', and figs from Jurjan were noted for their outstanding quality. In Ifriqiya women purchased figs 'sold in earthenware jars wherein they were tightly packed'. Prunes were imported from Balkh, and al-Tha'alibi considered Syrian apples 'excellent'. Ibn Battuta saw in the Damascus *suq*, 'shops of the candlemakers and a gallery for the sale of fruit'. A Maghrebi account around the beginning of the fifteenth century mentioned an astonishing number of varieties of figs, grapes, pears and apricots. All of these depended on the skill of irrigation by men and the harvesting by women and their children, but one must ask how much of these products were available to ordinary women?

Women used sesame or olive oil according to local availability. In Baghdad and Old Cairo, Iran and Turkestan cooking in sesame oil was the norm. Elsewhere, in Syria and Tunisia for example, olives were grown and there were numerous pressing mills.[61] One point should be noted concerning non-Muslims. Jews were prohibited from using animal fat, so yoghurt and butter were absent from their diet. Cooking oil was sold around the doors from donkey-carts. It would be interesting to know if the absence of animal fat among the Jewish community positively affected their health, and if their Muslim neighbours suffered adverse effects. Or was the general level of sustenance and therefore the fat content rather low in any event? The Jewish Sabbath was also different to the Muslim weekend, and Jewish women could not cook on Saturdays, so if hot food was required it had to be prepared the night before and somehow kept warm. Did they call on servants or neighbours of another faith to tend the fire for them on the Sabbath, as certainly happened later in Europe? Generally speaking, Jewish and Christian women probably cooked similar dishes to their Muslim neighbours, but special foods exclusive to their communities were served at ritual meals and religious festivals, for example the biscuits known as 'Haman's ears' for Jewish children at the festival of Purim.

Iraqi women considered Tigris fish most superior, but that even fish from the Euphrates was better than that from the Nile. How were the rivers of populous cities kept free from sewage contamination? Fish was fried, roasted or pickled, or salted, and small fish (*sumayka*') were dried. Dried, crushed and sieved *sumac* was used instead of vinegar or lemon when cooking fish, and its colouring qualities made it particularly useful for white fish.

Women made soft drinks at home. These must have been freshly prepared, given the high sugar content, because fermentation very quickly took place. A wide choice of brightly-coloured cold drinks was available in the market-place from stalls with coloured drapes, gaily lit with lanterns. They sold sherbets, yoghurt and beer. 'Sherbet' is from the Arabic root 'to drink' and has passed into English.

The availability of many food items varied according to location and climate, proximity to the extensive trading networks which by the tenth century the Muslims had made their own, and the like. By this time too prosperity was such that gold was established as the currency standard in Baghdad. Trade obviously offered and reflected a comfortable lifestyle for some. The estate of one notable in 904 included shops at the Damascus Gate worth three thousand dinars.

Sometimes there was a room for animals near the house, perhaps a donkey, cow or goat, and fowl would have run around scraping in many a courtyard, perhaps fed by women and children on almonds, other shelled nuts and milk. Fresh milk and eggs were always available for those families. Eleventh- and twelfth-century accounts noted that hens were cheap in the market;[62] again one must bear in mind the writer's audience. Fowls could never have been reasonably priced for many housewives and for some, a chicken was a real luxury. A Tunisian folk-tale told how a man of modest means asked his wife to cook a plump fowl with saffron and cardomom until nicely browned. She demanded to know, 'How can we think of indulging ourselves like princes?' Nevertheless he presented it to the ruler, and set it out on two flat loaves.

For women in the countryside and the outskirts of towns, their land provided at least a level of subsistence by way of vegetables, milk, cheese, eggs and meat. Their diet was arguably better and more varied than that of many townspeople, although this would have depended on the severity of the prevailing land-tax in kind (*kharaj*) which they paid to the state, the amount of produce they were forced to sell in the market and family size. Women travelled to the markets to sell their home-grown produce, and probably took children to help them. Perhaps there was an element of barter with city-dwellers for essential items unavailable in the country? But city women sold cinders from their fires as fertiliser to market-gardeners in the suburbs. Animal droppings were also utilised, and one wonders if the contents of cesspools and privies which were usually collected at night in large urban areas were also used as fertiliser? Finding fuel would not have been such a major concern for country women, and it is possible that they cooked more to satisfy the taxing physical labour of life on the land.

Courgettes, melons, cucumbers and watermelons were all grown in market gardens, as well as many fragrant herbs and plants to vary the diet, for example mustard, rue (which was something of an all-purpose remedy) aniseed, cumin, basil, oregano, marjoram, coriander and absinthe. Pepper and ginger were added to the usual repertoire of mint, lettuce, coriander and so forth. Aubergine, as now, was widely used. Townswomen therefore had a large variety of everyday culinary ingredients at their disposal, but did they themselves do the shopping, or was this done by their menfolk? Whatever the case, they would have decided what they needed. Even today in the *suq* many men on their return from work buy produce to take home. There were undoubtedly peddlers hawking foodstuffs at fairs and in the market-place. It would have been fairly easy for a woman to do a large batch of baking or sweet-making, take as many items as it was possible to carry, and dispose of them fairly quickly before the inspectors made their rounds.

Confectionery was very popular, and there were booths in all towns. Excellent *halwa*, a very rich dish based on flour, yeast and honey, contained a base of wild white honey from Persia from particular tamarind trees, and chopped almonds and pistachios. Ordinary *halwa* had nuts in it, but the cheapest kind was mixed with poppy seeds. The name indicates 'pleasantness', 'agreeableness' and it was a treat. Women made their own sweetmeats at home from the assorted ingredients in the market. Honey, which was expensive, rice flour, sugared almonds and barley sugar were all displayed on leather plates. Sugarcane had been introduced from eastern lands and was cultivated in Iraq, India and Gurgan. One reads too of the sugar from Ahwaz province 'whose excellence and extensive production are without equal in the rest of the world'. The versatile chick pea was also used in sweet-making.

Acetic acid was produced by a fairly lengthy technical process. Medieval dictionaries described vinegar *(khall)* variously as being the 'expressed juice of grapes' and also 'of dates'. Women and others who were not ultra-pious would have agreed with Ibn Durayd in the eighth century that 'the best is that of wine'. Vinegar formed the basis of many sauces served between courses and it was very useful in tenderising tough meaty fibres; this had the additional advantage of reducing the cooking time. *Na'na' mukhallal*, a sauce prepared with mint, celery leaves, garlic, vinegar and saffron, was ready when the vinegar lost its tartness. Spices, both indigenous and imported from Asia, were also invaluable in food preservation. They were not necessarily cheap, but many women and families in the poorest classes literally lived from hand to mouth and day to day, and food for immediate consumption would only have been bought as money came in. These women simply had not the means to put something by for hard times or as a convenience.

Al-Tha'alibi reported that Jamila, daughter of Nasir al-Dawla, took fresh green vegetables in earthenware containers on her journey from Baghdad to Mecca on the pilgrimage. This journey took a considerable time by camel, and one wonders how they were preserved? They were probably regularly topped up with water which cooled by evaporation through the porous surface of the vessels.

While other condiments were dispensable, salt *(milh)* as a preservative and adjunct to taste was not. Salt, like bread 'the staff of life' was proverbial. Even the term in English 'worth one's salt' implies it was highly valued. Salt also had many entries in the ancient Arabic dictionaries, with connotations of suckling an infant, that is something basic and vital; one's inviolable bond, and the rites and obligations of friendship which rated so highly in the old Bedouin values.[63] Salt was also a theme in early Arabic poetry.

Al-Jahiz, refererring to the citizens of Baghdad, mentioned 'a kind of jar or jug bored with a hole in the middle in which was inserted a tube of silver or lead, through which they drank'. This muffled crock (*muzammala*) was so-called because:

> It was wrapped in sackcloth or some other material which held in place a layer of straw tight against the body of the earthenware; this was much used in summer days. Water stored at night in cool places was then poured into such 'muffled crocks', where it stayed chilled.[64]

Fetching and carrying water was women's work. The 'cool places' probably referred to the huge earthenware jars of water which were placed in a through draught, perhaps under a staircase or wind-shaft. As the water evaporated, it cooled itself and the surrounding circulating air. Another cool place was the *mashrabiyya*, literally 'place of drinking' in houses, a sort of oriel window with carved wooden latticework where the ladies sat in comfort, unseen, and watched the street life.

Many of the classic dishes of Arab cuisine evolved from basic foodstuffs and the cooking methods of ordinary women everywhere via the bourgeoisie and the court and the great variety of ingredients increasingly available. Persian and other influences were evident from the names of dishes, and slave women from other regions added literally to the 'melting-pot' at court and in ordinary households. Pilgrims and scholars from diverse Muslim lands also played their part, to the extent that the cosmopolitan cooking of Mecca reflected their presence.

Hospitality and etiquette

We turn now to *qira al-dayf*, 'the nourishment of guests'. The principle of hospitality which ruled in the desert was elevated in society in general almost to the rank of sacred duty. It was originally borne out of the recognition by the traveller in the hostile environment that 'There but for the grace of God . . .' Hospitality was an ever-present reminder of Allah as Protector and Provider, and the prophet Abraham, he who entertained the angels and the poor, was the paradigm for the liberal host. The personal example of the Prophet Muhammad enshrined in the *Traditions* also played a major role in Arab etiquette and hospitality. For example, he paid particular care to posture when eating, to aid digestion, and sat 'simply' and ate 'as a servant'.[65] Tradition has it that, 'The most excellent way of eating is that adopted by the Prophet and those who follow him, with three fingers.'[66]

'Eating with one finger or with two does not allow the one eating to derive pleasure'. Muhammad always ate something in the evening, if only a few dates, and pronounced that, 'To abandon the evening meal is a cause of ageing'. According to a *Tradition*, 'He who loves Allah and His messenger should be generous to his guest'. Allah 'loves generosity'[67] and the stingy host was much deprecated. The Prophet asked Duba'a bint al-Zubayr to feed a group of people. She 'slaughtered a sheep in her house' (presumably this referred to the precincts), but was ashamed that all that remained for the Messenger of God was the neck. The Prophet reassured her: 'Send it to me, for it is the front part of the sheep, the nearest to what is good and the furthest from harm.'[68]

This probably alludes, to ritual purity and was a sympathetic gesture to alleviate the woman's embarrassment. The Prophet enjoined:

God loves kindness in all (human) actions. Let the man who is to slaughter a sheep therefore sharpen his knife, so that he may deliver that living creature from pain sooner.[69]

Under the Islamic rules of ritual slaughter, Duba'a would have invoked the name of Allah over the lamb. Women in nineteenth-century Egypt intoned over the beast: 'In the name of God! God is most Great! God give thee patience to endure the affliction which He hath allotted thee!'[70]

Meanness was the subject of many an aphorism in literature and al-Jahiz of Basra collected numerous tales on this theme. An early poem summed up popular sentiment, 'May Allah curse the ungiving even if he fasts and prays'. One should note that this literature was for public, male consumption; nevertheless the rules of etiquette and right conduct prevailed in any social gathering. Women were similarly constrained and were always under pressure to prepare a good spread for visitors.

Guests were offered shelter and hospitality whether or not it was convenient, and it followed that social custom dictated the design of the Arab home. *Bayt* was used both for 'house' and by the Bedouin to describe their tented home. A notable feature was the division into private (female) and public (male) spheres when offering hospitality to people who were not closely related. Entertainment, as elsewhere, was done in the 'best room', and the guest no less than the host or hostess was bound by a strict set of rules prescribed by canon law.

A *Tradition* confirmed that among the Bedouin, where life itself depended on food and shelter, a visitor was at liberty to approach the nearest tent, whether or not there were men of the family present, and the womenfolk immediately settled the guest and prepared food. No questions were asked by either party, and even the unexpected guest was welcomed profusely. A contemporary manuscript illustrated this to perfection; it depicted unveiled women bustling in and out of a tent with large trays of food, while outside their menfolk were slaughtering a camel to honour the travellers.[71] In the event, there was always a number of women around and any visitor who overstepped the mark and abused his host's household did so in peril of his life.

Imad al-Isfahani discovered when he joined Sultan Salah al-Din in Damascus:

> The tablecloth was spread out; the carpet rolled out, tables were made ready; deep dishes were lined up. The cooks presented sheep, fowls, very sweet, fiery, acidic, with no particular flavour, stinging, boiled, roasted, already-made, fried foods.[72]

All this came from the equivalent of a field kitchen. This incident, of course, took place in illustrious company, but a touching tale in al-Hariri's *Maqamat* is reminiscent of the parable of the widow's mite. The meanness of the indigent old man's home, 'narrower than the booth of Moses, more fragile than a spider's web', was in inverse proportion to his hospitality, and he offered the narrator a dish of fresh ripe dates and rich cream. This bears out what many westerners know from personal experience, that the hospitality of the Arabs is rightly renowned.

Social status based on such behaviour and the extent of one's hospitality was closely related to the honour of the family. Hospitality bound together host and guest in mutual obligation. Nothing was more welcome to the hungry wayfarer than the sight of a fire, and in some cases whole tribes became proverbial for their liberality. Ibn Khallikan's *Biographical Dictionary (Wafayat al-a'yan wa anba' abna' al-zaman)* cited a poem by Ibn Mammati in praise of the hospitality of the Bani Muhallab.

> How brightly his fires burn at night to attract the tardy guest! He who draweth to the light of his fire will not have reason to complain, provided he never received hospitality from the family of Muhallab.[73]

That was the desert context, where the women's presence and contributions to the entertainment of male guests were openly acknowledged, but the situation was very different in the settled lands. Men entertained in the *majlis* in their homes, the 'place of sitting', which on that occasion was for their exclusive use. One is struck by the meat content of meals served at male gatherings. These indicated the host's social status, and underlined his role as generous and honourable provider. However, there is no doubt that the power of women, albeit unseen, held sway here, for they were ultimately responsible for the spread. Platters of food were set on a floor covering. This was often simply of woven matting, but leather mats were also used to prevent food spillages on expensive rugs. In official accounts, at least, men consumed alcohol, despite religious condemnation. The Prophet reportedly said, 'All evil was assembled in one room and locked in and the key to it was drunkenness'.[74] It is unlikely that respectable women drank alcohol, but the situation was probably different with singing-girls and others at court.

After the fabulously wealthy jeweller Ibn al-Jassas was arrested by the Caliph al-Muqtadir, an inventory of the contents of his house revealed seven hundred water coolers (these were apparently reed-covered). The compiler exclaimed admiringly: 'Think of the hospitality of a man among whose goods such a quantity of these articles is to be found!'[75] (He might have commented on the women's work behind the scenes to entertain on such a scale.) Such anecdotes were appreciatively traded at refined male social gatherings. They were not invariably complimentary, and it is ironic to think that when transposed to female settings they were probably condemned by men as 'gossip'.

Women's visits were also closely linked to food and drink, with the addition of the reciprocal exchange of small gifts, but there was apparently a much greater variety of dishes and meat was not served. Did everyone take some food along to the gathering? Men did not provide the wherewithal for these events, which were much more informal than male gatherings. This was women's entertainment for women, and they set great store on the appearance of food, presumably using fancy garnishes and colouring agents. There were set ways of arranging assorted dried fruits and a wide selection of nuts and fresh fruit, for example in pyramids, in bowls or on metal or pottery platters with indentations. These can be seen in contemporaty illustrated manuscripts. Alcohol was not served at women's gatherings, but sherbets made from sugar, fruit juices and water were to hand.

There was undoubtedly an element of competition concerning women's culinary offerings which would, in time, contribute to the refinement of the local diet. This would also be apparent in the time women spent on their appearance, and their display of cosmetics and jewellery. Refined women did not offer their visitors fruit with stones, chestnuts, figs or dried raisins (known colloquially as 'goat droppings'). Men, apparently, had no such qualms; *ta'ifi* raisins from Herat were a great delicacy, praised by a poet in the following words:

> How often do the topers enjoy a dessert of *ta'ifi* raisins brought in with the wine! When they are placed in a flagon, it appears like a flask of garnet filled with honey.[76]

When such effort was expended on a guest's behalf, the guest was no less expected to reciprocate.

Women burned aromatics including incense and aloe wood (*'ud*) in pierced metal braziers to create a pleasing ambience when emtertaining in their homes. Fragrances were believed to be overt expressions of purification and reinforced the state of ritual purity. The Prophet recommended the use of scent. His perfume (*sukka*) was ground, and generally made from musk and *ramik*, a black pitch-like substance. There was one further important quality of perfume, it had 'this special characteristic that the angels like it, but the demons flee from it'.[77] On arrival, guests were offered braziers to perfume their clothes and hair.

In large houses the scene was set by the light of candles, often perfumed, in heavy, floor-based candlesticks, and guests washed their hands in a ewer and basin set. The basin had a perforated removable cover to ensure that the water used for handwashing would not be seen by subsequent guests, underscoring once more notions of impurity.

The use of a toothpick was not obligatory; it was, however, commended as one of the prescriptions of 'natural religion'. According to the Prophet, 'The *siwak* is a means of purifying the mouth, pleasing to the Lord' and he recommended its use before prayer. A *Tradition* related that as the Prophet lay dying with his head in 'A'isha's lap, her cousin came to visit, bringing a sliver of green wood as a toothpick which the Prophet took and used.[78] Ibn Battuta noticed women in fourteenth-century Mecca using toothpicks of green *arak* wood; this is interesting – did he share a meal in female company? Al-Hariri's silver-tongued Abu Zayd even described a toothpick metaphorically as a refined woman: 'Elegant in form, attractive, provocative of appetite, delicate as an emaciated lover, polished as a sword, and supple as a green bough.'[79]

The passing round of rosewater sprinklers for the hands at the end of a

meal signalled that the guests should leave. Al-Sari sang the praises of glass
rosewater flasks from Jur:

> How many slender (flagons) like doe-eyed virgins, with their shifts
> wound round them,
> as if they were sweet-scented wallflowers![80]
>
> I am the rose of Damascus, queen among flowers
> I weep that my tears become an essence in your long-necked bottles.

These bottles were attractive household ornaments.

The perfect guest (and the host) was mindful of the injunction in Sura 33:
'When you are invited, enter; and when you have taken your meal, disperse,
not seeking familiar talk.' Visitors were again invited to perfume their hair
and clothes. What might seem a pleasant ritual to banish the odours of food
and freshen one's clothes and person was possibly also connected to a notion
of pollution. At smart hotels around the Arabian Gulf today incense burners
are brought forward by waiters.

Food and ritual

The sociability and co-operation of women and their binding together by
food was given great rein at rites of passage. Special dishes were prepared and
formally offered as a condolence, and a *hadith* concerning the Prophet's wife
'A'isha told how:

> Whensoever someone from her own people died, the women would
> gather together for that reason; when all had dispersed except for her
> family and close friends, she would order an earthenware pot of *talbina*
> to be cooked, then a soup *(tharid)* would be made, and the *talbina* poured
> over it.[81]

Talbina was the nutritious thin gruel cooked with ground barley
recommended by Ibn Qayyim al-Jawziyya the physician. It resembled
yoghurt, and it was poured over the *tharid*. One Arab folk-tale poignantly
held that there was 'no cauldron but has cooked the meal of mourning', with
the implication of communality, while another ran: 'Sister we used the large
cauldron to cook the rice for the people who came to weep with us when my
husband died.'[82]

Other foods, such as the gourd *dubba'*, were recognised as being appropriate on these occasions, and the Prophet one day reminded 'A'isha: 'When you cook a cauldron of food, put in plenty of *dubba'*, for it strengthens the heart of the sad.'[83]

Blue herb tea (*ward mawi*) was also served during mourning. These accounts confirm that at life-crises, women used food as a means to show their concern and sympathy and to create an occasion when, through the small-talk of intimates, solace was offered.

Ibn Sahnun reported that in ninth-century Qayrawan, the custom when large gatherings of families and friends gathered for weddings, the birth and circumcision of a son and so forth, was that women banded together to produce the food and defray the costs of the host.

> Then his neighbours and friends will assist him with all manner of foods and all that might be eaten with bread, and with grain, and with flour, and with foods dressed and cooked; and he shall return the like . . . all that we have mentioned of similar provision.[84]

According to the fourteenth-century dictionary, the *Qamus*, dishes of dates cooked with fenugreek (*fariqa*) were prepared 'for the woman following the state of childbirth'. The *Qamus* elaborated that it was 'the kind of food which is given to women when childbearing'. Although this was very nourishing, the term is surely symbolic, since the verbal root of *fariqa* has connotations of 'separation',[85] in this case the child from the mother. After a birth, usually on the fourth or fifth day, food was sent by the women of the household to female relatives and friends. They included eggs (everywhere a symbol of fertility, with perhaps an unspoken blessing here for the recipients) prepared with cumin to celebrate the cutting of the baby's umbilical cord. *Mufattaka*, a mixture of honey, clarified butter, sesame oil, ground spices and aromatic herbs, was also given and again the term has connotations of 'separation'.

Libaba was a dish of crumbled bread, rosewater, honey and clarified butter. Butter was melted in a pan and the crumbed bread and honey added. *Hulba*, a tonic of dried fenugreek, was boiled and sweetened with honey. This may also be symbolic, since the verbal root is related to milk (*halib*) and thus to female fertility; further, when fenugreek was used medicinally, its yellow grain was soaked in water 'to germinate'. The new mother was also given *masluqa*, 'a skinned fowl cooked with water, by itself'. *Saliqa*, from the same root, was grain cooked with sugar, cinnamon and fennel, possibly from

Syria, or a broth with grain and vegetables. It is striking how much emphasis was placed on sweetness in these foods prepared by women for women. Was this in some sense a comfort?

Ritual food was also cooked for the naming ceremony of a child ('aqiqa) on the seventh day after the birth, when the infant's hair was cut. A sheep or, more commonly a goat, was sacrificed and the animals' legs were stewed and distributed to the poor as a pious act of thanksgiving, always remembering that there were others less fortunate in the world. One wonders if this was done both for a boy and girl infant?

Kashk, a dish of pounded wheat or barley, or barley water, appeared in a medieval dictionary as an arabicized Persian word. An Egyptian recipe from last century gave a very full description of the preparation of '*kishk*', which sounds rather similar. It was made

> from wheat, first moistened, then dried, trodden in a vessel to separate the husks, and coarsely ground with a hand-mill; the meal is mixed with milk, and about six hours afterwards is spooned out upon a little straw or bran, and left for two or three days to dry. When required for use, it is either soaked or pounded, and put into a sieve, over a vessel, and then boiling water is poured on it. What remains in the sieve is thrown away; what passes through is generally poured into a saucepan of boiled meat or fowl, over the fire. Some leaves of white beet, fried in butter, are usually added to each plate of it.[86]

This was a large-scale and time-consuming operation, possibly performed by a group of women, but it was also time-saving, since some of the soured dried product could be stored for future use under whatever circumstances, as it kept indefinitely. *Kishk* was eaten in Lebanon at the festival of *Muharram*.

Ramadhan, the fifth month of the Muslim calendar, was chosen for the Fast because it was in this month that the first revelation to the Prophet Muhammad occurred on the 'Night of Power' (*laylat al-qadr*). The Fast, one of the five Pillars of Islam incumbent on all adults (with certain exceptions) was a very rigorous physical and mental test of the individual. One fasted from dawn to dusk, which meant very late nights and long, hungry and thirsty days. This was particularly onerous when Ramadhan fell at the height of summer. The unique merit of fasting was that it was visible only to God Himself.

Ramadhan was a period of extreme social dislocation of the normal activities of eating, sleeping and working. It was a very stressful time for the women of the household, since the Qur'anic exhortation in *Sura* 2 to 'eat and drink until so much of the dawn appears that a white thread may be distinguished from a black, then keep the fast completely until night,' necessarily meant that they had a very short period of time in which to ensure that the family ate sufficiently from prodigious quantities of food to last out until sunset. It was surely likely, towards the end of a very long month of abstinence, that sufficient food was left over from the previous evening's meal with which to start the next day, with perhaps some fresh dates and tea, hence the *Tradition*, 'Hasten the *iftar* (the breaking of the fast) and delay the *sahur* (fast).' The richness of the sweet pastry *halwa* was sustaining during a long day.

'*Id al-Fitr*, the breaking of the fast, was celebrated with pomp and ceremony and great rejoicing and gifts of new clothing, confectionery and money were exchanged. Even the animals in the ruler's cavalcade in the famous illustration for al-Hariri's seventh *Maqama* were caught up in the excitement and anticipation surrounding the official announcement of the end of Ramadhan.[87] In one way or another, Ramadhan truly embraced every individual in the community within the bosom of their own homes, while the *hajj* stressed the efforts of the individual who was able to journey to Mecca. The abstinence from food ensured it acquired a symbolic aspect at this time. One's mind and stomach were so much concentrated on food and drink during Ramadhan that women's great contributions to meals could not go unnoticed. Ramadhan also served as a powerful reminder of the less fortunate in this world and that God was the ultimate provider. At '*Id al-adha* (the Festival of Sacrifice) at the end of the Pilgrimage, a sheep or goat, or a bovine or camel was sacrificed as a religious obligation and distributed to the poor and again gifts were exchanged.

Whole roast lamb was served with rice and side dishes at the feast of the Prophet's birthday (*Mawlid al-Nabi*), and on the tenth day of Muharram ('*Ashura*') the Shi'a community's remembrance of the martyrdom of the Prophet's grandson Husayn at Kerbala. The women made '*ashuriyya*, a sweet dish, and as the name suggests, made from ten different types of grain.[88] These feasts were occasions when the neighbourhood oven was well used, given the quantities involved, when few private homes had sufficient facilities or utensils for cooking large animals whole and stuffed. The communal meals stressed women's solidarity and unity, and renewed family ties. One is struck how men and meat feature so prominently at these great public events in the religious calendar, while women's contributions were confined to home and hearth and mostly unseen.

Al-Baghdadi, al-Warraq and others have left us a glimpse of the distinctive fusion of Arab and Persian cultural traditions, a valuable guide to etiquette in the Muslim world, and an insight into the reciprocal responsibilities of host or hostess and guest. Underlying all the ceremonies was the collectivity of women commemorating a significant life-event, and the supplementary information gleaned from contemporary dictionaries confirmed the ritual aspects of food served at these times.

Disease and high mortality rates ensured that food in the medieval Near East remained a high priority in the minds of most women, whatever their circumstances. Food was a beacon of social status, cultural background and changes in sophistication and taste, and the contribution of women in this field should not be underestimated.

CHAPTER 5

Costume

Tradition

It had long been the custom in the Near East for both men and women to
cover the head for reasons of modesty. Even within – or perhaps because of
– the familiar confines of the tribe, where there was a high incidence of
intermarriage, Arab women dressed conservatively. By the dawn of Islam,
everyday, functional costume compatible with climate and the limited
material resources of the Arabian Peninsula was the norm, but with some
modification in line with religious stricture and the personal example of the
Prophet and his family.

Women's entire bodies fell under the category of *'awra* – strictly
speaking, the pudenda – except for their heads, necks and the forearms[1] but
even they had to be covered to a degree. For men, *'awra* applied to the area
of the body situated between the navel and the knees; in effect, in the
language of the jurists those parts reserved for spouses (and concubines). Al-
Albani, a specialist in *Hadith*, carefully considered the matter of women's
clothing and ruled that:

> It must cover the body, except the face and hands (although he personally
> preferred them to be covered.) It must be thick, not transparent. Costume
> must not be an ornament, and be neither perfumed nor smoked with
> incense. It should resemble neither that of men, nor the Unbelievers.[2]

Al-Tabari confirmed that male clothing could be altered to suit women
and described the cloak known as *ghilala* as of 'women's cut'. At a later
period, in Egypt, the *bughlutaq*, a military jacket with short sleeves, was re-
styled to fit women; it was popular to the extent that it is listed in Jewish
trousseaux lists from Cairo.[3] Al-Ghazali also recommended that men and
women should dress and behave differently; to do otherwise was contrary to
God's will.[4] The *Qamus* dictionary defined clothing (*libas*), as 'the covering

of that portion of the person which modesty forbids one to expose'.[5] Since Islam proscribed figural representation, it is arguable that these prescriptions had some effect on the notion of personal adornment; indeed the term for clothes implied an additional purpose, 'to beautify and adorn oneself'.

Whether a desert, country or city dweller, a veil of some sort, a chemise-like gown (qamis) and a long, enveloping outer wrap were obligatory when an Arab woman left the confines of her home. There are two classifications of apparel in Arabic; shi'ar, clothes worn next to the skin, and the cut and sewn outer robes known as dithar. The terms used, the fabric, its cut, colour and pattern were dictated by economic and domestic circumstances, personal taste, and region. 'Arab' covered a huge geographical area, and the fashions of Syria and Egypt, for example, varied considerably, even if the name remained the same. Local custom and practice persisted in other Muslim territories.

The qamis (a shift)

The all-enveloping qamis, a simple, sewn, sleeved shift of varying length with no front opening, merely a round neck-hole, was charmingly defined in some dictionaries as 'the membrane that encloses a child in the womb'.[6] The woman's version was slit as far as the breast and sometimes sported a fancy embroidered band, while the man's opened to the shoulder. There were variations of the basic type of chemise, known variously as sidar, itb, shawdar and qarqur. Methods of draping, gathering and so on would be at the dictates of fashion and in theory all of these garments should have been long, according to legal prescription, but by the fourteenth-century they were reportedly frequently only knee-length. For women, any disapproval would be counteracted by the knee-length boots which they donned in contemporary illustrations, and of course by an outer wrap. Were these boots a fashion response to male disapproval?

Ornamental patterns, sewn or woven by the women according to personal preference, reflected the environment, whether of desert, country or town. For example nomads might have chosen fairly simple, abstract designs in a limited range of hues on fabrics which had to be quickly packed up at the dictates of climate and the grazing flocks, and where the availability of dyestuffs was an unknown factor. These were in sharp contrast to the delicate floral patterns found in more sophisticated environments where the weaving was done in controlled surroundings on upright looms under supervision.

Individual tribes likely made particular motifs their own, so their womenfolk would have been readily identifiable. Decoration would also reflect the traditions of the diverse Muslim lands. Many of the motifs were likely apotropaic in function. The hand of Fatima, the Prophet's daughter, was a very popular prophylactic symbol known as the *khamsa*, literally 'five', referring to the fingers of the hand. This was an Islamic symbol, but other superstitious charms were undoubtedly in existence in the *jahiliyya* period and may well have been carried over. It is interesting to see how aspects of a dominant culture were adopted by minorities; this was demonstrated by Hebrew legal documents from Cairo which show that Jewish women, at least, also wore the *khamsa* as a talisman.

Al-Kayyim and others described the *qamis* as a well-known sleeved undergarment of cotton or linen, but never of wool. However, al-Kayyim wrote in the urban context, and Bedouin and peasant women did not always have access to other materials. Indeed in many cases one woollen robe was the only garment some possessed.

Some tenth-century Bedouin women wore a body wrap as their only garment, and dispensed with the *qamis*.[7] For those who were breast-feeding and constantly on the move, a wrap was much more practical than a garment with a slit neck and no fastenings. Further, as with their country sisters, Bedouin women had to gather firewood (and thorns), tend domestic animals and undertake other tasks, so a loose-fitting wrap was cooler and more comfortable than the *qamis*. The ends could be thrown quickly over the head and around the face should male strangers approach.

Outer cloaks

The *Book of Songs* particularly mentioned the *kisa'*, an outer wrap usually of wool, with regard to the Bedouins. This was a multi-purpose garment doubling as a blanket in cool weather, which sounds similar to the *shamla*, a very thick cloak made from goat's hair or wool. The outer '*aba*', defined by the *Taj al-'arus* as, 'A well-known sort of woollen garment of the kind called *kisa'*, in which are (generally) stripes; and said to be a *jubba* of wool', was also worn. In the Arabian Gulf countries, for example, women still wear the '*aba*', the long black cloak in cotton, or today in a synthetic fabric, which is not so comfortable. It is donned in public by women of all classes, from the palace downwards, and offers anonymity and little or no indication whatever of the quality or personal style of the clothing underneath.

The thawb *(a robe)*

The *thawb*, was another ample, enveloping robe, with connotations of 'protection'. It had wide sleeves and was worn by women (and men) and is still worn today. When dyed a very dark blue-black, it functioned as a mourning garment known as *thawb al-hidad*. For a woman, the *thawb al-hidad* signified an important rite of passage, the entering into widowhood, a temporary withdrawal from society and the preparation for a new lifestyle. Hamda bint Ziyad, a poet in twelfth-century al-Andalus, wrote: 'When she unpins her hair you see the moon in a dark horizon, as though the dawn has lost his brother and worn his mourning dress.'[8]

Here, as well as praising the darkness of the hair, there is a reference to the literally black-as-iron *thawb al-hidad*.

Proscribed clothing

It would be fair to say that the basic rules and modes of dress were followed even in the cities. Fitted clothes set the city-dweller apart from others, but an outer wrap was always a prerequisite. Piety and respect for tradition also played a part. The Prophet personally disliked wearing silk and brightly coloured clothes, hence perhaps the religious proscription of silk for men, on the grounds that 'silk, like adornment of gold, was forbidden to men because of its evil effect of making men resemble women'; others held that 'it was forbidden because it gives rise to conceit, pride and vainglory'.[9] The Prophet only wore woollen garments in the latter part of his life. A *hadith* ran, 'Allah loves white clothes, and He has created Paradise white'.[10] In time, green was reserved for descendants of the Prophet, even females. This made them immediately identifiable, and earmarked them for appropriate respect. Al-Jahiz related how Rabi'a al-'Adawiyya, the eighth-century extremely other-worldly mystic, gave a man three silver dirhams to buy a garment she needed. When he asked which colour she desired she said, 'Since it is a question of colour, give me the money back', and threw it in the Tigris.[11] If one compares the sum here and the enormous amounts bandied about as the cost of clothing at court, it follows that Rabi'a's garment was of the simplest in every sense of the word and demonstrated her total disregard for the material world. Rabi'a, of course was an exception. Al-Muqaddisi and Ibn Hawqal left accounts which demonstrated that as late as the ninth century the ordinary people in the Muslim world still followed a conservative lifestyle and dressed accordingly.

Al-Albani decreed that women's costume 'should not denote prestige'. This is interesting, since men in at least one category were excluded from censure. Judges wore the *taylasan*, the distinctive white or black head covering seen in thirteenth-century manuscript illustrations.[12] This particular item is obviously not an Arabic word, and the implication is that the *taylasan* was an import from Persia. In any event, it came to be a mark of high office and was not confined to Arabs. Al-Suyuti, who produced *Fine Hadiths on the Excellence of the Taylasan (Al-ahadith al-hisan fi fadl al-taylasan)* mentioned that the distinctive and socially superior headgear of religious scholars had its parallel among Jewish scholars from Iraq to al-Andalus.[13]

Women, on the contrary, enjoyed no such public licence. Shortness in the length of male clothing came to be associated with piety and the poverty of asceticism, and this is well attested to in thirteenth-century miniatures.[14] However, although there was no apparent censure of men revealing much of their bare legs, it was totally unacceptable for women to do so. The earlier Umayyad practice of wearing clothes which covered the heel was officially overturned in the 'Abbasid period, for whatever reason. Did this signal a diminution in piety in general or did footwear styles adapt to accommodate pious strictures, hence women's apparent predilection for boots in contemporary paintings?[15]

Theologians also looked with disfavour upon yellow garments such as half-silk (*mulham*), and al-Hariri described gold as, 'yellow, two-faced, like the hypocrite'. The source of al-Washsha''s disapproval seems to be that yellow robes were, as he sniffily put it, 'the dress of dancing-girls and serving-girls', not his refined audience. Unfortunately, he wrote for the very people who owned, patronized and exploited these girls.

Hammad, a famous court-singer, recounted his first visit to the caliph al-Walid, whom he found 'on a settee wearing two yellow garments, a cloak and a waistband, both having been dipped in saffron.'[16]

The Arabic term *mughammar* was applied to fabrics dyed with saffron. Saffron was exceedingly expensive, and one can only imagine the amount of crocuses needed to deep dye a fabric. Shamsa al-Mawsiliyya, an esteemed thirteenth-century poetess and scholar, wrote: 'She sways in a saffron dress bathed in camphor, ambergris and sandalwood like a narcissus in the garden, a rose in the sun or an image in the temple.'[17]

The expensively clad and perfumed subject of the poem was probably a slave-girl at court. Such ostentation, especially in a singer, was particularly reprehensible to the pious; given the generally-held imputation of immorality to entertainers, they undoubtedly viewed the dress as payment for sexual favours.

According to a tenth-century source, red was 'only worn by Nabatean women and singing-girls of the slave class'.[18] The theological proscription of red clothing was modified by al-Washsha' with the proviso: 'Except that which is by nature . . . red, such as the red silk stuff called *ladh*, silk (*harir*), brocade, *washi*, being a kind of variegated, or figured cloth, of diverse colours.'[19]

Medical prescriptions

Physicians such as al-Majusi were interested in the medical applications of textiles. Cotton was said to warm the body and constituted winter wear. This probably needs qualification, in that several different layers of cotton clothing would have to be worn at that season to achieve any degree of warmth, thus far beyond the purse of ordinary people. Ibn Qayyim al-Jawziyya was of the opinion that, 'Clothing of hair and woollen material heats and warms, while clothing of linen, silk and cotton warms, but does not heat'.[20] These writers by their calling dealt specifically with so-called 'refined' society, and their views mirror al-Idrisi's twelfth-century comment that 'rich people wear cotton clothes and short cloaks', while the poorest wore wool.[21] In fact as it was the poorest, women and men, who did all the manual labour, one would have thought that, in time, there would have been a strong demand for a very cheap, cool type of cotton, and one that could be easily washed. *Ibrisim* silk (raw silk), according to al-Razi, was 'warmer than flax but cooler than cotton'.[22]

External influences

As Islam spread, Muslim rulers took foreign wives who introduced their own fashions. The Arabs had to rely on experienced administrators for their empire, and who more so than Persians, with their long tradition of kingship? The Persian names for many garments revealed a very strong influence from the earliest days of the caliphate, and it is likely that at this time too the seclusion and veiling of women became the norm. Yet another important factor was the circle of poets, singers and musicians – male and female – who were enticed from court to court by royal patrons. For example Ziryab, probably the greatest Muslim musician of all times, moved from the court of Harun al-Rashid first of all to north west Africa, then to Cordova,[23] where he became the arbiter of fashion and refined living in al-Andalus. Resources were exploited, trade flourished and a prosperous and growing bourgeoisie was able to emulate the aristocracy and lead an increasingly hedonistic lifestyle. Tensions inevitably developed between them and the religious class, who sought to reinforce tradition, and for this reason, perhaps, women were increasingly less visible in society.

When women's outfits were deemed too costly, too distinctive or too provocative (to men) they provoked decrees from the palace itself. Given the excesses of some royal establishments, this was somewhat hypocritical. For example, Al-Salih Isma'il, the successor of Sultan Ahmad al-Nasar who ruled briefly in Egypt in 1342, went out riding accompanied by two hundred concubines wearing precious silk clothing. We know from the indignant recording of a judge that the wife of the Egyptian Sultan Barsbay reportedly paid thirty thousand dinars for one dress for her son's circumcision feast. This was a public occasion, and she could not have failed to impress. Was there a more fundamental, worrying concern for the authorities? One must ask to what extent the luxurious clothing flaunted by the upper echelons of society fomented social discontent among the masses?

Nevertheless, ostentation in clothing became the rule for the better-off, who had no compunction in citing the Prophet when seeking to justify their wearing of luxurious garments in the face of religious disapprobation. The Prophet reportedly said: 'When Allah gives riches to a man, He wants it to be seen on him.'[24]

It followed that luxurious clothing was by no means confined to men. Ibn Battuta reported from his far-flung travels on the ermine, sable and minever from 'the Land of Darkness', some forty days' journey from Bulgha,[25] and al-Nuwayri's classification of furs also included Bulghar sable as well as marten from Kashgar and fine Herati skins. Brocade had been widely available in the Roman world, and Kirmizi was one version noted.

The court and refined society

Baghdad lay at the hub of the Islamic world, and even late in the ninth century al-Ya'qubi reported that there was more merchandise there than in countries of origin such as China, Tibet and India.[26] Earlier that century fine embroidered silks with bird motifs in the Sasanian tradition and others in geometrical patterns were being produced in caliphal workshops.[27] There is a certain irony here, in that this period of unmitigated luxury in Baghdad coincided with the beginning of the decline in 'Abbasid power. Some one hundred years later, al-Muqaddisi noted that Iraqis had a keen interest in fashion,[28] which was not confined to men. The pious and learned daughter of Abu 'Umar ibn Qudama criticised her brother Shams al-Din for wearing worldly clothes. (Despite being well-known, she was designated only by the name of her father, 'the father of 'Umar'.)

The wardrobes of affluent women comprised a *qamis*, a *rida'* of silk or linen, wraps and long underpants with broad hems, the *sarawil*. Strictly speaking, non-Muslims were not supposed to wear the *rida'*, which was a type of cloak and a single, uncut garment characteristic of the Arabs.[29] It was fairly voluminous and women wore it when venturing outside their homes.

The word for trousers, *sarawil*, was patently not Arabic, and medieval dictionaries classed it as originally Persian; it is reasonable therefore to assume that trousers were yet another import from Persia. *Sarawil* was a lightweight female version of the male garment. *Sarawil* were certainly required by women from polite society when outdoors, and represented a response to notions of 'respectability' and the covering of the lower leg. They were probably discarded in the privacy of one's home on the grounds of comfort and coolness. *Sarawil* were secured by a waist-cord (*tikka*), and a fashion-conscious lady would surely have had a version in *ibrism*, a variety of silk. Men were no exception; Hisham ibn 'Abd al-Malik allegedly had ten thousand silken waist-cords. He also had twelve thousand embroidered robes. Were these an investment, a realisable form of wealth?

Contemporary illustrations showed *sarawil* as light and flowing. They were depicted in manuscripts in the fashionable smokey-grey colour and because of their fineness they clung to the leg. *Sarawil* were eloquently and aptly likened in a contemporary dictionary to 'a bird whose plumage clothes its legs'.[30] The wife of one Egyptian *amir* reputedly owned trousers valued at ten thousand dinars in 1341.

Who did women dress for? Men? Or to vie with other females? There is probably an element of each, but one can imagine the competitive atmosphere in the royal apartments, with women vying with each other to be favourites. However, not all women were enamoured of the so-called 'high life'. Some women, like Maysun, the mother of the caliph al-Yazid no less, might have chosen a simpler life, given the opportunity. Maysun wrote wistfully: 'I'd rather have a pleasing smock (*'aba' wa taqarra*) than a chiffon dress (*shufuuf*).'[31] The term for chiffon denoted great delicacy and translucency.

Clothing functioned as a barometer of wealth. It was itemised in marriage contracts and trousseaux lists, and garments were carefully stored. Henna blossoms *(faghiya)* and citrus peel were useful as moth-deterrents, and a prerequisite for fine textiles. It is plausible to suggest that there was a ready market in second-hand clothes which had been sold on or cast off, and one imagines that seamstresses were retained to maintain and repair elaborate textiles in royal and upper class households.

*Robes of honour (*al-khila'*)*

Powerful incentives for the demand for costly garments were the highly-valued customs in Islam of bestowing a full set of robes of honour *(khila')* by the ruler on those appointed to high office or to personal favourites, and the exchange of diplomatic gifts. In 997 in al-Andalus, for example, the Caliph al-Mansur gifted silk robes with *tiraz* bands to Christian allies.[32] The narrow *tiraz* embroidered bands would have mentioned al-Mansur and his pious honorifics, in the style of 'Pillar of Religion' or 'Light of Religion'. These bands had an underlying ideological function; they served as a personal advertisement for both the donor and recipient, and indicated to the onlooker that the wearer had been honoured by no less than the ruler himself. In other words, clothing with *tiraz* bands was a prized status symbol or trophy. Women were similarly honoured. According to al-Maqrizi (1364-1442) women and even lesser functionaries in Egypt, such as the carpet-spreaders, were presented with silken robes.

Al-Washsha', the tenth-century *belle-lettrist,* outlined a 'Section on fashionable ladies, concerning those clothes which differ from those of fashionable men', as well as a 'Section on the dress of the elegant' for 'men of position'. Al-Washsha' described the best fashions:

> They do not pass beyond the limits which we have demarcated . . . The best taste in dress is to wear clothes which suit one another, with a graduated range of colour, and materials which have something in common and do not clash.[33]

Veils

The issues of honour and shame and leaving the home have been explored at length in Chapter 1, and the discussion now centres on different varieties of veil. Veils were *de rigueur* for girls from the onset of puberty and for all women, regardless of class, and were the subject of fashion concerning material, colour, pattern and availability. There were various types of veil, each with its own name according to region and particular style, for example *mizna'a*, and *qina'*. In Egypt the *qina'* was about a metre long and rather less wide. It was placed partly on the head, beneath the wrap (*izar*) and the remainder trailed down over the face and breast. It had eye pieces covered in net.[34] Another was the the outdoor veil (*niqab*), described in contemporary dictionaries as a veil 'that is upon (or covers) the pliable part of the nose' or which 'extends as high as the circuit of the eye.' This was admirably defined by the root of the verb, which means 'to bore, to pierce', in this connection to make eye holes. There is an extended meaning here and a suggestion that showing the circuit of the eye was an innovation. It may be that the *niqab* was a response to fashion, and possibly also some modification of the rules of modesty in a particular period.

The *burqu'* was also worn outdoors. Some were merely a piece of black net covering the whole face; others were similar, but with eye-holes, such as seen in an illustration of Bedouin women in a *Maqamat* miniature.[35] Anselmo Adorno, a Genoese merchant travelling in the Middle East in 1470, remarked upon the pieces of silk with two cut eye-holes which Alexandrian women wore, and added that women in Cairo and Damascus also dressed in like manner.[36] Similar veils in ordinary fabrics were available. These varieties gave women much scope for individuality in the manner in which they draped their veils, and one can appreciate the dramatic, highlighting effects of *kohl* when only the eyes were seen. In the *Romance of Warqa and Gulshah*, Gulshah rode unveiled into battle with her head 'covered in Kufa silk' (interpreted in one illustration as a headband), and the two armies were 'stupefied' by the sight of her face.

The *mi'jar*, a black veil, usually of muslin, was bound around the head and described by al-Washsha' as perfumed with hyacinth. This may be the fine, probably silk, item worn by a matriarchal matron in a mosque gallery clearly depicted in a *Maqamat* illustration from Baghdad, dated 1237.[37] The *mi'jar* was a desirable item in any bride's trousseau, and black versions, some with borders, were still popular in the fourteenth century. Documents from the Cairo *geniza* (storeroom for Hebrew religious and legal documents) confirmed that versions of the *mi'jar* were made in silk, as well as fine Dabiqi linen, with gilt ornamentation; as such, they were the preserve of the well-off, and prices ranging from two to fifteen dinars were recorded. It should be borne in mind that these were Hebrew documents, referring to Jewish women in a Muslim country; they testify that they, too, wore not just veils, but the other everyday garments of their Muslim neighbours. Christian women probably followed suit. It is likely though that non-Muslims had their own discreet community way of wearing certain garments, although they probably did not wear symbols of their religious affiliation outdoors. However, a manual on the regulation of the Cairo markets contained a protest at richly attired non-Muslim women, and the welcome accorded them by merchants who did not recognise them as being of another faith. How did the official identify them?

A fifteenth-century account from Tunis confirmed that veiling there was not the preserve of Muslims:

It is the custom with us . . . for the women of the Nazarenes to take the veil like unto Muslim women, and most often without any distinction – although some do observe distinction in the manner required of Nazarenes.[38]

One commentator described Egyptian women at an early period going outdoors, either on the back of a mule or in a litter, but rarely on foot. They apparently resembled nothing less than large, well-wrapped and tied-up parcels, in a great veil in two pieces to cover the back and front which came in various colours.[39] It was generally recognised as a sign of great distress when a respectable woman appeared in public unveiled. This is interesting – does it mean that only a woman who was unhinged would discard something so fundamental to Islamic society as the veil? Appearing in public unveiled could be a powerful manipulative force on a woman's behalf to embarrass authority and elicit compassionate influence in her favour. This much is suggested in another thirteenth-century *Maqamat* illustration from Baghdad.[40] Yet from fourteenth-century Anatolia Ibn Battuta reported that, 'whether at a hospice or a private house, our neighbours both men and women (these do not veil themselves) came to ask after us',[41] which is surprising, given these were Sunni, literally 'orthodox' Muslims. During a period of great civil unrest and house raids in ninth-century Baghdad, women fled into the streets without even throwing the *izar* over their indoor clothes; this, too, was evidence of 'great distress'.

Did Bedouin women wear the veil at all times? Strictly speaking, since marriage between first cousins was preferred, this meant that many of them were part of large extended families, whose menfolk were in any case exempt from the proscription of viewing a woman's face, on grounds of consanguinity. A headdress could quickly be pulled over to conceal most of the face. Bedouin women decorated the edges of their headdresses with jewellery, or silver or gold coins. One sees these even today and the coins look particularly attractive against the black fabric. Coins also weighed down the edge of the veil, kept it in place and accorded a certain financial status to the wearer, even if she were otherwise publicly anonymous.

The veil arguably gave women some advantage over men; their anonymity was guaranteed in tortuous, narrow alleyways and the proximity of strange men, and it incidentally gave them the freedom openly to scrutinise men while their own privacy was maintained. In this sense, veiling could be a form of personal empowerment.

The khimar (a headcovering)

The *khimar* was a head and shoulder covering worn under a wrap, and seems to have been a modification of the turban (*'imama*). Strictly speaking, as the male turban was widely recognised as 'a badge of Islam' and 'a divider between belief and unbelief',[42] the *khimar* should not have been worn by non-Muslims, so one wonders if Christian and Jewish women wore the *khimar* over their modified headdress? Again we are fortunate to see a version in a contemporary *Maqamat* illustration, where it is obvious that it lent a heavy look to the head.[43] Similar headgear can be seen today in Syria.

The 'isaba (a cap)

Harun al-Rashid's half sister, 'Ulayya is credited with setting a fashion late in the eighth century for the *'isaba*, a close-fitting cap with a lower border which could be embellished with jewels.[44] Small girls in Mamluk Egypt were unveiled, but wore little caps (*al-kawafi wa al-tawaqi*), which were sold in the special market, the *Suq al-bakhaniqiyyin*.[45]

A thirteenth-century illustration of a singing-girl in the *Maqamat* surely furnishes for us the epitome of an 'elegant woman'.[46] She is clearly wearing both an *'isaba* and a headband. The *'isaba* is tight fitting, with a frame of pearls which encircle her face and chin, so it would possibly the *'isaba ma'ila*, which had connotations of wealth, in particular gold and silver. This is also confirmed by the gold circlets on the cap, which could be gold dinars, or a form of decoration printed directly on the fabric. Her *'isaba* is close-fitting and seems to be silk, in which case it was the *harir al-mu'ayyan*, the silken fabric with embroidered circlets much favoured by discerning ladies. Ibn 'Abd

Rabbih mentioned girls at al-Rashid's court who also wore headdresses decorated with jacinth (*yaqut*) from Ceylon, and pearls. The term *yaqut*, strictly speaking, was a blue gemstone, possibly sapphire, but it also embraced a variety of gems such as quartz, topaz, garnet or pearls (*lu'lu'*) from Oman and the Gulf around Bahrain.

A Persian variation of the *'isaba* appears on the base of a Persian polychrome pottery bowl dated around 1200, which showed a noble lady being bled.[47] It however was heavier and of rather more elaborate design with a fringe of pearls at the forehead and what may be small ornaments of gold or silver sewn on the sides. The Persian example conformed rather more to the literal translation of *'isaba ma'ila* in this respect and confirmed variations in style in different lands.

'Ulayya apparently had a birthmark which she concealed with a headband, and she also popularised this accessory. The headband was probably the *wikaya* which, like armbands and borders on other garments, was frequently adorned with amatory verses by young women. For example, a spirited slave-girl in Harun al-Rashid's *harim* allegedly daringly sported a headband with the following embroidery: 'Tyrant, you were cruel to me in love. May God judge what happened between us!'[48]

One hopes she had fallen so far from favour that there was no possibility of the Caliph seeing this. It is fair to say that while outspokenness in women of her ilk was frequently admired, it would not have been tolerated in the home. The *wikaya* was formed by a strip of material, folded several times into a narrow band, which suggests it was very fine and probably silk.

Headbands came in various colours and fabrics; a band of black silk was very popular and al-Washsha' mentioned fashionable headscarves dyed black with spikenard, an Indian plant of the valerian variety.

The *Maqamat* singing-girl's headband was tied behind her left ear in a manner reminiscent of the Persian ribbon denoting royalty from Sasanian times. From its lightness and delicacy, this fabric also appears to be silk. Again one is struck by the pervasive influence Persia exerted on fashions in the Arab world from the 'Abbasid period onwards. Although the head-tie was also known as *zunnar wikaya*, the *zunnar* more exactly referred to the belt prescribed for the People of the Book, the Jews and Christians.

Other headgear

Ribbons and lace were also used, and various head ornaments were worn.

Syrian records told how a prince of Aleppo, al-Malik al-Zahir (who ruled from 1186-1216) handed over twenty-seven dinars to a courtesan for a *baqyar*, a headdress.[49] From an early period, al-Maqrizi cited examples of great female extravagance in clothing among Egyptian women. Fashions at times became extreme, for example, the Mongol *boqtaq*, a tall feathered headdress, required one to walk so carefully that movements were restricted to a stilted gait.

These examples, of course, are in the context of the royal court, but overly-ostentatious women's headdresses, as well as wide sleeves, periodically raised the wrath of officialdom. One can only assume that many well-to-do women appeared out in the streets on some occasions. In 1471 women in Cairo, for example, were forbidden on pain of beating by police to wear a distinctive, tall head-covering. Some women were so afraid that they chose to go bareheaded.[50] They were risking social disgrace, as their reputations were impugned and their menfolk shamed, but nevertheless demonstrated that they were not necessarily meek and submissive.

The ghilala *(a wrap)*

Al-Albani maintained that female costume had to be ample, not figure-revealing, so he would undoubtedly have disapproved of the wispy garment which Abu Zayd's unveiled buxom wife in a *Maqamat* illustration wore when pleading her case before a judge.[51] This was a fine, long outer robe of a smokey-grey hue with gold edging. It conformed exactly in description to the fashionable *ghilala dukhaniyya*, or 'smokey-grey' *ghilala* mentioned by al-Washsha'. It seems to be an example of women conforming to notions of 'respectable' dress so far as its function, but subtly undermining them by the sheerness of the clingy material. The lexicographer al-Saghani's alternative thirteenth-century description of the *ghilala* was: 'A piece of cloth with which a woman makes her posterior (to appear) large, binding it upon her hinder-part, beneath her waist-wrapper'.

Was this a fashion whim on women's part, and did some women consider an ample build desirable? The text described Abu Zayd's wife admiringly as 'the mother of children', which increased her worth in society's eyes, or alternatively as 'a woman of enticing beauty'. The term for a woman heavy around the hips was *mikfal*; this had connotations of responsibility, and may, in fact, have been perceived by women themselves as a great compliment.

Although these writers addressed the large and influential upper and middle classes, it represented a relatively small section of the total population and their recommendations could only have been taken up by a minority of women in general.

The jubba *(a brocaded robe)*

The *Maqamat* singing-girl provides a fascinating glimpse of another variation of a male garment, the *jubba*. Her heavily brocaded blue robe, with golden bird motifs, must be the *tiraz farajiyya. Farajiyya* literally denoted that it was 'split', without closures. There are *tiraz* bands on the sleeves, and she is undoubtedly modelled on a court entertainer. Al-Tabari reported that the Caliph Amin offered a gold-figured *jubba* to a singer who pleased him. He later regretted his rashness and petulantly spoilt it; presumably his initial regret was on grounds of cost. In the illustration the robe is of a blue-green material, with heavy gold edging, *tiraz* bands, a red lining and birds in figured gold. Because it rarely appeared in marriage contracts from Egypt and Tunisia, Stillman concluded that the *jubba* was more popular in Syria than in Egypt in the medieval period.

The sleeves of the singing-girl's robe were extremely deep and extended from her breast to below the knee. A further point here is that this was a costly garment and Abu Zayd therefore implied that a very generous cut meant that no expense was too much for his paragon of a slave-girl of whom he boasted:

> Now I had a maiden, who was unrivalled in perfection; if she unveiled, the two lamps of heaven were put to shame, and all hearts were inflamed with the fires of desire.[52]

Unfortunately, she was otherwise a chattel. Her robe also sounded similar to the fourteenth-century fashionable Mamluk *bahtala* or shift with a long train and sleeves three ells wide which so incurred the wrath of the *wazir* Amir Manjak and led to the punishment of women who wore it.

Apart from ostentation, immodesty was a consideration, since wide sleeves would reveal much of a woman's arm and, incidentally, reveal her jewellery. Any woman wearing such a garment would have been doubly condemned, but this had little effect on popular fashion. Sleeves had become wide even by the ninth century and al-Mas'udi later mentioned 'three hand spans'. (Men also found them useful for doubling as pockets.)

The mintaq *(a girdle)*

The *mintaq* was a belt or girdle fastened with a clasp or buckle. A fourteenth-century dictionary elaborated that when worn by wealthy women it was: 'Generally adorned with jewels, etc, and having also two plates of silver or gold, also generally jewelled, which clasp together.'[53]

The peripatetic Ibn Battuta described his visit to the Ghazan bazaar, 'one of the finest bazaars I have seen the world over', where he saw wonderful jewellery displayed for sale on beautiful slaves who were 'wearing rich garments with a waist-sash of silk'.

The wishah *(a double belt or girdle)*

The *wishah* was a double belt or girdle worn from shoulder to hip. In al-Andalus it was sometimes ornamented with pearls of various colours, and a similar girdle is mentioned in the *Thousand and One Nights*. The term itself suggests ornateness. A European traveller of the early eighteenth century confirmed the durability of some fashions, noting Persian ladies of status who wore belts 'two or three inches wide ... ornamented with precious stones and pearls'.[54]

Coloured textiles

Brightly coloured textiles were always in vogue and women were spoiled for choice. A large variety of dyestuffs was produced, and the names related to the bright plumage of birds, spices, fruits and vegetables. The growth of the cultivation of textile plants closely paralleled that of the bourgeoisie, many of whom were engaged in the manufacture of and trade in luxury items, in particular silk. Blue was obtained from the leaves of the indigo plant (*nil*) cultivated in Syria and Iraq and it was much in demand throughout the Muslim world. In 1396 in Alexandria one *qintar* of indigo imported from Baghdad cost thirty five dinars, and East Africa and India exported indigo to Muslim Spain. (Indigo differed from the mollusc-based blue *halazun* from the cuttlefish found on the shores of Palestine.)

Red was obtained from *baqam*, an Indian wood, and a twelfth-century record revealed that the price in Egypt fluctuated between thirty and forty dinars per *qintar*, on a par with indigo. In his late tenth-century *Rules and*

Regulations of the 'Abbasid Court (Rusum dar al-khilafa), the secretary al-Sabi' recorded both 'red Susi cloth, gilded or plain embroidery' and a fine crimson luminous fabric from Armenia, adding: 'The more gold is woven into (these varieties), the better the quality and the higher the price.'[55]

It is clear that at the highest levels of society scant attention was frequently paid to religious strictures.

The hero in the *Maqama* of Sinjar was inspired to eulogise a high-born weeping maiden, who bit her hand in anguish on parting from her lover. He asked her to remove her crimson veil: 'So she removed the red light which had dimmed the radiance of the moon and dropped pearls from a perfumed ring.'[56]

When 'A'isha married the Prophet her wedding gown was of a striped red cloth from Bahrain, and other Medinese brides later borrowed this. In the Saljuq era red was also associated with brides.

There is some ambiguity in the various meanings accorded the Arabic terms for indigo and woad. Woad, known as *wasma* in Arabic, was defined in the fourteenth-century *Misbah* as 'a certain plant with the leaves of which one tinges or dyes (the hands etc.)'.[57] Ibn al-Jawziyya amplified *wasma* as: 'A plant with long leaves, of a colour tending to blue, larger than the leaves of poplar, resembling leaves of the bean but larger; it is brought from the Hijaz and Yemen.'[58]

The Talmud of the Babylonian period mentioned blueish-black garments.[59] The dyer (*al-sabbagh*) used various colouring materials, essences and spices as bases. Among these were prickly pear, pomegranate and onion skin, and ordinary women probably prepared their own dyes from these domestic plants for their home-spun fabrics.

From the eleventh century onwards in al-Andalus plants used in textile manufacture and dyeing were actively cultivated. Ibn al-Awwam's *Book of Agriculture* specifically mentioned madder, henna, woad and saffron.[60] The markets were strictly supervised, and dyers were forbidden to use unstable dyes. Given the high cost of the genuine materials, it is easy to see why some merchants and dyers were tempted to pass off woad as indigo, but they risked being charged with fraud and punished in twelfth-century Seville. Woad mixed with henna was called 'fool's henna' (*hinna-l-majnun*), for obvious reasons. The unscrupulous in al-Andalus – and elsewhere – also substituted mustard or henna for saffron, as unsuspecting women would have discovered after the first wash. These practices were probably fairly widespread.

Bedouin women had a predilection for dark colours, which is surprising, as they do not reflect the heat. This is undoubtedly explained by practicality in the absence of an abundant water supply, as well as the colour of the animal hair or wool most easily available for clothing.

Women's costume may have conformed to basic tenets of modesty, but even the colours used were highly visible indicators of social standing. The theme of colour symbolism is also discussed in Chapter 8, which deals with non-Muslim females and others on the periphery of society.

Textile production

Textiles among the Bedouin were of the most rudimentary, the loom consisting of wooden pegs driven into the ground. The availability of materials and the constant moving on probably resulted in a hurriedly-made fairly coarse fabric, uneven in tension, colour and design, and showing clear evidence of several 'hands', or at least that the material was worked on at different times. Were children sometimes allowed to weave with their mothers? These fabrics would not be entirely lacking in charm and would certainly have meant much to the users. Nomads were not totally isolated, and had intermittent contact with the settled lands, where sheep were run on nearby areas and their wool utilised. Goat's hair was also used. Ibn Battuta mentioned the Bedouin of the district of Samira on the road to Mecca who 'come there with sheep, melted butter, and milk, which they sell to the pilgrims for pieces of coarse cotton cloth,'[61] and there was apparently an element of barter.

Women spun clothing for themselves and their families. Spinning was their prerogative, and had the blessing of the Prophet, who said:

> Sitting for an hour employed with the distaff is better for women than a year's worship; and for every piece of cloth woven of the thread spun by them, they shall receive the reward of a martyr.

Another Tradition tells us that the Prophet received a wrap (*burda*) from a woman who had woven it herself. In the early days of Islam women provided all the family's clothes, and the Prophet's wife 'A'isha averred:

> There is no woman who spins until she has clothed herself but all the angels in the Seven Heavens pray for forgiveness of her sins.

This notion of woman sitting with her spindle, at the centre of the home, is thus a very potent image of virtue and duty and strongly reminiscent of the biblical 'woman of worth, who can find, for her price is far above rubies?' in *Proverbs* 31.

The spinning-woman fastened the distaff in a girdle or else held it in one hand, or under the arm. Her other hand drew out or twisted the fibres and attached them to a spindle, which revolved rapidly and was controlled by a small wheel. This is shown in great detail in an illustrated Hariri manuscript.[62] The *Suq al-ghazal* or Thread Market was naturally a magnet for Baghdadi women in the 'Abbasid period, who sold the items they had spun there, and women thronged the haberdashers' shops in Cairo. Women decorated their own clothes. In Cordova, Wallada, the great poetess and beauty, penned the following on the right hand side of her robe, 'By Allah, I'm made for higher goals and I walk with grace and style', while the verse on the other side read: 'I blow kisses to anyone but reserve my cheeks for my man'.[63]

Egypt was famed for the quality of its linen and cotton and al-Maqrizi mentioned a factory in Cairo which produced both summer and winter clothes. Scant information exists concerning the production of textiles in Baghdad itself, although Marco Polo reported that many varieties of silks were manufactured there. 'Attabiyya was the quarter of Baghdad where striped silk and cotton fabric was manufactured, hence the term 'tabby' in the West to describe a striped cat. Fine silks from Syria and Persia were highly regarded, but again there was a relative lack of documentation regarding Syrian centres. There was much inter-regional trade; textiles from Rayy were as well-known as those from Yemen, and indeed were described as *'adaniyyat*, that is alluding to Aden. Was this a sincere form of flattery, or a powerful marketing ploy? Another Rayy speciality was woven silk known as *munayyar*, run through with double thread. Rayy fabrics were costly, as one description of a peregrine falcon confirmed: 'You would imagine that when it shakes off the dew from its wings, it was showering pearls from off one of the mantles of Rayy.'[64]

Relatively few women could afford such a garment. Cambric, finely woven white linen or cotton, was another favourite of the well-to-do, and it was a delightful irony apparently lost on the rich that weaving had long been a despised craft. Al-Tha'alibi's *Book of Curious and Entertaining Information* reported that the Yemenis were contemptuously called 'weavers'.

Women played a prominent role in the huge demand for fine fabrics, whether as consumers or in the growing and preparation of the raw materials. They were therefore an integral part of the economy and contributed greatly to the general prosperity. Cotton, linen, indigo, henna, saffron and poppies were all important industrial plants. Cotton was extensively cultivated in well irrigated soil in springtime and harvested in the summer. Seasons obviously varied throughout the Muslim world, according to climate, for example cotton was picked in Iraq in July, but not until September in al-Andalus. This is the theory; in practice one was dependent on the climate, pests and the inundation or otherwise of great rivers. In springtime, women and children weeded the young shoots, while the men attended to the heavier duties of creating and maintaining irrigation systems, which required great skill and was thus an exceedingly expensive production factor.[65] The whole village participated and one wonders if this branch of agriculture, at least, was run on a co-operative basis? Women helped cultivate and pick the plants, and they shelled the cotton buds and one presumes that their manual dexterity played some part.

It is probable that women's costume and veiling in the countryside, like that of Bedouin women, was necessarily modified from that of their urban sisters. That consideration apart, if this was arguably an element of social freedom for women, was it not also a measure of their equality, and a tacit recognition of their financial contribution to the family? In Spain, local custom and practice before the arrival of the Muslims may have been retained to some extent, and one wonders if all Muslim women wore veils? Women poets there seemed to have enjoyed greater artistic licence than elsewhere in the Muslim world, and it may be that, apart from the very strict Almoravid and Almohad periods, there was some relaxation in rules of dress.

Sericulture was practised in the Middle East from the sixth century onwards. It was extremely labour intensive and involved great care against the elements and natural predators such as ants and rats. Women were very actively engaged in silk production. In hot climates, the eggs were placed in earthenware pots while in colder climes they were laid in sachets surrounded by fur, as insulation. In springtime, the women placed the sachets under their armpits to speed up hatching, which took place over four or five days.[66] The worms were then transferred to fresh mulberry leaves on a type of riddle which presumably kept them free from infection from their own waste materials.

Families depended on the successful raising and hatching of silkworms for their livelihoods, and vermin and insects were not the only threats. Cultivators could not risk using leaves from trees belonging to others, in case of ill intent by rivals. Ibn Irshad 's fifteenth-century account revealed that peasant women placed a turquoise or a pearl beside their precious charges, as a precaution against the evil eye and out of fear of envy and malice aforethought.

Textile prices

It is extremely difficult to approximate prices in one area with those in another. Available records reveal that quality textiles and clothing were always very costly in Muslim lands up to the end of the Middle Ages. Other considerations aside, the raw materials grown in one climate were exported elsewhere. For example, linen was plentiful in Egypt, but rarely cultivated in Syria, and therefore more expensive there.

Vanity was not the prerogative of women. Given that the law was grounded in the Qur'an and *Traditions*, it is surprising that the renowned eighth-century juriconsult Abu Hanifa reportedly paid some four hundred dinars for one robe. As he was also a merchant, one supposes that this represented the cost price. Women's clothing could be equally costly, but there would be something to suit most pockets. In any event, in such a prosperous era, many women had independent means, either from successful business enterprises on their own account or through inheritance, and were not necessarily dependent on their husbands' purses.

Silk was extremely valuable, even at the basic level of production, and it would be interesting to know what remuneration the primary producers received, in comparison to the prices of the finished articles in the market place after the costs of transportation, weaving and decoration, middle-men, the retailer and supply and demand were taken into account. Silk merchants were among the wealthiest in society.

Clean linen was cool and much favoured by those who could afford it. Even in tenth-century Egypt, a good male tunic from Dabiq cost fifty dinars, a very large sum indeed. Women's linen clothes were correspondingly expensive, and these prices excluded the bulk of the population from wearing linen. In 1134 a *thawb* of the famous Dabiqi linen cost ten dinars, yet during the same period a half-silk (*mulham*) *thawb* cost only three-quarters of a dinar. Al-Nuwayri mentioned half-silk from Merv, Sus and China.[67] A muslin *rida'* cost two and a half dinars in 1115 in Egypt, and a half-*rida'*, costing three dinars in 1134, was evidently of a superior fabric.[68] One *izar* mentioned in a marriage contract dated 1083 was priced at one and a quarter dinars.[69] Since this item, and others, were deemed worthy of mention in legal documents, the implication is that these were of good quality and that here we are dealing not with the majority of women. One should note that a *dinar* was a gold coin, and a considerable sum of money.

Inventories were not necessarily an accurate guides to price. For example a probate list might undervalue property for tax reasons, while trousseaux lists possibly sometimes exaggerated the generosity of the donors, to satisfy the bride's parents and inflate the groom's family wealth, but fine textiles were always costly. Extravagant female purchases are not a modern, consumer-driven prerogative. The mother of Harun al-Rashid paid fifty thousand dinars for a silken-brocaded robe.[70] Even if these somewhat-suspiciously rounded figures had been exaggerated, the evidence is nevertheless that textiles in the medieval Middle East were extremely expensive.

Bearing in mind fluctuations in price and period and from area to area, how could the wife of a mason in eleventh-century Baghdad earning one and a half dinars a month or a female nurse in the same period in Damascus taking home a comparable sum afford such goods? They could not. These were regularly employed and skilled persons, possibly with large families, but there was a huge teeming underclass in the cities, who patently had to turn to utilitarian versions, from whatever source. Cheaper versions must have been found in the market place to suit the pockets of all women.

Footwear

Given the harsh terrain and heat and the long distances travelled, comfortable sandals for all were a necessity in the desert and countryside. The shoemakers' market was an important fixture in any town, and along its length all kinds of footwear was made.[71] Yemen was proverbial for the quality of its leather, but in the twelfth and thirteenth centuries, for whatever reason, much leather footwear was apparently of poor quality and the soles were stuffed with rags. The majority of the people wore some kind of shoe, sandal or leather slipper made from the skin of various animals, from the humble donkey to the exotic giraffe. Footwear conformed to climate, and sandals were widely worn. The poor sometimes wore wooden overshoes, and one ascetic in ninth-century Baghdad, the aptly-named Bishr al-Hafi ('barefeet') mentioned shoes costing one third of a dirham.[72] These were extremely cheap, befitting his calling.

All classes of society were catered for, and a common complaint was the tardiness of shoemakers, who invariably promised but seldom delivered on time. This implied that shoes were made to measure and that many women visited the market-place to order and purchase them. As with the fitting of clothes, there would be no question of a man measuring up a woman's feet. Perhaps they provided him with a paper pattern. Soles of good quality slippers comprised several layers of leather, and were stitched with linen thread. In Egypt and Syria the hair of the wild boar was forbidden for sewing, and this obviously is connected with the interdiction on the eating of *khinzir*, swine.[73] This was apparently not so in the eastern empire, under Hanifi legal jurisdiction.

The subject of pollution was an important consideration in footwear, as well as the ease with which it could be slipped on and off, to conform to religious and social practice. Shoes were removed before entering the mosque and at the entrance to a house (and before greeting the hostess or host). Good manners dictated that one always put on and took off the right shoe before the left, and entered upon the right foot. This was connected with the notion of the ritual impurity of the left-hand side. It is likely that in the privacy of their own homes women went about barefoot, only donning footwear when going out. In any event, indoor footwear ensured that no 'pollution' entered the home.

Around the year 1000 al-Hakim, a notoriously cruel and profligate Egyptian ruler, under the guise of underpinning traditional Islamic practice, decreed that women could not leave their houses and that shoemakers should not make women's footwear. Women undoubtedly heard and paid no notice, as has been demonstrated on other occasions when men's public disapproval was aired, whatever the motives. Egyptian women seem to have been subject to great restrictions concerning their dress codes from time to time. Did this necessarily mean that they had more freedom to appear in public or were they less timid than women elsewhere in Muslim lands?

Fashionable ladies wore the *maqsur*, a split kind of shoe, or a light Rahawi shoe from Edessa in the summer, and a fur-lined winter shoe (*musha'ara*) for wear in colder areas. Ibn Battuta, en route to Astrakhan, wore 'woollen boots, with a pair of linen-lined boots on top of these and a pair of horse skin boots lined with bearskin on top of these again.'[74] That was an extreme case.

Thirteenth-century Arabic manuscripts show ladies wearing fine black leather boots (*khifaf zaniyya*), which were, as the term indicated, 'narrow'. Elsewhere one finds mention of elegant ladies' calf or suede boots, as well as riding boots. It is plausible to suggest that boots came into fashion literally to 'bridge the gap' between ankle and calf when women wore shorter clothes. Elegant women and men were evidently amused by shoes made specifically to squeak and were 'intent on crackling their way through the markets and public cross-roads'.[75] Did this also command men's disapproval, in the same way that the tinkling of women's anklets which drew attention to women's legs raised the ire of theologians?

The urban markets

How did knowledge of fabrics and the latest fashions become apparent to ordinary women? A 'very beautiful, finely woven cloth of a very good colour' named after the Caliph al-Mutawakkil, became popular, hence the report that 'lengths of this Mutawakkili material fetched high prices'.[76] This suggests that lesser mortals in society were now within the orbit of the court's influence. Trade was extensive between far flung countries of the Muslim world, as was travel by scholars, merchants, pilgrims and others, indeed to an amazing extent, given the huge distances and lack of modern conveniences. Renowned geographers and historians recorded their lavish entertainment at foreign courts. Homecoming heads of household had some influence in setting taste, perhaps bringing back tales of the latest styles of costume or samples of fabric from other lands as souvenirs for their wives and daughters.

Merchants did not confine their business dealings to royal circles, however lucrative. Rulers frequently acted on a whim, and traders had to ensure that their enterprise was covered and all stock realised. Much of their merchandise would be unloaded into the main market-place. In time, a demand for cheaper versions for ordinary people arose. For those women who did not venture outside the *harim*, agents in turn sold the goods on, and women brokers plied their trade around private homes and ensured that fabrics, articles of clothing and other fashion accessories had the maximum possible exposure.

Where would women find these and other more plebeian materials, and who made them up? Cotton, silk and brocade were all readily available, and the thirteenth-century geographer Yaqut noted that cloth merchants had moved over to the eastern side of Baghdad from the western side. Women frequented the *suq al-thalatha* on Tuesdays, since Yaqut says it was the busiest, and it also housed the clothmakers' market (*suq al-bazzazin*). In Cairo Ibn al-Hajj strongly disapproved of women visiting material shops and being on familiar terms with the male shopkeepers. This familiarity presupposed frequent visits.

The Silk Market was one of the most important in the cities, and *crêpe de chine* and satin were also on sale.[77] Many other locally-made materials imitating Chinese silk were available. In the twelfth and thirteenth centuries fabrics were sold by weight, not length. Apparently some were lightly starched to add 'body' in imitation of the real thing, always assuming that the merchants escaped the sharp eyes of the market superintendent (*muhtasib*). Imported textiles were more expensive due not only to transportation costs, but to supply and demand, fuelled by the desire of some women for the exotic. Their motifs likely betrayed their origins, and women would have been well aware of how costs reflected place of origin and quality. Home-produced fabrics and patterns drew on the indigenous culture but, as in other areas of Islamic art, there was much adaptation of external influences by local artists and craftspeople.

Cotton was a valuable commodity and as such, was under tight quality controls in the *suq* in Muslim Spain in the eleventh century. It was probably introduced to Iraq from East Asia via Persia.

While tailors for men's clothing probably worked from their shops, it is unthinkable that men would measure up women. Did seamstresses have shops in the market, or did women buy the material themselves and either do their own sewing, or have a seamstress call at their homes for fittings, to return later with the finished garments? Since good clothes were expensive, there would have been a market for women who could sew and repair clothes and provide 'uniforms' for household help. In these cases, merchants probably sent bales of textiles to the palaces for inspection and approval. It is plausible to suggest that, in view of the very high cost of many garments, there was a thriving market in second-hand clothing. Who better to exploit it than women brokers?

It is evident that there was a social hierarchy in costume in terms of fabric, cut and ornamentation, and silk, fine linen, brocade and furs, for example, were the mark of the wealthy. The court escaped much of the opprobrium heaped by theologians on lesser mortals, and many royal edicts were of the 'Do as I say' and not 'Do as I do' variety. The flaunting of wealth in general was considered unseemly, somehow 'beyond one's station', and clerics and others in authority rightly feared that it was conducive to social discontent.

Colours, too, and their combinations, set the classes and the sexes apart; they also indicated life-stages such as the married state, and reflected a tendency for older women to choose darker clothes. Plain white was worn by women who had been abandoned. Unfortunately this served to make them stand out in society when many might have preferred to keep a low profile and hide their shame. These are involuntary rites of passage in any woman's life, and linked to this theme of transition is the consecrated white robe worn in the sacred precincts at Mecca, as well as the traditional dark robes of mourning. Colours were also employed as a prop to the belief system of Islam, and this theme is elaborated upon in Chapter 8 in the context of women on the periphery of society.

Clothing, therefore, was an important bearer of meaning in the medieval period. As such, it begs the question of where and before whom women wore their finery, and surely suggests that many women appeared in the public eye with or without their families' approval and were well able to deal with male hostility and harassment on the streets.

Not all Muslim women were interested in fashion. While Ibn Battuta was heartened by the assiduous devotion of the Muslim negroes of Mali, he was shocked to observe among their 'bad qualities' the fact that:

> The women servants, slave-girls, and young girls go about in front of everyone naked, without a stitch of clothing on them. Women go into the sultan's presence naked and without coverings.[78]

This practice was not confined to the lower classes, for even the sultan's daughters went around naked.

CHAPTER 6

Cosmetics, Jewellery and Fashion Accessories

The twelfth-century poetess Safiyya al-Baghdadiyya wrote:

> I am the wonder of the world, the ravisher of hearts and minds. Once you've seen my stunning looks, you're a fallen man.[1]

Most women could only aspire to her beauty. Her contemporary, the lovely Salma bint al-Qaratisi, 'the chastest of all people', was nevertheless also well aware of her allure:

> My eyes outshine the oryx's eyes, my neck outfines the gazelle's neck, and my neckline sparkles my necklaces.[2]

It is striking that Safiyya and Salma, after some five hundred years, still used the metaphors associated with the early Bedouin poetry to describe their physical charms, and that their self-confidence was boundless.

The face

In the medieval period the Arab ideal of female beauty favoured a full face and rouged cheeks. Beauty spots were considered particularly attractive attributes and likened to quince seeds. Hakam, a poet and singer at the court of al-Walid, was captivated by one girl whom he described in glowing terms:

> Her garland's all colours; her face a seduction.
> The mole on her cheek is without a companion.
> Shimmering, swaying, she moves like a serpent.
> She's a cord round my heart, and I'm caught in her bridle.[3]

Dhat al-khal, 'the possessor of the mole', was a favourite of Harun al-

Rashid. He had paid seventy thousand dirhams for her, but her allure evidently faded, and he handed her over to a male servant in a fit of pique. In the 'Tale of the Ebony Horse' in the *Thousand and One Nights* the prince compared a sleeping slave-girl to a full moon, with a flower-white brow and cheeks with moles like blood-red anemones. One besotted Persian ruler even considered the beauty spot on his beloved's face above the prized cities of Bukhara and Samarqand with all their riches.[4] In the absence of these natural features, did women pencil or paint them in?

Mihrab's daughter Rudaba, was described in Firdawsi's *Book of Kings* (*Shahname*) as:

Like ivory from head to toe, with a face like Paradise and a figure as graceful as a tree. Her cheeks were as red as pomegranate blossoms and her lips like its seeds, while two pomegranates grew from her silver breast.

Her eyes were 'twin narcissi in a garden',[5] and her lover Zal predictably found her irresistible. Arab poets used similar colourful metaphors in the language of love, and the chin was compared to a drop of alabaster on a ruby, denoting the smoothness and translucency of skin against red lips. These were descriptions of women by men, moreover women who were cossetted and pampered and enjoyed a lifestyle far removed from the lot of the majority in society. Many of them were not Arabs.

A twelfth-century poem by al-Tarabulusi illustrated well the extent of the influx of foreign women. It described someone's daughter who had vanquished him 'by the variety of her perfections (charms)':

The sound of her voice and the aspect of her form, the haughty pose of the Persian, the voluptuousness of Syria, glances like those of the maids of Iraq and language (sweet as that) spoken in the Hijaz.[6]

Within two hundred years the old Arab aristocratic lines had been diluted through intermarriage and al-Amin was the last Caliph born to an Arab mother.

The poets wrote of pale beauties in the *harim*, all of whom had at their disposal a wide array of cosmetics, extensive wardrobes and costly jewellery as complement. Of other, more ordinary Arab women, Bedouin and peasant women and girls who spent long hours outdoors in the harsh sun, we hear little. How could they live up to such lofty ideals? However, cosmetic preparations could be concocted at home from a variety of easily obtained ingredients and natural recipes handed down in families from mother to daughter and between friends. Fruit juices and rosewater, honey and watercress and poppies were used to soften the skin.[7] Women stained their lips red with iron oxide and other substances. Face creams were produced from powdered stones and crushed flowers, spices and dried herbs. Rose petals, moss, herbs and plants from many a garden were mixed with a little water and pounded in a mortar and pestle, then put out to dry in the sun.[8] The result was *ghasul*, a paste which had a variety of cosmetic applications, including adding the desirable reddish glow to cheeks.

Freckles, unlike beauty spots, were frequently considered unsightly, and lemon juice was used to lighten them. Women seeking an ivory-like complexion also used the skin bleaching agent *batikha*, a paste made from pounded white marble, borax, pulses and other ingredients sun-dried to a powdery consistency.[9] This desire for pale skin was undoubtedly a fashion influenced by the presence of so many foreign women and acknowledged as a marker of social status. The 'Abbasid court poet Abu Tammam sang:

Women marble-white and fair,
Trailing gold-fringed raiment rare,
Opulence, luxurious ease
With the lute's soft melodies,
Such delights hath our brief span;
Time is Change, Time's fool is Man.[10]

The face-lotion *ghumra* was prepared from *wars*, a yellow dyestuff which resembled sesame from a plant uniquely cultivated in Yemen. It was apparently used by brides, and there may be an association here with Ibn al-Jawziyya's comment, that 'A robe dyed with *wars* has an aphrodisiac effect'.[11] Melon juice and milk were good for dry skin, always a hazard in extremely hot climates, and face masks were made with fresh fruit. Some of these cosmetics are concocted by women to this day in Saudi Arabia, according to their personal preferments.

Eyes

Dark eyes, preferably large and almond-shaped, were much admired and highly desirable. Beautiful eyes were among the attributes of the virginal *houris* in Paradise, and the term *houri* has connotations of intense whiteness.

The ideal beauty 'had '*hawar al-'ayn*', that is, a strong contrast between the blackness of her eye and the white, in the words of the *Qamus* dictionary: 'Intense whiteness of the white of the eye and intense blackness of the black thereof, with roundness of the black, and thinness of the eyelids'.

The description in *The Thousand and One Nights* of the eyes of Princess Jawhara conformed exactly, 'blackest black and whitest white'. Eyes were frequently compared with those of does, with drooping eyelids. Qasmuna, a poetess, seeing a gazelle in her garden, sadly wrote: 'Gazelle, roam and nibble in the ever-fresh garden, for I'm like you, houri-eyed and alone.'[12]

The tenth-century Syrian poet al-Mutanabbi's ideal Bedouin woman:

Shone like a moon,
and swayed like a moringa-bough,
and shed fragrance like ambergris,
and gazed like a gazelle.[13]

To enhance the illusion and add lustre, women applied *kohl* made from pulverised antimony or other materials to the inside of their eyelids. *Kohl* made eyes appear lustrous and appealing. It is debatable if this was cause or effect, since *kohl* caused irritation, and the resultant watering of the eye had a beneficial therapeutic function in hot, dry climates, where flies were a constant source of infection and endemic disease. The practice had long gone on in the Near East, and the Old Testament prophet Ezekiel railed against women who 'painted' their eyes. Antimony from Isfahan was well-known for its excellence. It was also produced in the Maghrib and *kohl* was prescribed particularly 'for old people and those whose sight has grown weak'.[14]

The first Arab woman recorded as using *kohl* was Zarqa, for whom the proverb, 'More keen-sighted than Zarqa al-Yamama' was coined.[15] Zarqa was, unusually, a blue-eyed girl from Bahrain, who had given a warning to her kinsfolk of approaching heavily-camouflaged soldiers in the third century.[16] Her advice was ignored, since nobody else could see anything, and her kin were massacred. The victorious enemy ruler Hassan, keen to discover how Zarqa came by her exceptional gift, gouged out her eyes, and found that her eye-veins were black. On asking Zarqa why this was so, she said she applied *kohl*.

Zarqa may have used *kohl* for other than therapeutic purposes. Blue eyes reminded many Arabs of their traditional, northern enemies. Al-Jahiz personally found the 'whiteness of their eyebrows and eyelashes' loathsome and ugly, and slaves dyed their eyebrows, eyelashes and hair black to conform to the Arab ideal of beauty. They perhaps used a similar infusion to an old recipe from Persia, where walnut leaves were boiled up and reduced to a dark viscous mix and then applied to eyelashes and eyebrows.[17] The hagiography of the Prophet holds that one of his distinguishing marks was that when he was born his eyes were already 'kohled' (*makuhl*).

Imagine the effect of a well-highlighted eye when wearing the *niqab*, the veil worn outdoors described by contemporary dictionaries as extending 'as high as the circuit of the eye'. A spirited girl from a clan of the Banu Kalb caught the eye of a poet, who recalled :

I passed by women of Minjab,
Bright flashing eyes.[18]

In the same vein a modern Saudi poet writes,

Eyes naked
As a knife-blade,
You are a rose,
Drained by butterflies
Flirting.[19]

With such emphasis on the eyes, even an otherwise plain girl could emphasise hers with *kohl*. If she wore a veil she could still captivate; this would also allow her to use her eyes as a heightened means of communication, as 'Ulayya the poetess sister of Harun al-Rashid demonstrated: 'We hint our missives and our eyes are the go-betweens, for letters can be read and contacts let you down.'[20]

In other words, women had to rely on themselves for discretion in matters of the heart. It is sad that betrayal and disappointment were so often the lot of the lover and represent other themes which underpin Arabic love poetry.

Kohl was stored in a special container made of glass, ivory, silver or bronze, with a blunt applicator which tapered towards the end doubling as a decorative stopper. These receptacles had cylindrical necks, sloping shoulders and conical bodies and their design excluded air and prevented the *kohl* from drying out. Its application required great care and a steady hand, as the stick was moistened with rosewater or water then drawn along the inside of the eyelid. There were undoubtedly flasks in other materials available in the *suq* within the means of all women.

The ingredients of *kohl* varied from area to area, and pounded olive stones and the soot from assorted resins and seeds were all used. Some were cosmetic, others therapeutic and it is possible that its use as a cosmetic followed on from the medical application. One had to beware of charlatans. The underworld 'hero' Gharib in one of Ibn Daniyal's popular shadow plays practised magic and boasted: 'I give treatment for their eyes, and how many eyelids will never sleep any more after my application of *kohl*!'[21]

Men, too, applied *kohl* for cosmetic purposes. A dream interpretation of Ibn Sirin read:

> If someone puts on *kohl* with the attention of adorning himself, that means that he will achieve a work of religious character which will attract women's esteem.[22]

This sounds a rather worldy endeavour for one of religious disposition.

Teeth

White, gleaming teeth were also highly desirable physical attractions. Elaborate metaphors such as teeth like 'pearls set in coral' frequently appeared in Arabic literature and 'snowy crystals' or 'white pearls' also emphasised their lustre and brilliance. It should be remembered that literary references to the ideal of female beauty were usually within the context of the court and the upper classes, and applied more particularly to singing girls. An ordinary woman was probably diet-deficient. In addition she had likely had multiple pregnancies and breast-fed her children. All of these factors affected the state of her teeth, certainly as she aged. What could a woman do to improve her appearance?

Teeth-spacing

Teeth-spacing had been practised in Arabia since at least the advent of Islam, but the Prophet said God cursed those who spaced out their teeth, 'thus deforming Allah's creation'. After the murder of the Caliph 'Uthman, his successor Mu'awiya sought the hand in marriage of 'Uthman's widow, the tall striking daughter of Farafisa from the Banu Kalb. Men in the early community, following the Prophet's injunction, naturally found the practice of teeth-spacing reprehensible. To prove her fidelity to her dead husband, the widow extracted her front teeth, so that no other man would want her, despite her prized pale skin.[23]

Were teeth extracted to a pattern in the pursuit of fashion, or how much of this was initially due to decay? The practice sounds somewhat extreme, and could not have been painless, and one assumes that powerful narcotics derived from plants in some form were administered. The dissolute caliph Al-Walid II noticed among the girls from Minjab, 'a tender sylph, a pretty flirt, with slender waist and sharp eye teeth' who 'graced her desert-dwellers' tents'.[24] Perhaps she had undergone extractions to emphasise her eye teeth, or even sharpened them for emphasis. Fashion may even have been behind teeth-spacing in the better-fed upper classes. The mother of the Egyptian vizier 'Alam al-Din, (appointed in 1351) reportedly carried it out. She would not have needed to earn money, and most likely applied her expertise to friends and acquaintances in her own social circle. Perhaps she also whitened teeth. Teeth-spacing in the early days may simply have been a pragmatic response to the problem of dental decay, and an effort to balance unsightly gaps.

Ghasul, a type of paste made from marshmallow or other plants, was useful as toothpaste, but served many functions. Cleaning the teeth formed part of the ritual ablutions before prayer, and was carried out several times a day; indeed the term *ghasul* is derived from the verbal root 'to wash'. Hariri's impudent Abu Zayd in the seventh *maqama* requested *ghasul* to: 'Cleanse my hands, and smoothe my skin, and perfume my breath, and brace my gums, and strengthen my stomach'.

With the stipulation that it should be newly pounded, in fine powder form and fragrant. However revealing this request, it was a gross breach of etiquette on the part of a guest. Lemon grass (*idhkhir*) was also useful in dental care, since, 'its root strengthens the bases of the teeth'.[25] The Prophet personally recommended:

> Cleanse your mouth with toothpicks, for your mouths are the abode of the guardian angels, whose pens are the tongues, and whose ink is the spittle of men; and to whom nothing is more intolerable than the relics of food in the mouth.[26]

Care was taken to keep the breath sweet, and lemon peel was used as a bleaching agent.

Hair

Framing all of these ideal physical features was a woman's crowning glory, her hair. Hair was worn long and then, as now, it was dressed in a variety of styles. It could be waved, curled, or rolled into ringlets. Rayy, a Persian town between Hamadhan and Tehran, was known for the quality of its combs. Fashions would come and go. Aromatic shampoos such as an extract from the plant *khatmi* or marsh mallow, kept hair lustrous and herbal and floral rinses added fragrance. Wigs were worn by Arab women in the seventh century at least, but the practice was condemned by theologians.[27]

Individual scented plants had particular significance in the language of poets. For example, the hyacinth recalled the beloved's curly hair, and musk described something black and fragrant, such as night-time or the lover's hair. The violet also represented the hair in this genre, and an Umayyad poet mentioned 'curls with saffron drenched' where saffron was used to perfume the hair. Plaits hung down the back of the neck and the celebrated Basran poet, Abu'l-Ayna, remarked admiringly that: 'If Umm Ja'far were to unbraid her plaits, they would be bound to touch some caliph or heir to the caliphate.'

The length of her hair evidently alluded to her blood ties to twelve caliphs. Women in Spain, at least, wore hair nets, and this suggests that it was worn long and perhaps back, off the face.[28]

Women had their hair braided with black string, and this must have been a time-consuming business, giving the opportunity for much social chit-chat and companionship between friends. Hairdressers also visited homes and would keep their clients up to date with the latest styles and types of hair decoration, not to mention gossip. Even numbers were considered unlucky, so the braids were invariably of an uneven number. Small flat gold ornaments (*barq*) were attached to each strand and staggered between braids, to give an all-over effect.[29] The name *barq* is apt, as it denotes 'glistening, gleaming, and flashing', as of lightning. A small tube (*masura*) was attached to each braid. It measured some three eights of an inch long, and seems to be related to the word for bracelet, implying encircling or enclosing. Finials of jewels or small gold coins were sometimes hung on tiny rings below the *masura*. The total effect against black hair would be most attractive, and the ornaments undoubtedly tinkled as women walked along. Not all women had gold hair ornamentation, but they would have decorated their tresses according to their means, with beads and silver or other accessories.

Girls and women dyed their hair with henna. The flowers of the herb were perfumed, and its roots were red, but the leaves contained the tint.

Henna from North Africa tended towards an orange hue, while that from Persia produced a rich red.[30] First of all a smooth paste was prepared with boiling water, a dash of lemon juice added, and the solution applied when cool. For a really deep colour, many women left it on overnight, and then carefully wrapped their head in muslin. The addition of a beaten egg acted as a conditioner. There must have been initially an element of trial and error with such a strong agent, and women doubtless added other ingredients to modify the shades. Henna was also used by Nubian women as deodorant. Among the multiple uses of henna enumerated in Ibn Qayyim al-Jawziyya's medical compendium *Medicine of the Prophet*, (*Tibb al-Nabawi*), was that 'It causes the hair to grow, strengthens and beautifies it, and strengthens the head'.[31] Again the therapeutic aspects may have preceded the cosmetic.

Men, too, used hair dyes. The first male recorded in Mecca as using black dye was the Prophet's grandfather, 'Abd al-Muttalib ibn Hashim; other Meccans, who had previously used red henna, imitated him. *Katam*, a plant which grew in the plains, produced a very deep black colour. Fittingly, *katam* had literal connotations of 'concealment', so its Arabic meaning is unequivocal, and its use on its own to dye the hair black was proscribed by the jurists, whose ruling was intended to eliminate deception in order to gain advantage. For instance, older women or men might dye their hair to deceive a prospective partner; this was construed as fraud.[32]

There could be other hazards in inappropriate 'concealment'. The eighth-century caliph al-Hisham was extremely unprepossessing both in manner and looks, and had a very noticeable squint. One scholar found him in splendid perfumed robes and noticed that he had dyed his hair black. It is, of course, arguable Hisham was anxious to deflect attention from his physical blemishes, but the fact that his black hair was worthy of mention suggests that he merely looked incongruous.[33] The Prophet personally recommended henna used with *katam* as 'the best you can use for changing the colour of white hair'[34] and this mixture produced a warmer shade of brown. Men, and probably women, in al-Andalus in the fourteenth century also used henna, unless the hair had become totally white.

Other hair preparations were available. Al-Tanukhi passed on the prescription of a physician given in a dream to a man with a greying beard which contained coconut, something called 'yellow myrobalan' and sal ammoniac. After pounding and mixing it well and rubbing it in, the user reported with satisfaction, 'My hair became black and it was a long time before it began to turn grey'.[35] Preparations of indigo or walnut oil enhanced the blackness of the hair. There were likely other, common-or-garden herbs

and plants for hair dyes and tinted rinses known to women and passed down
to each other in recipes.

Perfumes

Perfume had always played an important role in Arab society among both
women and men. According to a *Tradition* of the Prophet, Adam brought
three things from Paradise – the myrtle, 'the chief of sweet-scented flowers in
this world', the narcissus and the hyacinth. The Umayyad Caliph Yazid I was
able to reinforce his Medinese forces against the Syrian army in 683 by calling
up some four hundred perfumiers. As early as the ninth century, Arab
scientists had devised means to make perfumes synthetically, and one wrote
that they could be sold 'for good money without anyone noticing the
deception'.[36] Al-Tirmidhi drew a distinction between perfume for men, which
should be colourless but fragrant, and that for women:

> Perfume for men is manifested in its smell and its colour is concealed:
> perfume for women is manifested by its colour and its smell is concealed.[37]

Obviously one could only be aware of a woman's perfume at close
quarters, which was generally reprehensible in any case between non-relatives.
There seems to be an implicit notion here that women used strong perfume
as an agent of sexual attraction, but surely some women considered male
perfume in the same light?

Ghaliya, like ambergris and musk, was a very costly fragrance frequently
associated with amorous pursuits, and references to them could only ever be
in the context of the upper classes. Ambergris, incense and saffron, myrrh and
balms were imported via Yemen and transported in camel caravans along the
Red Sea coast to Egypt and Syria, then made their way onwards to Europe
along the Mediterranean.

Muhammad ibn Sulayman ibn 'Ali al-Hashimi, a prosperous resident of
Basra, had 'a large urn of porcelain filled with the perfume *ghaliya*'. The old
dictionaries defined this as 'a perfume composed of musk and ambergris and
camphor and oil of ben *(moringa aptera)*'[38] and its root meaning referred to
boiling and thickening to a dark salve. Scientific textbooks mentioned
variations which were concocted for well-known historical people by
professional perfumiers. A poor visitor to al-Hashimi's home scooped out a
large amount with his hand and hid it under his turban. Guilt at the enormity

of his 'crime' (in every sense) then overcame the man, and he became blind. A doctor was called and after all trace of the *ghaliya* had been removed with cold water his sight returned.[39] It is to be hoped that that was punishment enough.

From the beginning of the tenth century onwards, *ghaliya* was a particularly prized gift to singing-girls, who used it and other costly fragrances to write amorous verses on cheeks and foreheads. One lover wrote of his mistress: 'Across her brow with musk three lines I traced, as stray soft moon-entangled clouds; 'God curse those who betray'.'[40]

Some 'boy-girls' also used it as a 'moustache'. Al-Washsha', the arbiter of refinement, decried *ghaliya* precisely because of its association with singing-girls and homosexual boys. Although perfume was used on the body, applying it to garments was reprehensible to the genteel. Al-Washsha' had mentioned fine linen from Dabiq in Egypt 'impregnated with ambergris' and again he associated perfumed clothing with dancing-girls and entertainers, who were of low social standing among the righteous. Since he also recommended that the elegant person never wear soiled clothing with newly-laundered, one wonders whether he implied that the personal hygiene of singing-girls and their ilk was not what it might have been and that they used perfume as a mask? Or did he merely regard such a practice as 'common'?

Perfumes were stored in glass phials or bottles, with ground glass stoppers. A contemporary dictionary describes *khazma*, as a receptacle 'for their perfumes and other similar things' made from palm leaf for storing perfumes and so on; this must have been for storing the receptacle itself, that is, a glass bottle. The palm leaf acted as a good insulator against heating and evaporation, and the name indicates that the outer container was made by splitting and tying the leaf.

Rosewater was used extensively as perfume. It also featured largely in entertainment, etiquette and cookery. The rosewater from the town of Jur in Persia was proverbial for its excellence. A suggestive tribal song from the southwest of Iran sung for a bride mirrors well the sentiments of many women: 'If you want your husband to like you, swing your hips, and early in the morning sprinkle rosewater on the bed.'[41]

Home-made beauty preparations using flowers and aromatics were doubtless handed down from generation to generation, and the water-lily, violet, and lemon and orange blossom were all popular. Ziryab, the great and influential Persian musician, had introduced deodorants made from lead monoxide to Arab society.[42]

All of these would have been available in the market-place, or from gardens, and many women who were affluent in their own right personally shopped for jewellery and perfume. The perfumier ('attar) in his shop pounding the precious ingredients with a stone pestle was a familiar sight in the suq. One writer complained that in the markets of Cairo of old on Thursdays there were more women than men, and one could hardly move for them. That was the weekend, after all, and women might have taken the opportunity of shopping. According to one authority, there were many marital disputes betwen husbands and wives over such outings.

Jewellery

Women and small girls wore jewellery. Ibn Sirin was of the opinion that, 'Jewellery worn by women is synonymous with beauty, charm and good circumstances'[43] and al-Washsha' catalogued the fashionable jewellery of the Baghdad ladies of his time. Gold chains, amulets linked with gold and silver braiding, precious minerals such as amber, black obsidian, pearls, coral and rock crystal all appeared on his list. Expensive turquoise came from Nishapur and according to al-Jahiz: 'The price of a setting of one of these jewels often reaches two hundred dinars, provided that it weighs over a mithqal.'[44]

This presupposed that it was in perfect condition. Crystal, rubies and pearls were imported from Ceylon, and local pearls were fished in the Arabian Gulf around Bahrain. (The place-name indicates the 'two seas', that is the salt and sweet water springs bubbling up from the sea-bed from which the fishermen could replenish their water supplies.)

Clothes and jewels were complementary, and women's penchant for ostentation highly indulged. Zubayda, the wife of Harun al-Rashid, was literally weighed down by her finery, and 'could scarcely walk under the weight of her jewellery and dresses'.[45] A poet fulsomely described the adornment of a singing-girl in eleventh-century al-Andalus:

The jewel on her breast flashes like lightning in clouds dark, like in the night the lamp's spark, like flowers in full bloom in the meadow of spring or in the June sky's nightly blue the Pleiades' ring. Her bangles shine like the half-moon the same, her anklets like rings of flame.[46]

Ibn Sirin, the interpreter of men's dreams, said that to dream of bracelets and pearls on the feet and hands symbolised 'the husband, brother or father'. Was he referring to gifts made to women from their families on marriage?

The goldsmiths' and jewellers' *suq* was one of the most beautiful, and even today one can become rather *blasé* at the rows of shops in Middle Eastern markets with windows gleaming with gold. It is fair to say that by the twelfth century rubies were very common and within the reach of many, to the extent that the richest could have the largest specimens fashioned into perfume containers. Diamonds in the medieval period were of the industrial variety and were frequently used as poison, or a means of committing suicide when ground up. Ibn al-Hajj expressed the opinion that it was up to a husband to buy his wife's jewellery and costumes. He found it reprehensible that women entered jewellers' and material shops, conversing animatedly with men – apparently often with deplorable consequences.[47] Women also frequented other types of business.

Necklaces were always popular, and the *tawq* was literally 'a neck ring' of heavy gold. The *labba* reached down to the breast bone. The *sha'ir* was another type, and its name suggests that the beads resembled grains of barley. Several colourful strings of beads were often worn together, and amber was another favourite. Dictionaries described the *'iqd* as 'a string upon which beads are strung'. More commonly, a string or strings of graded glass beads, with a large one at the centre, were worn. But there was something to suit every purse, whether jewels worth a king's ransom or, for those of more modest means, cut and painted glass. Costume jewellery was manufactured under Indian influence from the eleventh century onwards, and versions of gold jewellery in silver or base materials, even iron, were available. Lane described the jewellery of poorer women in Egypt: 'Some are of gold and precious stones, but the more common of brass; and many of the latter have coloured beads attached to them. A few are of silver.'[48]

Many women probably made their own jewellery from whatever was to hand. For example, even bone could be fashioned into bracelets and beads and carved and painted.

Earrings

Earrings were very popular, highly visible, ornaments, and a gold pair would always have been expensive. The type known as *halqa* was literally a 'ring', and could only have been worn in pierced ears. In eleventh-century al-Andalus Ibn Hazm wrote of the plaint by the lover of a 'lissom maid':

Deep in his heart the lover hears,
The pendants hanging from her ears,
Ring out a tender melody,
'I love thee dearly: lov'st thou me'?[49]

There is the suggestion of onomatopoiea, of repetition and refrain which seem to mimic the swaying and tinkling as she walked. Medieval dictionaries described the *qurt* as: 'The thing that is suspended to the lobe of the ear, (such as) a silver bead fashioned like a pearl, or a pendant of gold,'[50] and mentioned the proverbial Mariya, the first Arab woman to wear ear-rings, 'said to have been of great value'. The *tuma* was variously described as a silver earring with a large bead, possibly a pearl, at its centre, or a silver bead 'fashioned like a pearl', which a girl 'puts in her ear'. In these instances the ears were probably pierced, which was prudent in the case of expensive jewellery. More elaborate earrings were correspondingly expensive, and many were worked in elegant filigree.

Rings

Women wore rings of all descriptions and materials. Strictly speaking the term for ring, *khatim*, referred to a signet ring, but the meaning could include inset gems and other stones. Were particular items of jewellery always universally worn and did Arab women in the medieval period wear nose-rings? Nose-rings, which sounded very much like those worn by Bedouin women, were among the items of female jewellery deplored by the prophet Isaiah, all of which had been worn from time immemorial. Poorer women in the cities and in country areas of nineteenth-century Egypt certainly favoured the nose ring (*khizam*, commonly called *khuzam*), usually made of brass, but occasionally in gold. It measured from one to one and a half inches in diameter and had at least three coloured glass beads in blue and red attached. It was worn in the right nostril, and its name came from the root 'to pierce'. Its initial insertion must have been unpleasant, and the risk of infection high. Small children surely presented a major – and potentially extremely painful – hazard, and nose rings would snag on full face veils. Given poorer women wore these rings, the inference may be that they went out in public unveiled.

Chardin reported from Persia that well-to-do women in the middle of the seventeenth century sometimes wore a nose-ring in the left nostril; this was suspended like an earring and decorated with gemstones. These women were strictly secluded and did not leave the *harim*, so had no need for a full face veil. They could also call on servants to care for their small children. Overall, it may be that many women found the nose-ring uncomfortable and 'lower class'.

Bracelets

Bracelets (*asawir*) were crafted in silver, gold or other materials. They were sometimes encrusted with precious stones, and prices varied accordingly. As in so many aspects of the fashion of Arab women, *asawir* is an arabicised Persian word. Marriage contracts from Egypt were useful in revealing prices, but would necessarily detail only relatively costly items. The name in the singular, *siwar* simply means to encircle; there is an extended meaning of springing together, and many bracelets were jointed and fastened with a clasp.[51] This seems to imply a degree of workmanship and an urban workshop background, while more prosaic versions simply slipped on the arm.

Bracelets decorated with pearls cost from two to five dinars in Egypt, and one bourgeois woman received a pair of bangles valued at twenty eight dinars.[52] More ornate types had precious stones set in gold, came in plain gold or were sometimes made in a simple twist. Some women wore an armlet (*dumluj*) on the upper arm. While this was larger and presumably more costly, it could only have been seen by the immediate family and close friends, so many women and girls may have preferred an assortment of small wrist bracelets for their ease of public display.

At least some portion of women's jewellery came in the form of gifts on marriage and was regarded by women as their own personal wealth. It represented a financial safeguard in the event of divorce and abandonment as well as inflation. An important point was that if jewellery formed part of the marriage settlement, it belonged solely to the woman, unless she instituted divorce proceedings, committed adultery or in any way contravened the terms of that contract. Jewellery was portable, and where more safe than on one's person, particularly in the case of bracelets and anklets? Women therefore found jewellery desirable for reasons other than personal adornment or as evidence of one's place in society.

The early eighteenth-century Dutch traveller Le Brun commented on the appearance of Persian ladies, which sounds little different to earlier periods: 'They (also) have a white, gold-embroidered veil hanging down over their shoulders, necklaces of precious stones and pearls.'[53]

A small phial of perfume was often suspended on a long gold chain, and upper class women had belts 'two or three inches wide . . . ornamented with precious stones and pearls'. Le Brun also commented on rings and 'bracelets of precious stones' and obviously wrote about well-off women.

Anklets

Anklets are apparently no longer worn, but in the seventh century the Qur'an exhorted women believers never to knock their ankles together and draw attention to themselves by walking provocatively. The Arabic for anklet is *khalkhal*, a bracelet in silver or gold worn on each leg. *Khalkhal* is again onomatopoeic and charmingly suggestive of the clinking noise produced by the rhythmic, swaying walk of the women and girls. Men found this distracting, as the Arab song confirmed, 'The ringing of thine anklets has deprived me of my reason'.[54]

Arab men were not alone in their disapproval of female ornamentation and the perceived flaunting of their sexuality, but there seems to be an underlying denial that they themselves were inherently weak and capable of succumbing to female charms. The Prophet Isaiah castigated the haughty daughters of Zion 'who walked with stretched forth necks and wanton eyes, walking and mincing as they go, and making a tinkling with their feet.'[55]

Isaiah disapproved equally of bracelets, headbands, earrings, rings and nose jewels, so all these forms of personal adornment were evidently of long standing in the area. The disapprobation of Muslim theologians stemmed in part also from the wish to abandon practices which had been current among Arabs in the pre-Islamic period.

Henna and tattooing

Women decorated their hands and feet with henna. The dark grey strain was used on the fingers and hands, while red henna was applied to the nails. Abu Zayd may have referred to the former variety when he waxed eloquent in the *maqama* of Halwan on a beautiful singing-girl:

> Her fingers that, with henna dyed,
> Seem purple grapes in cluster bright[56]

Abu Zayd also likened her nails to the 'onyx' and 'beryl'. Other women preferred not to stain their nails. Ibn Qayyim al-Jawziyya recommended, 'When finger-nails are smeared with henna paste, it improves and benefits them'.[57] One assumes that women were aware of this and prepared henna and other common plants for cosmetic and therapeutic purposes. Henna from the banks of the Nile had a long pedigree in Ancient Egypt, where it was also included in the mummification process, and it was still exported from Egypt up to the nineteenth century.

Lane noted that upper class Egyptian women painted their nails, hands and feet with henna paste in the evening; they were then bound tightly in a cloth which was removed the next morning. The process was repeated every two to three weeks as 'an embellishment'. The colour could be darkened afterwards with other materials.

The word sani'a referred to a woman who used her hands skilfully. A tattoist appeared as a character in one of Ibn Daniyal's shadow plays. It is not clear if the design she produced was permanent, by dyeing the skin, or temporary, using henna. Either is possible, and both procedures certainly involved pricking the skin; indeed a toothpick or something similar is used to mark out a pattern up to the present day. Needles were required for permanent designs. These would reflect tradition and changes in fashion. It is likely that many were originally intended to deflect the evil eye and that different areas and tribes had their own particular patterns. This imparted a notion of group solidarity, as well as revealing tribal affiliation. Tattoos apparently had erotic overtones. Was their permanence a rebellious act by women against official condemnation? Al-Raziq was of the opinion that the Egyptian tattooist in the Mamluk period was a gypsy woman, and possibly not pure Egyptian.[58] Was this because Muslim jurists condemned tattooists (and those who removed body-hair) on the grounds that they were cursed by God, and that Muslim women did not carry out these functions?

Lane recorded the practices in the countryside and among the lower classes where tattooing in a blue or greenish shade replaced staining with henna. The cost of frequent applications of henna may have encouraged poorer women to opt for the permanent tattoo. Other factors, such as regional, district or social class preferences possibly came into play. According to Lane the skin was pricked in a pattern and, 'some smoke-black (of wood or oil) mixed with milk from the breast of a woman'[59] was then rubbed in and left for a week. This was done around five or six years of age, again 'by a gypsy woman', but neither al-Raziq nor Lane mentioned the origin or religion of those gypsies. A fourteenth-century dictionary said that women also dyed their hands with the leaves of the woad plant (*wasm*). Lane's and other nineteenth-century descriptions confirm earlier historical accounts, and henna continues to be an important cosmetic embellishment. Women's visits to the *hammam* are discussed extensively here in the chapter on women's occupations.

Mirrors

One necessary accessory for the application of cosmetics was a mirror. These were simple discs of bronze or iron, and the latter were about half the price of mirrors in glass, steel or porcelain. Some were very elaborate and encrusted with gemstones and other decoration. Mirrors usually had figurative designs in relief and, in common with other metalwork and pottery of the period, blessings to its owner of a general nature on the obverse. Relief casting did not appear on mirrors much before the thirteenth century and probably arrived via Chinese influence.

Fans

Fans, apparently, apart from their suitability for the climate, were also considered *de rigueur* for fashionable ladies, by day or night. In Mecca in the second half of the tenth century, at the end of Ramadhan:

> After the *'Id al-Fitr* prayer young girls wearing splendid decorated clothes and holding fans in their hands visited the houses of the people and collected *'Id* money from the elders.[60]

Palm leaves were plaited and coloured then mounted on a handle of palm or figured orange-wood. Fans were peddled around houses by fan-makers, who were invariably blind in order to allow them entry to the *harim*.[61] While this would certainly prevent them seeing the women and the inside of the home, it was surely no guarantee of their morality. Male thinking presumably was that they could not be attracted and tempted by the women's looks; what if the women were attracted to these men? The fan-maker could obviously plait the leaves, but one wonders if the 'figured' orange wood was decorated by someone else, perhaps the women in his family?

The mandil

One indispensable fashion accessory for the fashion-conscious lady was the *mandil*, a multi-functional oblong textile item with connotations of 'wiping' and meanings as varied as 'napkin', 'kerchief', 'towel' and 'covering'; its size was in proportion to its function. The *mandil* was a symbol of rank and refinement, and one Arabic saying allegedly ran, 'They are people who have made their money *mandils* for their honour',[62] meaning 'they protect their honour with their money.' One should not be surprised that the *mandil* appeared in illustrations in the context of royal courts; from this naturally followed carousing scenes. Literary references abounded in *belles-lettres* and poetry, where *mandil* is referred to in admiring terms, and it was frequently perfumed.

It is obvious that *mandil* prices fluctuated widely according to fabric, ornamentation and rarity value, and that, for example, the most expensive was likely the speciality from China described as made from 'the down of phoenix *(samandal)* feathers'; these were cleaned by fire, yet remained unscathed.[63] They could measure some two metres in length and were evidently used as napkins. They sound rather large, but when one considers that they were used by a large group of drinkers – a ruler and his boon-companions – the cleansing by fire in a brazier would have been very convenient, hygienic and most effective. Discussion of the *mandil* is confined from now on to its use as a desirable accessory to a woman's wardrobe, and in all likelihood the preserve of the court and the well-to-do.

One *mandil* bore the inscription, 'I am good only in the hands of coquettish (maidens)'.[64] This defined but one of its functions, to make signals to an admirer, perhaps to emphasise a point made by a singer or attract a man's attention. The material, colour and pattern were defined by usage, and one found it variously described as being of 'brocade', a velvety cloth, silk, wool, linen and cotton. These fabrics were manufactured in different areas of the Muslim world, and the type frequently indicated the place of origin. For example a Dabiqi *mandil* was of the finest Egyptian linen from Dabiq. The best quality *mandil* was of any sheer material and some Egyptian examples were so fine that comparison was even made in the *Book of Songs* with the inner membrane of an egg; this also aptly confirmed their sheerness and luminosity. In *The Thousand and One Nights* the white *mandil* dropped by 'Aziza to her lover was 'softer than the zephyr and more pleasant to the eye than his cure is to a sick person'.[65]

Camphor was used metaphorically to emphasise whiteness, and a

Tabaristani poet fittingly compared a narcissus to 'a goblet of gold in a *mandil* of camphor'. One mandil delightfully 'spoke' thus, 'My sheerness has turned me into a zephyr, and I pass by meadows constituted by faces'. The *mandil* was also manufactured in Iran, Iraq and the Yemen.

All sources seem to agree that the item had a fringed or gold decorative border at the shorter ends. Gold ornamentation and other shades of stripes and coloured dots appeared in *mandil* borders in medieval manuscripts, and most contemporary illustrations suggested that the majority of these cloths were white. Ibn Battuta noted the 'matchless cotton fabrics with gold embroidered edges, which have a very long life on account of the excellence of the cotton and of the spinning,'[66] of Ladhiq in Anatolia. He did not specifically refer to '*mandil*' but the similarity is striking. Most of the spinners there were Greek women. Technically, the weaving of a *mandil* was difficult, and this affected its price. Flirtatious slave-girls and other young women were given to penning amatory verses for their paramours which they then frequently laboriously embroidered or painted, sometimes in gold, in these borders. One literary opinion was that :

A *mandil* is not good until it is provided with a striped border
And the iron (needle) hits it, and it is wounded.[67]

Embroidery on a fine *mandil* was necessarily a very skilled task. This was so because a *mandil* was a luxurious item. Great care had to be taken when using gold or other metallic thread, to avoid damaging the very fine material. The allusion to pain in the above verse is also apposite to the sewer, because metallic thread was sharp and cutting. Al-Hamadhani's merchant boasted: 'And this kerchief? Ask me about its story! It was woven in Jurgan and worked in Arrajan . . . I gave it to an embroiderer who worked it and embroidered it as you see.'[68]

One account told how in ninth-century Baghdad a woman took a *mandil* to a Sufi silk weaver, Khayr al-Nassaj, to have it embellished – presumably by adding embroidery or other ornamentation or fringing – for the cost of two pieces of silver.[69]

The man's name is interesting; '*nassaj*' is the occupational title 'weaver', and '*khayr*' implies that his work was of superior quality. He evidently supplemented his income from plain silk weaving by adding decoration. Two dirhams does not sound an excessive amount for excellent, careful workmanship on an already-expensive item, and one wonders if this included the cost of metallic thread? It is striking that the embroiderer was male; to what extent was this in keeping with the *hadith*, 'The work of pious men is sewing, of pious women, spinning'?[70] However, many women and girls must have embroidered their own *manadil*; this was literally a labour of love, since they frequently gave the finished item to the objects of their love-poems. A discerning lover, 'pining, consumed by desire, a prisoner of separation' or 'deeply, passionately in love' used a *mandil* to wipe his tears, to 'guard him from slanderous accusations and the eyes of humanity'.[71] It is striking to note how frequently gossip related to shame is mentioned in the context of affairs of the heart. One *mandil* 'lamented' that it had been the best type, but 'the tears of the lovers have changed me.' The *mandil* was therefore a symbol of joy, or a lover's token of affection which professed loyalty and steadfastness. It even served as an admonition by an aggrieved lover to a faithless one:

> I am the *mandil* of the one who keeps agreements. I am the *mandil* of (maidens) with pure cheeks. She embroidered me with her hand. Then she said: 'May God curse those (maidens) who break agreements'.[72]

In *The Thousand and One Nights* 'Aziza was privy to the secret gestures of her brother's lover. In time-honoured tradition, she acted as go-between and interpreted them for 'Aziz, 'As for the kerchief, it betokeneth that her breath of life is bound up in thee'.[73] Gestures by *mandil* were but one means of secret communication in the codes of love between lovers and married couples. It is fitting that the title of Ibn Hazm's account of courtly love in tenth-century Cordova, *Tawq al-hamama* was an allusion to the carrier-pigeon, 'the necklace of the dove' referring to its feathered neck-ring. Sadly, a *mandil* was also a symbol of grief at the loss of love. These verses are good illustrations of the custom at an early period to personalize objects such as textiles and metal-work, as demonstrated elsewhere.

One could also tuck a *mandil* into a belt, or carry it in the hand. Although veils and headcoverings have been discussed at length in the chapter on textiles, most had their individual Arabic names. The term *mandil* appeared in the twelfth-century dictionary *al-Mughrib* but, tellingly, it was also included in the Arabic-Persian *Kanz al-Lu'gha*, which suggested it was originally a cloth bound around the head.[74] Versions in different colours and patterns offset particular garments, and it is likely that both the colour and the manner in which a *mandil* was folded, held or tucked gave off the appropriate signals of the flirtatious, the unmarried, or the married woman, and conveyed a secret message to a lover. The greatest modern exponent of the *mandil* as trademark and theatrical prop was undoubtedly the late, lamented Egyptian singer, Umm Kulthum who used it extensively in her expressive renditions.

It is perhaps taking the concept of honour and refinement a little too far in reporting that the term '*mandil*' was also used for the bloodstained cloth produced as proof of a new bride's virginity,[75] but it does underscore the erotic aspects of this fashion accessory.

Poets and singers sang in lyrical terms of the praises of desirable beauties, but these were ideals, far removed from the realm of the mundane. In the absence of today's intensive media advertising, how were ordinary women made aware of cosmetic and fashion trends? Were they fairly static in a conservative society, passed down from mother to daughter, friend to friend, hence the descriptions of later European travellers which confirmed definitions in medieval dictionaries?

It is arguable that the ban on figural representation and the norms of society concerning personal modesty and virtue stimulated women's interest in their bodily enhancement and adornment, for example the widespread use of *kohl* to highlight the eyes, the only part of the face visible. This incidentally was validated by the allusion to the *houris* of the Qur'an, and was a potent reminder of the reward of the righteous. Perfumes and fragrances were prescribed in Islam as an adjunct to ritual purification and in time came to be a benchmark of high civilization which permeated society at all levels.

It was striking to note that many plants and herbs which formed the bases of cosmetics were also prescribed in medical manuals, and the therapeutic aspects may have preceded their cosmetic applications. Is it not strange that despite a *Tradition* that every eye is adulterous, (which seems to concede that women also had desires), blame was laid firmly on women as sexual temptresses? This view, however, was by no means confined to Arabs, for the *Kama Sutra* spoke of 'voluptuous women (who) inflame the hearts of all men with their lascivious graces; they chat with one man, dart provocative glances at another and a third occupies their heart.'[76]

There were two other aspects to cosmetics; the aesthetic and the prophylactic. Perfumes and fragrances created ambience and ease and stimulated the senses. As we have seen, there was an element of hypocrisy on the part of some men concerning women and perfume. In fact was this not a tacit recognition by men of the heightened physical allure of women who wore perfume, but a denial that men found them attractive?

Tattooing was frowned upon, and was also linked with prostitutes and slaves, that is, people who were not considered respectable. However, it is also likely that patterns applied as tattoos or with henna paste incorporated good luck symbols. Charms and amulets with sacred writing, and coloured beads to avert the evil eye were also worn.

Jewellery was a barometer of wealth, setting apart rich and poor, in many cases to an obscene extent, given tales of women literally laden down with jewels and finery. Accounts of excess must have filtered down through society to street level, for example popular entertainments such as *The Thousand and One Nights* and the shadow play, and the authorities rightly identified public ostentation with the fomentation of social unrest. Apart from adornment, jewellery was a demonstration of and reminder to men of women's independence. It was also, of course, frequently a token of real affection and respect from men.

At the most basic level, women applied cosmetics to improve their appearance, as a mark of self-esteem and to feel good. Were they wearing make-up for themselves, or for men? It is likely that they had a variety of reasons for doing so, but it is undeniable that the cloying, even suffocating, atmosphere of the *harim* system fostered a spirit of great competition among upper class women. In order to compete for the master's attention, one had to stand out, and make-up and fashion were one way of doing so. Time and money did not enter the equation in this hedonistic lifestyle.

How successful were women in subtly persuading men that their own ideas of beauty and fashion were acceptable in society? Ibn Battuta was been very impressed with Berber women: 'The most perfect in beauty and the most shapely in figure of all women, of a pure white colour and very stout; nowhere in the world have I seen any who equal them in stoutness.'[77]

But the self-assured poetess Salma bint al-Qaratisi, she of the 'stunning looks', also boasted, 'I have no problem with my hips, and my breasts don't weigh me down'.[78] If Salma meant by this that she was proud to be slim, then she appears to be rebelling against the male ideal of the time of a comfortably-built, even stoutish, woman. In doing so, she incidentally fulfilled men's pre-conceived notions of women's capacity to cause discord.

CHAPTER 7

Women's Public Roles

The political arena

With the advent of Islam, the status of women in public life gradually declined, and the Prophet allegedly addressed women thus, 'I know nothing of lower rank in knowledge and religion which overpowers intelligent people more than you!'[1] There is little evidence of 'A'isha's intervention in any major political decisions taken by the Prophet. Nizam al-Mulk the powerful vizier to the Saljuq sultans for more than thirty years, produced his *Book of Government* (*Siyar al-muluk*) towards the end of his career. He advocated, political reform and outlined the duties of kingship and the ruler's relations with his subjects, and was of the opinion that, 'in spite of all the nobility, the learning, the devotion and the piety of 'A'isha, the Prophet did the opposite of what she wanted'.[2]

Opinions varied as to whether women could be appointed ministers of state. The famous jurist al-Mawardi ruled 'On Appointment to the Post of Minister' in his *Rules of Government* (*Al-Ahkam al-sultaniyya*), as follows:

> A woman may not undertake this position, even though information she transmits is acceptable, because of the implication of the (sovereign) powers it involves, which the Prophet declared to be foreign to women.[3]

This did not deter other women from promoting their own interests. Many were able to exert a real measure of influence in the political sphere, in particular in matters of succession. Polygamy ensured much intrigue and infighting in the *harim* as sundry wives pressed the claims of their own sons or plotted to retain or acquire the title of 'queen' for themselves; both of these aspects are relevant up to the present day in Arab lands. Even 'A'isha, the Prophet's favourite wife, and other wives sought to promote the interests of their own kinsfolk in the events surrounding the Prophet's dying days.

The Traditions of al-Bukhari and Ibn Hanbal further revealed a somewhat hardline view of powerful women, for example, 'When men obey women, ruin is certain', and al-Mawardi also quoted the Prophet, 'A people who entrusts their affairs to a woman will not prosper'.[4] This is despite the uncritical mention in the Qur'an of Bilqis the beautiful Shunammite, better known as the Queen of Sheba.

In his section 'On the subject of those who wear the veil, and keeping underlings in their place', Nizam al-Mulk decreed that:

> The king's underlings must not be allowed to assume power, for this causes the utmost harm and destroys the king's splendour and majesty. This particularly applies to women, for they are wearers of the veil and have not complete intelligence . . . when the king's wives begin to assume the part of rulers, they base their orders on what interested parties tell them, because they are not able to see things with their own eyes in the way that men constantly look at the affairs of the outside world . . . mischief ensues.[5]

Nizam al-Mulk seemed blissfully unaware of the irony here; he might have been a wise and incredibly influential vizier, but he was nevertheless an 'underling', hardly a disinterested party in offering counsel, and his own attempts to run the show met opposition from the *harim*. Al-Mawardi considered women too 'frail' to exert the determination and independent reasoning necessary to manage affairs of state.[6]

There were objections on the question of women's jurisdiction over men. In *On administering the Judiciary* al-Mawardi ruled that, 'The person must be a man of legal majority' and quoted the jurist Abu Hanifa and the Qur'an in confirmation of this view:

> Women are permitted to act as judges in matters in which their testimony is admissible. Ibn Jarir al-Tabari alone permits them to act as judges in all cases.

> Men are in charge of women, because Allah hath made the one of them to excel the other.[7]

The Caliph al-Ma'mun was also against women in the judiciary, for, 'Inevitably people will resort to the women's court and present their needs to them since they can be more easily won over.'[8]

The old chestnut of women giving way 'to all sorts of vain desires' was thus resurrected.

In the eighth-century Caliph al-Mahdi bypassed his son by Khayzuran as his successor. His wife Khayzuran, who had been first of all his concubine, was a beautiful and talented poetess and singer, and she vigorously promoted the claim of her favourite son.[9] The 'Abbasid dynasty was plagued by ineffectual leadership and intermittent outbursts of public rebellion and in the mid-ninth century the mother of Al-Musta'in ruled in concert with two Turkish generals.[10] Al-Muqtadir, who became Caliph at the age of thirteen, remained as clay in his mother's hands throughout his reign. Not every son welcomed his mother's interference. The historian al-Tabari recorded that Musa, son of the same Khayzuran, allegedly sent his mother a dish of rice which was given to a dog; the dog died.[11] Many of these mothers were not Arabs, although married to Arabs; Hisham II's mother was a Basque named Aurora, in Arabic *Subh*. She acted as regent in al-Andalus when Hisham succeeded to the throne as a minor late in the tenth century, but the joint authority she exerted with her favourite, the minister al-Mansur, was not universally recognised, and state authority declined. Following the moral example of so many male rulers, Subh's young and ruthlessly promoted *protégé* was allegedly also her lover.[12]

Shajarat al-Durr, a Turkish slave, as sovereign regent in Egypt in 1250 assumed the title of Sultana, and was described by a contemporary Arab historian as a 'strong personality of great nobility' who led a blameless life. This is at odds with the knowledge that on learning that her second husband might take another wife, she had him murdered in his bath after a ball game. She in her turn was battered to death by slave women armed with the wooden shoes of the *hammam*. Shajarat became the first woman to have coinage minted in her own name. She had her name proclaimed in the Friday mosque, and reigned but three months. She later married the new Sultan, but her personal power continued unabated, since 'she dominated him, and he had nothing to say'.[13] The friction between Egypt and Syria was ascribed to her influence, and a contemporary Syrian historian described her as 'the most cunning woman of her age, unmatched in beauty among women and in determination among men'. Al-Musta'sim's message to the Egyptian princes on Shajarat's accession to the throne, was a sarcastic, 'If ye have no man to rule you, let us know and we will send you one'.[14]

Other non-Arab Muslim women also played important roles in public affairs. Sultana Raziyya, for example, was sovereign regent in Delhi for some three and a half years and an almost exact contemporary of Shajarat al-Durr. Raziyya exemplified the 'if you can't beat them, join them' spirit. In what must have been one of the earliest incidents of feminism anywhere, and in the face of outbursts of civil rebellion at her appointment, she assumed male costume and turban and appeared unveiled in public.

Unfortunately, women who ascended to the throne in the Muslim empire proved almost invariably as pitiless as men in political affairs, and arguably they had to be. However, there can be no excuse for the behaviour of some of them, who were not above plotting to usurp the rule of their own husbands, even to the extent of having them murdered. Despite having fabulous wealth and priceless jewels, the heartless mother of the 'Abbasid Caliph Al-Mu'tazz unbelievably sacrificed him for the sake of a ransom of fifty thousand dinars. Tandu, a fifteenth-century ruler of Southern Iraq and Khuzistan, then took the process one step further by having her stepson murdered.[15] All these examples tended to substantiate the widely held male view of women as personified in *The Thousand and One Nights* as amoral, wily, evil and a real threat to men, in whatever sphere.

Poetesses

Among the most famous Arabic poems are the elegies of arguably the greatest female poet, the highly influential Khansa' for her beloved brother Sakhr. Early women poets were also heavily influenced by the principles of liberality and bravery of the Bedouin of the pre-Islamic era. They, too, frequently wrote of love, but within the context of familial loss on the field of battle. Their extremely valuable ideological contribution towards the preservation of tribal memory and its effect on Arab society should not be underestimated.

Khansa, like so many women of her time, was spirited, and well able to defend herself against criticism from no less than the Caliph 'Umar and the Prophet's wife 'A'isha. Layla al-Akhyaliyya was another acclaimed poetess,[16] and an exponent of the elegy.

The leading figures at court were surrounded by a galaxy of entertainers – poets, singers and musicians – and many of these were multi-talented women. Women poets did not, however, confine their subject-matter to separation and panegyrics. One, Juhamiyya, penned an amusing verse at the expense of an extremely short vizier, Muhammad ibn al-Qasim of Karkh, in Baghdad, whose seat of honour at the celebrations for Nawruz, the Persian New Year, had to be reduced in height so that he could climb up.[17] In practice, this was an extremely dangerous course for poets to follow, but there was always the opportunity to redeem themselves in their ability to ridicule the rivals of their rulers.

Arabic literature and poetry also found a fertile breeding-ground among the Muslim women of al-Andalus. Al-Maqqari wrote of the well-known poetess Wallada in eleventh-century Cordova, in whom 'eloquence was a second instinct'. The beautiful and talented Wallada held literary salons at her home, and her circle at Cordova was a 'rendezvous for the noble minds of the region'.[18] Hitti called her 'the Sappho of Spain'; nevertheless several men sought her hand in marriage, and she was renowned for the very frank romantic verse she exchanged with the poet Ibn Zaydun. After a night spent with him, Wallada wrote:

> The nights now seem long to me, and I complain night after night,
> That only those were so short, which I once spent with you.[19]

Although society in al-Andalus may have been more liberally minded than in the eastern Muslim world, al-Maqqari nevertheless qualified his praise of Wallada, averring that, 'her unconcern and poems of sensuous openness were a source of gossip'.[20]

A century later, Wallada's star was eclipsed by Hafsa bint al-Hajj, who died in 1190-91. She too had a passionate love affair with a fellow poet, Abu Ja'far ibn Sa'id, and her poetry exposed her love for him. Despite her beauty, Hafsa was not immune to doubt, and openly expressed her insecurity.

> Jealousy fills me with pain, not only at my eyes, at you and me, but at the time and place where you may be. And if I locked up you in my eyes, until the Day of Judgment, it would not do.[21]

Hafsa's poetry was more restrained than Wallada's, perhaps conditioned by the prevailing morally severe Almohad tradition. Even so, it appears that there were no constraints on Hafsa openly visiting male admirers. This is pertinent comment on the ability of some women to flount custom.

The Prophet had disapproved of the poets of the early Islamic period because of their quite natural links with pagan practice, for example the music of religious rituals.[22] One Tradition reports that he said, 'Singing and hearing songs can cause hypocrisy to grow in the heart, as water promoteth the growth of corn'. Nor is music mentioned in the Qur'an as one of the delights of Paradise. The Prophet also reputedly said, 'Do not pray for a deceased person who owned a slave singer'. (Strictly speaking, entertainers should come under the *'Defects'* section in the literary genre, since music had no place in Muslim liturgy, and ordinary entertainers and singing-girls at court are dealt with in Chapter 8). Despite these views, in time the cantilation of the Qur'an itself evolved into an art form. Zubayda, patroness of poets and the wife of Harun al-Rashid, had one hundred female slaves who recited sections of the Quran, 'so that it sounded like the buzzing of a swarm of bees'.[23] Music too came to play a part in the call to prayer, so distinctive to each *muadhdhin*, as well as in the recitation of the name of God, (*dhikr*), in the Sufi religious orders.

Court entertainers

Songs were composed and handed down orally, so it is difficult to know their exact original contents. Abu Faraj al-Isfahani's early thirteenth-century *Book of Songs* (*Kitab al-Aghani*) named several professional women singers from the pre-Islamic period, and it is evident that at least some of their compositions were poems which were put to music. Jamila, a freed slave of the Banu Sulaym tribe who died around 720 was a renowned teacher of music. Indeed she was known as the 'Fount and Origin of Song' and taught many of the finest Hijazi singers, both male and female.[24] The doyen of love poetry, 'Umar ibn Abi Rabi'a, was an ardent admirer of the talented Jamila, whose *pièce de résistance* was when she headed a splendid group of entertainers, friends and admirers to Mecca.[25] In the early days of Islam at Mecca and Medina, singing became an art form under Byzantine and Persian influence. Rival schools of music then developed in the courts at Damascus and later in Baghdad.

By the Umayyad era Muslim society was inclining towards the aesthetic, and musicians, female and male, had become familiar figures in courtly circles where, surely with unintended irony given the norms of society, the ruler literally 'kept his distance' behind a curtain. Court music was primarily vocal and the vocalist was the star attraction; singers were accompanied by musicians, as were poets and dancers. Since the lute was a melodic instrument, eminently suitable for solo and ensemble pieces, it became known as 'the prince of entertainment' (*amir al-tarab*). The lutanist, who was frequently the singer and could equally be female, used a plectrum.

Jurists were divided in their opinions on music. Some deprecated it in all its forms, while others did not consider it especially blameworthy. Singing itself was not reprehensible, but if the content was indecent, then it was deemed so. Strictly speaking, it was forbidden in the Traditions to purchase women slaves and to train them and sell them on, but the aristocracy was a law unto itself on this issue. By the Mamluk era, (1250-1517), some theologians even penned their own elegies for singing by celebrated music-ians.[26]

A penurious master offered his slave-girl Tawaddud to Harun al-Rashid for one hundred thousand dinars. The Caliph agreed, with the proviso that the claims to her superior education were first put to the test by experts. Tawaddud was duly examined in philosophy, law, Qur'anic exegesis, theology, medicine, rhetoric and chess, all of which apparently, were the requisites of a 'good education' in the medieval Muslim world.[27] Shahrazad, the well-bred heroine of the *Thousand and One Nights* was equally impress-ively well-read. It is difficult at this remove to judge just how much of a polymath each of these women was, but there is no doubt that the more highly educated the slave, the more desirable her possession (in every sense) and the higher her monetary value. Such a slave-girl's education was long and arduous and undoubtedly expensive for the master, but in the context of the court, cost would be minimal. As such, a good and multi-talented singing-girl became in a sense a commodity, an item to be traded according to fashion or economic circumstances. One redeeming feature for her was the possibility of finding true love, manumission and lasting security.

The pursuit of singing-girls and other women in tandem with the abuse of power was a recurring theme in Arabic literature. In the early days of Islam, a Bedouin had been forced to hand over his beloved wife Suada to Marwan before he succeeded to the caliphate. Marwan imprisoned the husband and he offered the woman's father a large sum of gold and silver in return for his consent to marry Suada. Having received it, the spiteful Marwan had the wretched husband severely tortured.[28] On another occasion Harun al-Rashid demanded a beautiful slave named Da'ifa owned by one of his high officials, Sulayman. Sulayman agreed – had he any choice? – but fell ill through grief and appealed to God against the Caliph, saying, 'The world heareth of his justice, but he is a tyrant in the affair of Da'ifa. Love of her is fixed in my heart as ink upon the surface of paper'. On hearing of this, Harun returned her to Sulayman, in a misguided attempt to vindicate his reputation for justice

In al-Hariri's eighteenth *Maqama*, Abu Zayd recounted the loss of his personal singing-girl to trickery by a high official. He described her in the most fulsome terms, and his financial deficit was more than made up by his appreciative audience. (Unfortunately she was a figment of his fertile imagination, which he exploited for personal gain.) There is no doubt that the rewards for entertainers, and the stakes, in every sense of the word, were high, so long as they retained the favour of often-capricious rulers. For example, a tenth-century anecdote recalled how al-Muhallabi gave a group of entertainers fine clothes and cash to the tune of some five thousand dinars,[29] and *The Thousand and One Nights* mentioned a slave-girl 'whose ornaments are worth a mint of money'.

If the above accounts are reliable, there may be more than a grain of truth in al-Jahiz's opinion that, 'The singing-girl is hardly ever sincere in her passion or wholehearted in her affection' and that she set out to entrap the (male) 'victims'.[30] How could she be otherwise? Her role was to be pleasant, compliant and entertaining to a thoroughly indulged audience at court, in situations which were frequently fuelled by alcohol, when men were seen at their worst. It would be highly surprising if a marked degree of cynicism on her part did not prevail. A singing-girl's multiple charms were only good until a fresh face came along or she could be sold at a profit, or a loss, as may be. For example, one girl purchased by the Amir Baktimur for ten thousand dinars was then sold on by him for four thousand. It was in a singing-girl's own interest to consolidate her future to the best of her ability. Many rulers did fall deeply in love with slave-girls, for example Yazid, who was enchanted by 'Aliya, a sweet beautiful girl who accompanied herself on a tambourine.[31] Yazid unfortunately was in thrall to women in general, and became similarly captivated by Sallama and Habbaba, pupils of the great Jamila.

Other girls were persecuted by fathers, irate that their sons were involved with singers, and slaves to boot. In some cases there was the opportunity to enter the ruler's *harim* – sometimes a doubtful privilege – and successful marriages could be made. Bayad, for example, the wife of sultan Ahmad al-Nasar, who ruled briefly in Egypt in 1342, had been a singer in Ahmad's father's *harim* and Ittifaq, one of the most famous Egyptian singers, was recorded by Maqrizi and other historians as the wife of three Bahrite sultans.[32]

Musical traditions in al-Andalus developed quite independently of the Persian influence of the eastern courts. The racy *muwashsha*, a type of folk-song invented in al-Andalus in the early eleventh century (although continuing somewhat in the Persian tradition), was concerned with sensual pleasures of all kinds, and women in particular were associated with that genre. Given the content, one wonders how these singers in Spain were regarded in society, and whether they were considered socially inferior to the poetesses. Maimonides (who died around 1203-4) wrote a tract *On listening to music* in which he reiterated the much-discussed theme in al-Andalus: 'Is it lawful to listen to the singing of the *muwashshahat* of the Arabs?'

The terms *raisa*, *mughaniya* and *qayna* were all used to describe the different classes of singing-girl at court in Egypt. The premier group belonged to the military class, and each sovereign had a personal orchestra at his disposal; for example that of al-Mansur Hajji was composed of fifteen musicians. Most musicians apparently were slaves who had been gifted to the rulers.[33] This is interesting so far as the musical tradition is concerned; presumably they were from different lands and introduced diverse influences. They were taught by celebrated practitioners also specially brought in from afar.

The stewardess (al-khazindara)

Husn, the stewardess at the late tenth-century court of al-Mustaqfi in Baghdad, was described in Miskawayh's *Experiences of the Nations (Tajarib al-Umam)* as 'strong-minded, astute and intellectual', and something of a power behind the throne. Such praise is praise indeed, for Husn lived in troubled times. While it is true that some women and their attendants exercised considerable influence on those in authority, it was generally at a personal level well below that of rulers and their *ahl al-qalam*, 'people of the pen', that is, the administration. Nonetheless real bonds of affection and trust were built up on long close acquaintanceship.

We know that under the Mamluk dynasty women were not permitted to hold military or administrative posts. However, the Sultan's wife had her own entourage of females who filled similar positions for her, including cup-bearers, guardians of the wardrobe and so on. There is some ambiguity surrounding the title of *khazindara*. The name has connotations of storing up, depositing, and suggests a highly-responsible person in charge of the treasures of the sultan's wife. However, one authority reported that when precious jewels and other valuables were kept in the *harim*, they were in charge of a male eunuch.[34] Ibn Taghribirdi reported that:

> One day the sultan (al-Nasir Muhammad ibn Qalawun) had summoned the judge (*Karim al-din*) to come to his home. Becoming aware of this, the wife of the sultan (Khawand Tughay) authorised her *khazindara* to transmit certain messages to the judge.[35]

The equivalent male post of *khazindar* ranked twelfth in the Mamluk military hierarchy. In India too, at the Mughal court of Akbar, women were employed to oversee expenditure in the private audience chamber.

The nursemaid (al-dada)

The *dada* was a woman employed in the education and upbringing of children in royal households and upper class homes. Al-Maqrizi told of one slave, Sitt Hadaq, who rose to the role of governess to the children of the Mamluk Sultan al-Nasir Muhammad ibn Qalawun. It has been suggested that this responsibility was conferred on loyal servants and, in particular, black women.[36] The esteem in which Hadaq was held is obvious from her honorific 'Sitt', meaning 'Lady' and she wielded great influence. In one law suit a petitioner successfully sought her intercession with the ruler himself. Great ties between children and their governesses were forged, and, according to Ibn Taghribirdi, the dethroned sultan al-Malik al-'Aziz was placed under house arrest in the home of his Ethiopian governess Sitt al-Nadim.

Yet another account recalled that the *dada* of al-Ashraf Sha'ban was also his confidante; a handwritten inventory of his estate in the Sultan's own hand was found in her home after his assassination.[37] This is revealing. Rulers on occasion became destitute; their governesses were frequently arrested and accused of misappropriation of items of wealth and treated harshly. Sometimes the accusations were well-founded, but it is likely that in anticipation of trouble, someone about to be bankrupted might secrete personal wealth with a trusted, loyal person, for example a very dependable female member of the household.

Women and religion

Turning now to the issue of women holding high religious office, early historians mentioned only Umm Warraqa bint 'Abdallah, a Companion of the Prophet. Ibn Sa'd reported that her clan was so large that it qualified to have its own *muadhdhin* for the call to prayer. It has been suggested that: 'Only in large harems, however (that is, before an exclusively female congregation) have women performed the office of the *imam*, the prayer leader.'[38] But the Prophet himself is said to have instructed Umm Warraqa in this capacity. Umm Warraqa recited the Qur'an and may even have been involved in 'Umar's collection of the sacred text.[39] She was extremely zealous in the cause and had aspirations to martyrdom; she was allowed to participate on the battlefield at Badr and tend the wounded. Another indomitable woman in the field of battle who proved herself the equal of men in a just cause was Hind, the mother of the first Umayyad Caliph, Mu'awiya. Before her conversion to Islam, Hind was implacable and one of the last formidable opponents of the Prophet. She rode fearlessly, wielded her sword in battle and tore out the liver of the corpse of the man who had killed her own father at the Battle of Badr, the Prophet's uncle, Hamza. In the Crusading period, the mother of Ibn Munqidh handed out weapons and encouraged the occupants of the Syrian castle of Shayzar to fight the enemy; indeed she was prepared to kill her own daughter rather than have her fall into the hands of the infidel.[40]

The Traditionist (al-musnida)

Many of the primary Traditionists were also women, and the Prophet's wives were central here; 'A'isha personally related some twelve hundred Traditions, more than two hundred of which are included in the definitive works of al-Bukhari and al-Muslim,[41] and she and Hafsa corrected scribal errors. Hafsa also participated in the rescension of the Caliph 'Uthman's text. Other women from the first Islamic communities were also instrumental in the transmission of Qur'anic texts. According to one authority, seventeen per cent of the first generation of reliable primary transmitters of traditions, numbering some one thousand, were female.

One tenth-century bondswoman checked the transcription of Muhammad ibn 'Abbas ibn al-Furat, the compiler of *hadith* and writer of exegetical commentaries on the Qur'an. Umm 'Abdallah, born in 1226, known by the honorific title *Shaykha Sitt al-Wuzara'*, was the foremost female Traditionist of her era. Her fame rested partly on her knowledge of al-Bukhari's *Sahih* and al-Shafi'i's *Musnad* from her father and Abu 'Abdallah ibn al-Zubaydi, and she appeared in the biographies of al-Dhahabi and other historians.[42] Umm 'Abdallah had had four husbands by the time she died in her nineties. She possibly outlived them all, but such a renowned personality would have posed a formidable challenge for many men. Amat al-Rahman was mentioned by al-Dhahabi. Her honorific title of *Shaykha Sitt al-Fuqaha'* seems to imply that she was also qualified in law.

The twelfth and final volume of al-Sakhawi's fifteenth-century biographical dictionary *The Brilliant Light* (*Al-daw al-lami'*) was devoted to women and recorded the largest number, with the greatest detail of any in the genre. The entry for Umm Hani, also known as 'Maryam, the Cairene' said her father was a judge, while on her mother's side she was the granddaughter of a judge. Umm Hani married and had sons, whose collective brilliance was noted, but of 'Fatima' her daughter, her mother or other female relations we hear nothing. Umm Hani inherited wealth and bought a 'great workshop, famous for its enormous size and many spinning wheels'. Al-Sakhawi reported:

She taught *hadith* for a long time, and many eminent scholars heard it from her; personally, everything I have learned from her teachers, I learned through her.[43]

Umm Hani 'obtained certificates of audition from a large number of masters', which legitimated her status. Following standard format, details of her pilgrimages, which she extended to teach and study in the holy cities, appeared. Despite having borne five children and making the *hajj* on thirteen occasions, she lived to a ripe old age. She was indeed strong in every sense of the word. Danger for pilgrims was ever present in Arabia. A flash flood in 960 wiped out Egyptian pilgrims who had unfortunately camped in a *wadi*. In 1004, pilgrims were forced to drink their own urine and many perished from thirst. Fifteen thousand deaths occurred when Qarmatians destroyed the water tanks en route and threw bushes in the wells. In 1014 some twenty thousand died of thirst and six thousand were saved only by drinking camel urine.

At least two other well-known Traditionists lived to a great age. Al-Sakhawi's entry revealed that Umm Hani was 'consistent in her fasting and night prayers . . . and especially concerned with ritual purity'. This latter point had a particular bearing on hygiene and health. It is suggested that piety, religious discipline and a relatively austere lifestyle produced spiritual and physical equilibrium.

Al-Sakhawi's inclusion of so many women in comparison with his successors may be explained by the fact that in fifteenth-century Egypt and Syria the Prophet's wife 'A'isha was being being actively promoted by the Sunni sect as the expert on matters pertaining to women.[44] Such was the esteem in which 'A'isha was held that many women sought to emulate her. Although the legitimacy of women's transmission was established, succeeding generations of women apparently produced fewer transmitters. Were they really fewer in number, or were their efforts deemed of no interest to contemporary chroniclers?

The evidence of the elevated status of such devout women in titles conferred by men, is reflected in a late sixteenth-century Turkish miniature showing the Prophet, his three distinguished wives Fatima, 'A'isha and Umm Salama, and female servants.[45] The Prophet and his wives were all given a flame nimbus to emphasise their religiosity; the women were veiled, but so was the Prophet, thus the women were elevated by the painter to the rank of the Prophet himself. It must be stressed that this is not sacrilegious. 'There is no god but God and Muhammad is his Messenger'. Their inviolability was stressed at the expense of the unveiled servants.

The scholar

Learning in Islam was much esteemed and was not viewed as the prerogative of men. In the earliest days, only three women and seventeen men of the Quraysh tribe, to which the Prophet was affiliated through the Banu Hashim clan, were literate. Scholars travelled vast distances to sit at the feet of great teachers. Apart from the honour, they in turn were perpetuating a chain in the transmission of learning from original source material and were able to capitalize on the reputation of their teachers to advance their own careers. Undoubtedly this led to competition among students and scholars. At the basic level, most elementary school pupils were boys, but there was some degree of mixing, and they were taught the basics. All this ceased at puberty. There were separate girls' schools, but it is likely that far fewer girls were educated. Only male teachers taught in the colleges, and women do not seem to have officially enrolled. However, some few may have sat in on lectures, in some capacity, and at least veiled.

Because of their relatively liberal property rights in law, many women were able to set up schools; even if they did not personally teach, they achieved public recognition and esteem and the satisfaction of playing a valuable role in society. If an injunction to (male) teachers to 'instruct the poor equally with the rich' can be taken to imply the expectation of gifts from grateful parents, then it is likely that successful women teachers were similarly rewarded. All teachers had to obtain a licence *(ijaza)* to practise. Religious institutions for men stipulated salaries and in kind payments of bread and firewood, but we do not know whether well-educated women in whatever field received salaries in their own right and how these approximated to those of male contemporaries, fathers and heads of households with responsibility for an extended family. Private study took place in the homes of teachers, or in women's own homes. These arrangements would suit many women teachers, particularly if they were mothers.

Women in the *harim* were frequently highly influential teachers. Ibn Hazm, the early eleventh-century writer from al-Andalus was taught mostly by women. A Muslim boy did not join the men of the household until puberty, and Ibn Hazm cultivated a keen interest in women – and affairs of the heart – from his experience of observing them at close quarters and forming some opinion of female psychology. Women taught him the Qur'an and the delights of poetry, and they also trained him in calligraphy. It would be wrong to assume that all scholars were of a serious frame of mind, or penurious. A certain twelfth-century scholar in the service of Salah al-Din amassed great wealth and owned twenty concubines worth one thousand dinars each.

A daughter's relationship with her father (and other male relatives) was crucial to her future in society, since his views of women in the wider world, their education, his assessment of her suitability and worth and so on would be honed from early childhood. Umm Hani's maternal grandfather, a distinguished judge, personally supervised her education from the age of seven. Other men set upper limits on the extent of a woman's education.

One expert in religious law, Fatima Bint Ahmad Ibn Yahya, held discussions with her father. Her husband, himself an *imam*, sought to clarify with her points which he wished to explain to his students. His wife evidently sat in on his classes, since one uncomprehending student boldly remarked, 'That does not come from you yourself but from (her) behind the curtain'.[46] Presumably some females attended classes with men, so long as they were unseen, although they were not formally enrolled in the colleges. This guaranteed anonymity and afforded them a degree of latitude in their opinions which might otherwise have been impossible in face-to-face situations.

Was there an element of conflict here for the pious between the law and verification? How could the authoritative opinion of an unseen woman be verified? How could one be certain of the identity of someone hidden behind a veil or curtain? There would have been no difficulty if she came from a family of respected male scholars, whose word was beyond doubt. What is evident is the esteem in which some women were held by male contemporaries and later biographers.

The pious endowment (al-waqf)
The endowment of property by *waqf* was a pious and charitable act which set aside the income from property and business for charity. Women were allowed to establish such trusts with their own property and many took advantage of this, sometimes out of benevolence, religious merit, a desire to be in control and possibly also for the cachet of having a public building named after them. For example, Zubayda, the wife of Harun al-Rashid, undertook to provide water and provisions for Iraqi pilgrims en route to Mecca and Medina, hence the 'Zubayda Road'.[47] Although women could draw up a deed, name the charitable foundation and stipulate many conditions, it seems that in the majority of cases they were thereafter not involved in the general administration. Indeed in a large majority of cases, men were named as the manager,[48] so in a sense women placed the property under the ultimate control of men. Typical endowments might be a college (*madrasa*) for male students only, a *hammam*, a business such as a *khan* for its income, a mosque, a hospital and so forth. All of these bore the name of the benefactress.

Other outstanding Arab women

Al-Tha'alibi included 'Atika bint Yazid, the grand-daughter of the Umayyad caliph Mu'awiya, in his section on *Outstanding Achievement or Character*. 'Atika boasted of twelve male relatives, all caliphs. It is not clear if this was due to extreme longevity on her part or of sudden, untimely deaths of the men. Her nearest 'Abbasid rival was Umm Ja'far, she of the long hair.

*The calligrapher (*al-khattata*)*

The Prophet asked Shafa' bint 'Abdallah al-'Adawiya to teach his daughter Hafsa to write. 'Ali ibn Abi Talib, one of the Companions, enjoined, 'Beautiful writing makes the truth clearer' and counselled sagely that writing was 'the key to livelihood'.[49] In later society, as the seclusion of women gathered apace, women's cultivation of calligraphy afforded them an *entrée* to society at large and an opportunity to branch out into the fields of letters, science and the arts. Some men perceived a threat to the status quo. In the eleventh century the Persian prince Kai Ka'us advised his son on how to treat a daughter, saying:

> Entrust her to chaste and virtuous nurses, and, when she is older, give her to a woman teacher so that she learns to pray and fast and to perform her religious duties, which are prescribed by the law of religion,

but 'Do not teach her to write!'[50]

Nevertheless, there was a particular cachet and religious merit attached to copyists and illuminators of the Qur'an, who were occupied throughout the Islamic world, from Spain in the west to India in the east. The library of the Caliph al-Hakam in Cordova held some four hundred thousand volumes, possibly the largest in the western mediaeval world, and in the eastern quarter one hundred and seventy women transcribed the Qur'an by day, and by the light of candles at night,[51] a far cry from solitary monks toiling in monasteries elsewhere. 'A'isha bint Ahmad, who died in 1009, was singled out for mention as a scribe. Sadly, the great libraries were destroyed by Christians at the Reconquista.

In early eleventh-century Qayrawan a woman named Durra copied a famous endowed Qur'an now in the great mosque for Fatima, 'the honourable nursemaid' of Abu Manad Badis. The colophon read:

This Qur'an was copied, diacritically marked, decorated, gilded by 'Ali ibn Ahmad al-Warraq . . . at the hand of Durra, the calligrapher'.[52]

Her Qur'an was extremely expensive to produce, and is a measure of the esteem in which Fatima was held by her employers. Durra's near contemporary in al-Andalus, 'A'isha bint Ahmad, was a bibliophile and poet and held in great esteem by rulers.

We know from the writing of al-Jahiz, that women in Baghdad also played their part in the court administration and worked with men of letters.

The kings and nobility had bondswomen who undertook all kinds of daily responsibilities joining the workforce or staff of the *diwans*.[53]

Al-Jahiz named Umm Ja'far's maids Sukkar and Turkiya among others, adding that 'women appeared in public stylishly dressed and nobody decried that or reproached it'.

Nuddar, a favourite at the court of the Caliph al-Hakam.[54] was another contemporary well-educated Andalusian calligrapher, poetess and mathematician. Right at the end of the 'Abbasid period the caliph, when his eyesight failed, delegated Sitt Nasim, whom he had taught calligraphy, to answer personally the petitions he received. Even without the honorific *'sitt'*, this post – and the trust it implied – was a great honour for a woman.

At the Mughal court of Akbar his secretary mentioned that five thousand women were in the *harim*, overseen in sections by 'chaste women'. Given the bureaucracy involved in such a hierarchical enterprise, one is not surprised to find 'a scribe'.[55] Female guards were stationed closest to the inner sanctum of the *harim*, literally as a sort of *cordon sanitaire* between the eunuchs, and furthest away were the trusted Rajputs. In other words, the people closest to the chief wife or wives were those (in theory) least able to do harm in the sexual sense.

It is clear that high-born women in the medieval Muslim world were well able to assert themselves in public life through close collaboration with male officialdom. In many cases they had to draw on those very female wiles imputed to them by men to subvert the restrictions imposed by legislation and social reality. It was men who recorded their achievements, and it is noticeable that the most respected women were particularly devout (and thus beyond moral reproach) and scholars, many of whom at least had sat at the feet of male teachers. This is not in any way to denigrate their great achievements, for there is more than a degree here of 'in spite of' and not 'because of', or to fail to acknowledge the liberal attitudes and active encouragement by some men of female education and social advancement.

Women in everyday life

In theory, Muslim women were not prohibited from working outside of their homes, for the Qur'an says, 'Men shall have a benefit from what they earn, and women shall have a benefit from what they earn', and 'I shall not lose sight of the labour of any of you who labours (in My way), be it man or woman: each of you is an issue of the other.'[56]

With the development of the literary genre of *'Merits and Defects'*, several medieval Arabic works contained lists of female occupations. These were mainly in petty trade, and included small business women servicing the community; dressmakers, embroiderers, a fishwife, an astrologist and hairdressers were all mentioned. More unusual and presupposing a decent education were 'a lady grammarian, a lady clerk, an expert in prosody' who comprised some of the female occupations under *'Merits'*; even in those days there was a 'counsellor'.[57] Not all women were or indeed could be virtuous, and the list also included a procuress and a robber.

The petty trader

It is possible that some women in the medieval period owned property in the *suq*, either as assets acquired by inheritance, or purchased by them as investments. Women were more frequently engaged in peddling goods around the neighbourhoods, for example milk, butter and oil, or offering personal services such as laundry, soothsaying and household duties. Indeed, the sale of home-produced products such as bread, dairy produce, fruit and vegetables may have been the prerogative of women for they were certainly involved with production, growth and gathering. Services to individual homes precluded males on the grounds of propriety.

The merchant (al-tajira)

The *tajira* was a business woman plying her trade far beyond the *suq*. Two Italian pilgrims visiting Egypt in 1384 observed that: 'Cairo is a very large town where many women are active in commerce. They go out to Alexandria . . . to Dimyata and all over Egypt.'[58] *The Thousand and One Nights*, where a female merchant considered hiring a ship to go to Basra, confirmed that Arab women elsewhere also engaged in long distance trade. An eleventh-century Moroccan Jewish merchant mentioned 'the boat of the Lady' in his letter home. Presumably a woman owned that vessel but had men conduct business on her behalf. Was she Muslim or Jewish? Trade for woman or man was hazardous in many respects, not least financially, for the same writer revealed that he stayed behind, hoping for a rise in prices, but 'the slump got worse'.[59] It is significant that in this context, letters home were almost invariably not from husband to wife, but between fathers and sons or brothers, with messages tacked on for wives and children. Although business was naturally discussed, there is the possibility that some women in this social class were illiterate, despite their relatively secure position in society.

Women who turned to this trade were well-travelled and highly respected and probably not young. Did they start trading on that scale when their children left home, or when widowed, perhaps using inherited money, or were they abandoned or unmarried and forced to earn a living? It is tempting to think that some dealt in textiles, the type of goods in which women would be particularly interested for their homes and persons. Egypt and other centres produced high quality fabrics, and goods were widely imported and exported across the empire. Being business women they undoubtedly turned their attention to any commodity on which they could produce a good profit. Nevertheless they, like male travellers and their loved ones on land, would have been prone to financial worries, and the perils of land and sea journeys, anxiety over family members left at home, and loneliness would bear heavily upon them. Many female merchants journeyed in great style, and who would blame them?

Cash in those days meant gold and silver, and when a merchant was away from home for long periods capital could not be tied up, because these precious metals were limited in supply at any one time. Cash had to work for itself. One Spanish Jewish merchant, quoting prices in Spain, wrote to another in Morocco:

> I desisted from further action: I did not buy and left the money. But between the time I bought and today the *mithqal* (unit of currency) lost some of its value and the goods are today more expensive, namely; peeled *khazaj* silk; first class *khazaj*; the very coarse *Khazz* silk.[60]

Frequently a merchant arranged – formally through a notary – for a business friend to make monthly payments to the family. Provision in kind was often made – for example firewood, oil and wheat, the bare necessities.

Women probably did not travel alone, but had a trusted male to accompany them. The Prophet's first wife Khadija had trading connections with Syria, and she employed the young Muhammad. Khadija was, of course, the exemplar *par excellence* for the later *tajira*. Any woman trader looking for a dependable male slave to accompany her on her travels could easily acquire one from the slave-market (*suq al-raqiq*); slaves were classified according to religion, race and skills. Abyssinians were cheap, and excellent cooks; Armenians, Berbers and Greeks were the 'white' slaves. One guide for employers counselled:

> Keep a complete tally of all your profit and loss, and have all written down in your own hand to protect yourself from oversight and error. Furthermore, always keep a reckoning with your slaves and those about you.[61]

Al-Harith, the narrator of al-Hariri's *Maqamat* was a well-travelled merchant who described his deep sense of loss at the death of a slave whom he had purchased as youth. Although the bond between owner and slave could be very strong, one trusts that one man's instruction to his agents: 'If you ever come across a Tukharistan draught horse, a Bardh'a mule, an Egyptian ass or a Samarqand slave, then buy it immediately, and don't bother referring back to me for a decision',[62] was not a typical attitude.

The broker (al-dallala)

Clearly there was a distinction between the *tajira* and the *dallala*, who conducted business on a small and localised scale, but exactly what the *dallala* traded in is not known. Medieval dictionaries, referred to 'the hire that one gives to the *dallala*', so she acted as an intermediary between the seller and buyer. It is interesting that the verbal root has connotations of 'directing', which is precisely what she did, pointing out her stock to her customers. *The Thousand and One Nights* mentioned a Christian broker.

It may be that a *dallala* did not purchase the goods which she offered, but was paid a commission by the wholesaler or manufacturer, who had to rely on her exclusive access to women's homes to capitalise on or even create a market. The astute wholesaler probably required a guarantee, in the event of her default. If this was the case, and the authorities were involved, the *dallala* would be licensed, on payment of a fee. A court archive from Jerusalem dated 1595 told how 'the woman Hanna the Jewess, daughter of Shu'a' was warned by a judge that:

From this day forth she may not engage in the broker's trade (*dilala*) in the noble city of Jerusalem, and may not take goods from anyone, and if she sells without a guarantor, she will be punished.[63]

Being paid on commission would be an excellent way for a resourceful woman to start out in business on her own behalf. There was no great initial outlay, and she would have the opportunity to accrue capital and cultivate her goodwill and contacts over a period of time.

Was there any sort of informal network conducted in homes, or did licensed people have an office or shop, some sort of agency, in the *suq*? In nineteenth-century Egypt, the *dallala* acted as intermediary between for example a textile merchant and a woman client, or acted independently.

The money-lender

It would surely be a small step from *dallala* to pawnbroker, or to money-lender, if only on an informal basis. It is suggested that a broker was arguably in a position to act in that capacity, or at least to buy back trinkets of which women had tired.

Another Jerusalem court document threw an interesting light on women's business activities. In Muharram 1572, a legal agent petitioned a judge on behalf of a daughter of a late governor, whose power of attorney he held. Among the items she had allegedly pawned to 'Bila, the Jewess, daughter of Shim'on', were 'a white, stitched, silk cloth as collateral for four gold coins', and 'one gold bracelet overlaid with metals as collateral for one and one half cubit Hurmuzi cloth valued at eleven silver *para* coins'.[64] A settlement was agreed upon. Both of these women were of some means; what is interesting is that 'the modest lady' petitioner did not appear in court. It is not clear if this was due to a tradition of seclusion in her particular social class, or the fact that her testimony was only equivalent to half of that of a man, hence the need for the power of attorney to a male.

Women of the lower classes apparently had no such qualms about appearing personally before judges, if several of al-Hariri's tales are to be believed.[65] These resourceful women were well aware of their legal rights, and keen to defend them. One wonders how they paid the legal expenses?

The marriage-broker (al-khatiba)

It is arguable also that the talents of the *dallala* could impinge to some extent on that of the *khatiba* or marriage-broker, who had a secondary role as purveyor of beauty products around the homes of Cairo. Both women had privileged access to homes and were shrewd enough to assess the characters of the women they met, their wealth or otherwise from their surroundings, and their expenditure on the goods they purchased. An entreprising *dallala* could easily capitalise on this knowledge, and indeed might have been consulted on such matters. Over the years brokers were privy to confidences and aspirations for their clients' daughters and sons alike and undoubtedly saw a means to deal in a businesslike fashion with them. However, both the terms *dallala* and *khatiba* were used to indicate different positions.

According to Ibn Daniyal, there was widespread use of the services of the *khatiba* in Cairo and Old Cairo in the Mamluk period. [66] He took care to point out that they were known for their elaboration of the facts; one wonders what this did for the future goodwill of their business? This strengthens the argument for employing a tried and trusted *dallala*. One honest matchmaker said, 'If the veil is lifted the suitor is not cheated.' Men no less than women had nasty experiences, for example one's promised 'bouquet of narcissi' was an unattractive old woman and he was furious. The broker imaginatively riposted, 'Her complexion is yellow, her hair is white, and her legs are dark in colour'. [67] What had the prospective groom expected? It was usually the mother of a young man who made the initial approach and his female relatives accompanied the *khabita* on visits to houses as ordinary visitors, when they could gauge for themselves whether the girl and her family were suitable. If that was the case, discreet enquiries concerning the financial circumstances of the girl's family were then made. The marriage-broker's fee undoubtedly reflected the means of the family who hired her, subject to negotiation, their opinion of the man selected, and the future prospects for their daughter.

Marriage brokers plied their trade in the pre-Islamic period, for Khadija's proposal to the Prophet was made through another woman. The handsome young Abu al-'Abbas, the first 'Abbasid caliph, caught the eye of the previously married Umayyad Umm Salama (Mother of Salama). She dispatched a proposal of marriage to him by a female servant, together with money for the dowry. He accepted, but found himself unable even to touch her on their wedding night since she was so laden down with jewellery. [68] A female marriage-broker also appeared in one of Ibn Daniyal's shadow-plays.

The phlebotomist's assistant (al-sani'a)

The medieval cupper or phlebotomist sometimes had a female assistant known as the *san'ia*, whose task was to prepare the skin by rubbing in an emollient such as camomile before he applied his lance; the term suggested skill with the hands. [69] The phlebotomist himself occupied an ambiguous place in society, for he was included in a list of those in occupations termed reprehensible (*makruha*) by the jurists, whose testimonies were not accepted in court. Given the connection between blood and ritual impurity, one wonders if theological disapproval of the phlebotomist and his woman assistant had any connection with the blood drawn off the patient, which rendered them both 'unclean' in terms of ritual purity? The bath attendant, tanner and weaver were also in that category.

The bath attendant (al-ballana)

The *ballana* was the female attendant at the *hammam*; the hot bath is specifically mentioned in this connection in medieval dictionaries. Ibn Bassam recommended that male attendants should pay particular attention to diet, so that their breath remained fresh, and avoid eating onions and garlic.[70] The same commonsense advice would apply to women who were in close physical contact with their customers. Baths, as with so many other institutions in Muslim cities, were strictly regulated, although there is scant early information on the tasks of the *ballana*.

A visit to the public bath, where they could escape their cares for a day, was a regular highlight for many women. The *hammam*, a conspicuous feature in all Muslim cities, offered the opportunity of employment to a great number of women. Women's sessions were held at specific times. Visits were not, however, purely social. They were circumscribed by religion, and a Prophetic tradition reminded one that 'Cleanliness is a part of the faith'. The number of these establishments mentioned in historical accounts fluctuated greatly, and al-Ya'qubi's figure of ten thousand shortly after Baghdad was founded is apparently relatively modest. It should, of course, be remembered that Baghdad was an enormous city.

The bath-attendant's work was very skilled, because extremely toxic materials were sometimes used in beauty preparations. *Nura*, the depilatory paste for pubic hair, was a mixture of quicklime with arsenic. It was applied and left on for some two minutes and was then well rinsed off and henna applied to counteract the burning sensation of the chemicals. Although there was some dispute if *nura* was a pure Arabic word, it sounds possible, for the verbal root referred to 'light', and the combination of quicklime and arsenic would certainly produce a 'lightening' of the surrounding skin. It goes without saying that *nura* was never applied to facial hair. In Cairo an inspector ensured that for each measure of orpiment (a bright yellow mineral used as a pigment) ten measures of lime were added.[71] This was also a hazardous mix, hence the supervision, but women felt the end result was worth it – a smooth, clean and light skin.

While in Syria in the early fourteenth century, Ibn Battuta called at Sarmin, where a particular kind of brick soap was manufactured and exported to Damascus and Cairo; the brick would have had an abrasive effect. Fragrancy played a large part of cosmetic ritual. Yellow and red perfumed soap, 'for washing hands' was also made in Sarmin and fragrant herbs and plants were placed in niches ventilated by hot air in the baths.

Ibn Battuta described the large number of private bathrooms with a corner washbasin and hot and cold taps in a *hammam* in Baghdad. Bathers were given three towels, which he considered an 'elaborate arrangement', although apparently in Damascus anything from six to ten towels were used as the bather had successive treatments. He also visited baths at Tiberias for men and women, and said the 'water is very hot'. A bride visited the bath the day before her wedding; afterwards her hands and feet were painted with henna, and her eyes made up.

The Maghrebi writer Ibn al-Hajj wrote scathingly of the custom in Egypt in the medieval period for women to be totally undressed while at the hands of the *ballana*; he was adamant that his wife could only be treated by a *ballana* when she covered up her private parts, as required by religion.

Lane reported that in Cairo women usually had their own personal attendant. She was highly skilled and offered a session of rubbing down and exfoliation, washing and depilation which lasted for more than one hour. Lane mentioned the 'cracking' of joints as she manipulated them.

The hairdresser (al-mashita)

Arab chroniclers had little to say about this occupation, but the mother of the illegitimate famous court singer Ibn 'A'isha was said to be a hairdresser. In Egypt the name *mashita* was given to the hairdresser as well as to the woman in charge of the preparations of the bride-to-be. There was a bizarre record of a female strangler who was arrested in 1263. She prepared brides for their wedding and took along outfits and jewellery which families in modest circumstances could hire.[72] This may have been fairly lucrative, since the criminal in question was accompanied by her young slave girl as far as the home where the crime took place. Then, as now, for the talented hairdresser, the rewards could be high, and the biography of one fifteenth-century woman recorded her immense fortune. Women's hairstyling has been dealt with at some length in Chapter 6.

The low life

From the ninth century onwards Arab writers had an abiding interest in the low life of the cities, in the form of wandering tricksters and beggars on the fringes of society, and often from the criminal class. There were well organized beggar confraternities, presided over by a chief who divided out the spoils. Beggars were expert in disguise and the feigning of medical disabilities, and the different character types were sufficiently easily recognisable to be given nicknames. Despite this, there were numerous gullible people around willing to give them alms. Such occupations were not the prerogative of men; one beggar chief's wife was described as strutting about 'like a noble mare'.[73] Another example was the female character, 'the breadwinner', who combined the two tricks of *al-bas*, 'the hawk', and *al-saqr*, 'the falcon'. She bandaged up one eye, saying she had lost it, or was suffering from ophthalmia. Or she tied up her hands so that it appeared she had no fingers, or feigned paralysis by drooping her hands. Presumably she touted herself as the family breadwinner but sadly, it is probable that in many cases that was indeed the case.

Beggars ingratiated themselves with the public by sprinkling rosewater on people, evidently to make the recipient feel guilty that the beggar had bought it, and so hand over money. They frequently worked around and in mosques, hoping to cash in on the gullibility of the pious. In one of al-Hariri's tales, a man and wife team are seen working the crowd in the main mosque at Barqaʿid on the great day of *ʿId al-Fitr*, when the fast was broken, preying on the religious sensibilities of the congregation.[74]

Abu Dulaf's *Qasida Sasaniyya*, a poem on the itinerant and roguish Banu Sasan clan, mentioned a trickster woman who feigned madness, and adorned herself with amulets and ornaments of polished iron. The Banu Sasan were self-styled rogues who embraced the various groups who felt themselves marginalised by society. 'Crafty Dalila', a confidence trickster type in al-Masʿudi's *Meadows of Gold*, also appeared the *The Thousand and One Nights* as a pigeon-trainer; her father had been an official in the pigeon post in Baghdad and Dalila passed on her expertise to her daughter. Her lowly position in society was predictable on two counts; she was a trickster but was also possibly tainted by the fact that her father's testimony as a pigeon-trainer was not acceptable to the jurists.

Women from the lower classes of society went out and about freely, and in many cases this social freedom was dictated by economics. Whatever the disadvantages of confinement in the *harim* may have presented, it is undeniable that the *harim* system afforded many ordinary women the opportunity of employment at all levels.

The relationship between the occupants of homes and those who called to offer services was mutually beneficial. The service-providers were an important cohesive force in society. They closed the circle, so to speak, of social relations and brought into the *harim* something of the world beyond closed doors. More importantly for them, the system provided those with sufficient talent and adaptability the real possibility of upward social mobility and the acquisition of wealth. For their part, the secluded women were, in a sense, role models for people from a lower social order who would never otherwise have the opportunity to observe the social graces and elegant lifestyles of their customers. It is not fanciful to suggest that itinerant traders upheld the *harim* system.

It is clear that women's business transactions were not confined to one's own religious communities – business was business. For example, in a lease from archieves in Jerusalem, 'Shaykh Ahmad al-Masmudi' rented out for three years a property forming part of a pious foundation belonging to North African Muslims in the Jewish neighbourhood to 'the woman Sara, daughter of Maymun'.[75] Sara, 'the North African Jewess' undertook to renovate the property, and was evidently another well-travelled, independent woman.

CHAPTER 8

Marginals in Society

A modern Muslim conservative interpretation of the alleged inferiority of woman's nature runs:

> The woman is afflicted with menstruation, childbirth, with pregnancy and delivery, with the raising of children . . . with a deficient constitution.[1]

It is striking to note how frequently foetal and menstrual blood were perceived to be in some way 'dangerous' in rites of passage in many societies, and the Muslim world was no exception. Menstruation, according to the Qur'an, was a vulnerable condition; these types of bleeding, in effect bodily rejects, were peculiar to women and temporarily set them apart from 'normal' society. While in this ritually impure state women were seen as particularly at the mercy of malign forces; further they could, voluntarily or otherwise, draw them down upon everyone else involved. This power, however, was quite distinct from the 'evil eye', which was deliberate in intent. The possibility of evil, sicknesss – even death – could only be averted by the carrying out of prescribed rituals as a means of imposing and maintaining order and averting social anarchy. This tied in well with the view of women as a source of *fitna* or rebellion in the sexual sense.

The new mother was impure (*nifas*) for a period of forty days after the birth, when she went to the *hammam* for purification. Interestingly, a pregnant woman could pray at that time, but if bleeding occurred, she had to refrain. The number forty had ritual significance in Semitic languages; Jesus spent forty days in the wilderness, by definition a place out of bounds and beyond the control of mankind. Among the Jews, a new mother was ritually impure for forty days following the birth of a male infant, but eighty days for a female.[2] Is there an underlying notion here that the female infant was twice as polluting as a male, and dangerous? Such perceptions had long been prevalent in the Near East.

Superstition also played its part, and it was believed that a new mother could not go outdoors; she was forbidden to wash her hair; she could not go near the fire nor touch objects of terracotta or wood. If she looked at a mountain, life-giving water could dry up, and so forth.[3]

There were many taboos and rites associated with childbirth guaranteed principally to keep the new-born baby – one of the delights of life according to tradition – safe from the *jinn*, who worked ceaselessly to undo the work of God; some of these are outlined elsewhere here in the chapter on childcare and health. Neglect of ritual was dangerous for all. Everyone who attended a birth had been in a sense 'polluted', and required to be ritually cleansed.

Such beliefs were deeply ingrained in societies, and persist even today. In Iraq, for example, some sixty years ago, anyone who came from a home in which there had been a recent death had to invalidate the danger by first calling at another house, or at least crossing another threshold before visiting the mother.[4] And a visitor calling in en route from the market had to be particularly careful concerning the colour of purchases. Something red might cause the infant to turn red and suffer convulsions, while a yellow item predisposed the child to jaundice. The antidotes for these ailments were items of the same colour pinned to the baby's clothes. A widow had to avoid a bride or a new infant until a year had passed from her bereavement. This would have been particularly sad for a grandmother in denying her some consolation in her loss. It is likely that similar beliefs were current elsewhere.

In nineteenth-century Egypt, at least, male dancers impersonating women were frequently employed in preference to female dancers at marriage, birth (and circumcision) festivities.[5] Was this because they were better performers than women? It is more likely that these men, who wore part male, part female clothing which emphasised their 'neither fish nor fowl' nature, were considered outside the bounds of the 'normal'. Perhaps they negated and absorbed the element of danger. Such ceremonies underscored the marginality of the participants in these rites of passage, all of which additionally involved blood.

It is arguable that the rules of major ritual purity discriminated against women, even if some also applied to men; they certainly defined sexual and role differences. Is it not ironic then that the notion of blood as impure did not apply in the necessity to provide a token of virginity after the marriage ceremony? This had positive connotations; it upheld the honour of the bride's family and legitimated the marital rights of the new husband, and without this sign the marriage contract might be rendered null and void. Further, the shedding of female blood (*ghasl al-'ar*) if a woman was sexually compromised, allegedly or otherwise, negated the ensuing (male) family dishonour and shame. Regrettably, this still takes place today. It is obvious that on these two occasions the issue of female blood was not involuntary, that men took the initiative to control it, and yet in doing so restored order in society.

Al-ghasila *(who washed and prepared a corpse for burial)*

Death, like birth and marriage, was hedged around with superstition and taboo, and women again were subject to prescribed behaviour. According to Islamic law, a corpse might only be washed prior to burial by a person of the same sex, preferably someone pious and informed on the points of law regarding funeral rites.[6] The female washer was called *al-ghasila*, and it is no coincidence that the word was derived from the same root as *ghusl* or full ritual washing.

Ibn al-Hajj, a Maghrebi writer, commented on the attitude and behaviour of women towards the *ghasila*; they hurled insults and blows at her and she often took precautions to avoid them. This is interesting and implies that because of her marginality through association with death, they were in some way setting themselves apart because she was ritually impure. It is likely that this was less to do with personal animosity than to reflect their desire to avert malign forces, since a person who had been in contact with a corpse was not only extremely vulnerable to evil influence, but could also transmit this to others.[7] It is suggested that another possible explanation of the attitude of other women was that the livelihood of the *ghasila* was dependent on death, and hence she might, so to speak, have a 'death-wish', a vested interest, so far as other individuals were concerned.

Everyone who had touched a corpse was classed as impure. When death was imminent, someone in attendance turned the head of the sick person to face Mecca, and closed the eyes, and thus it is likely that close family members would themselves have touched the body, even inadvertently, in their distress. The *ghasila* served as the scapegoat who absorbed their impurity, and their behaviour in effect was a prophylactic against the effects of death and a necessary ritual to mitigate their denial.

The wailing-woman *(al-naiha)*

Further confirmation of the marginality of those intimately concerned with Muslim rituals in connection with death is a *Tradition* that wailing women were cursed by God. Several medieval dictionaries mentioned *al-naiha*, the professional wailing woman,[8] and the term was a synonym for *al-nadiba*, one who deplored the loss of a deceased person. The Prophet personally decreed that wailing women and their entourage would go to Hell for eulogizing the dead, and Islamic law upheld the prohibitions. Nevertheless, these views were largely disregarded among ordinary people; indeed age-old expressions of grief at such an intimate rite of passage could probably never be completely eradicated in any society, at whatever level.

Al-Hamadhani described how in a Mosul household whose master had died:

> Hired women weepers did mourn by his side.
> The people crowded, pain seared their hearts and they cried:
> Anguish ripped all their bosoms to shreds
> And the women let down all the hair on their heads
> And beat on their bodices
> And tore on their necklaces
> And scratched on their faces.[9]

The women would have drawn blood, but this did not flow 'naturally' and perhaps herein lay the danger. The jurists also deprecated such goings-on, which they maintained harked back to the behaviour in the *Jahiliyya* 'period of ignorance' and should be set aside.

These deeply ingrained practices have an ancient pedigree. They were firmly rooted in the burial rites of Ancient Babylonia, they were documented in the Old Testament in connection with the Jews in the provinces of the Persian empire, and continue to this day. Lane reported that on several occasions in Egypt he saw unveiled lower-class women in funeral processions with mud smeared on their headcoverings and bosoms.

A will dated 1113 from Fustat (Old Cairo) made specific provision for funeral expenses and 'singers'. It is important to distinguish between an ordinary singer and these women, because it has been firmly demonstrated that the former were perceived as morally suspect, and their presence would have been totally inappropriate at such an important, intensely personal life event. Singers at funerals were, however, marginalized. The lead singer eulogized the deceased, and although many of her phrases were formulaic, she undoubtedly liaised with the family beforehand and filled in personal details. Her companions provided the appropriate responses, and the responder was the *mustafqiha*, defined by the *Taj al-'arus* as 'one who catches, retains quickly and understands'. This indicates a talent for improvisation on a standard lament.

Individuals composed eulogies for their loved ones. Umm Khalid al-Numayriyya early on wrote sorrowfully of the death of her son:

The morning south wind blew from my son's land his musk, ambergris and lavender-scented presence. I miss him and the thought of him tears my eyes like a prisoner recalling home under the shackles' painful grip, or the cries of a soul away from its love.[10]

And Lubana, the beautiful wife of the Caliph Amin (787-813) movingly lamented her husband, who had been killed before their marriage was consummated:

Oh hero lying dead in the open, betrayed by his commanders and guards. I cry over you not for the loss of my comfort and companionship, but for your spear, your horse and your dreams. I cry over my lord who widowed me before our wedding night.[11]

Lubana's emphasis on traditional Bedouin values of 'manliness' (*muru'ah*) is striking, since she wrote from the palatial comfort of the court.

Public demonstrations of grief also occurred. Al-Dhahabi reported that people in the streets of Baghdad ripped their clothing and wailed at the funeral of the Caliph al-Mustarshid bi Allah in 1134-35. Weeping women undid their hair and struck their faces; they also intoned the merits of the ruler. The Egyptian military classes availed themselves of the services of professional mourners. In 1294 the funeral ceremony for a lieutenant lasted three days, with soldiers and wives of the princes going round the town each night accompanied by tambourine-playing wailing women.[12] Their instruments doubtless helped orchestrate the proceedings and provided a sonorous counterpoint to musical instruments used on other, happier, occasions. (Some religious scholars ruled that tambourines should only be used at weddings.) Elsewhere, officers' wives publicly attended funerals.

However, it would be incorrect to think that the authorities invariably sanctioned wailing and eulogizing, for historical accounts prove that this was not so. For example the Prefect of Cairo punished women who disobeyed his instructions in 1419. Despite this, there seems to be no doubt that professional mourners were employed and subject to taxes similar to those paid by women in other spheres of public life, such as ordinary singers and entertainers.[13] This confirms their semi-sanctioned status at some time or another, depending on the prevalent religious viewpoint.

Wailing women were socially at the margins of society through their association with death and, like the *ghasila*, perceived as subject to malign forces and even possibly suspected of wishing for death upon others. They too were 'cursed by God' in tradition. However, they fulfilled a valuable role in a society where burial must take place within a very short time after death. The family would be so taken up with the practicalities of arranging the funeral that they had little or no time to come to terms with their loss. Uncontrolled grief, which was considered unseemly, was therefore largely channelled through the professional mourners and their eulogies.

It is likely that wailing women wore distinctive robes, to set them apart from the private mourners. A *Maqamat* illustration from Iraq of a funeral dated 1237 suggested this, and the singers wore red and green clothing, which we read that in the tenth-century was 'only worn by Nabatean women and singing-girls of the slave class'.[14] The Prophet proscribed dyed mourning robes for women (with one exception, a Yemeni cloth called *'asb.*) The significant forty days was again evident in the period of mourning which women adopted.

We know that in the days before Islam, women donned their worst garments for funerals. In the late eighth century at the funeral of the Caliph al-Mahdi his slave-girls 'went in figured silk, then came in sackcloth'. The later technical term for mourning garb, *'thawb al-hidad'* implied fabric dyed a very dark black.

'Usama ibn al-Munqidh, a Syrian prince and warrior described a mother whose son in 1113 was killed by 'a Frankish stone dropped from the citadel' as: 'A very old woman who used to chant dirges at our funerals and who would on every occasion sing a lamentation for her son.'[15]

She sounds not like a professional mourner, but merely an old woman overcome by grief and only too proud to create the opportunity to commemorate her son in her own very personal way.

A will, obviously the testament of a woman of modest means, left half a dinar each to her sister and cousin, but she stipulated six dinars for her funeral. This would have included the shroud, some provisions for the mourners among family and friends, and the hiring of professional mourners.[16] By comparison, a courtier set aside twenty dinars for his funeral, excluding the shroud; this implies that the poor set great store on a 'decent' and 'proper' funeral, and in western society at least, this notion is still prevalent among the elderly.

Hafsa bint al-Hajj al-Rakuniyya, tutor to the families of several Almohad Sultans of Granada was grief-stricken and sadly disappointed in love when her paramour, the vizier-poet Abu Ja'far ibn Sa'id, was put to death by the ruler, who hoped to have Hafsa himself.[17] (Ironically, the Almohads were a puritanically religious dynasty.) Hafsa wrote, 'They killed my love and threatened me for wearing my mourning clothes'.

In the early 'Abbasid period the raconteur al-Asma'i and a friend were astonished to see a well-turned out young woman weeping beside a grave, and reprimanded her for not wearing suitable mourning garments. She spoke out through her lover:

Grave tenant, my comfort and joy, I've come to visit you clothed and jewelled as though you're still around. I want you to see me as you knew me. Those who watch me weeping for my man ponder the clash of grieving tears with colourful attire.[18]

All the taboos surrounding birth, marriage and death were prophylactics against impurity and the particular vulnerability of those attending to mysterious dangers of sickness, envy and malign force. In each of these processes the involvement of women, and their blood, was noticeable.

Ritual purity

We turn now to women and religious practice. The ritual purity of women and menstruation were widely featured in the classical works of *Traditions* and the law, and are very much a concern of modern studies. For this reason, only a few aspects will be touched upon here.

Although the Prophet enjoined, 'Do not prevent the handmaids of God from access to the places where He is worshipped',[19] he believed that it was better that women prayed privately; they could attend the mosque, with their husbands' permission, but they were not actively encouraged to do so. Al-Suyuti quoted a *Tradition* from the time of the Caliph 'Umar, whose wife had been in the habit of attending prayers in the mosque with the men, much to her husband's annoyance. 'Umar apparently disapproved and was jealous. His wife, 'Atika bint Zayd bint 'Amr bint Nufayl, defiantly held her ground. When she requested his permission and he stubbornly remained silent she said, 'I shall go until you prevent me'.[20]

There were, however, constraints and women were excluded from the official religious life of the community on account of their ritual impurity at certain times. The definitive definition of women's religious 'deficiency' came from the Prophet who, on being asked by women what was their defect in religion, replied: 'When she is ceremonially impure, (that is, menstruating) she neither prays nor fasts. This is the defect in her religion.'[21]

The *Muwatta* of Malik ibn Anas (who died in 795), the earliest extant law book, contained a chapter on ritual purity. One of the rules of etiquette prescribed that a woman should cover the area from her groin to just above the knee during menstruation. This corroborated 'A'isha's report that the Prophet told her, 'Wrap your waist-wrapper lightly about you, and return to your sleeping-place'.[22] It may be surprising to a non-Muslim that such intimate details of the Prophet's life should be known, but so much of everyday living is predicated on the Prophet's own conduct and the example of his family and his Companions.

However, it was not only when menstruating that the presence of women in the mosque was frowned upon. They were doubtless considered a distraction and an impediment to the right conduct and worship rituals of the men. An additional proscription to that of menstruation was the use of perfume. According to Lane, nineteenth-century Egyptians believed that:

> The presence of females in the mosque inspires a very different kind of devotion from that which is requisite in a place dedicated to the worship of God.[23]

Again, it was the fault of women that men find them a distraction.

With their increasing seclusion in society, Muslim women became marginalised from formal religious observance. Practices obviously varied from country to country throughout the ages, for a thirteenth-century *Maqamat* illustration from Iraq depicted a well-dressed group of women, possibly from the ruler's entourage, in a mosque gallery, and a sixteenth-century Persian miniature showed women in the upper part of a mosque, their lower faces covered.[24] Despite this, it should be noted that some outstanding women Sufis, such as the justly revered Rab'ia al-'Adawiyya, attained saint-like status and were even believed to possess powers of intercession. We see here, as in many other aspects of life in other cultures, the difference between the pronouncements of clerics in general and prevailing customary practices among the population at grass-roots level. Devout women must have been particularly aware of their exclusion from society in religious matters, when even their young sons publicly accompanied their fathers to the Friday service.

Menstruating women were proscribed from touching holy objects such as the Qur'an, but the attitudes of Muslim society are by no means unique, for the Jewish woman in a state of impurity should similarly, 'touch no hallowed thing, nor come into the sanctuary'.[25]

Sexual relations were forbidden during menstruation (al-haydh) or the period immediately following, since menstruation was adhan,[26] which had connotations both of pollution and hurt. A popular misconception in the medieval period was that a man could contact leprosy after intercourse with a menstruating woman.

Early Muslim women personally consulted the Prophet on matters of ritual purity. Another hadith related that when asked, 'When menstrual blood gets onto our clothes how do you think we should deal with it?' He advised, 'If menstrual blood gets onto your clothes you should wash them, and sprinkle them with water before you pray in them'.[27]

Women had to refrain from prayer during menstruation. 'A'isha said that a woman in a state of major ritual impurity, 'should scoop water over her head with both hands three times and rub the roots of her hair with her hands'.[28] The water was stored in a faraq, a special type of vessel containing three measures. In the absence of water, other methods of cleaning oneself were acceptable. Women could make do with some sand, with which they rubbed the fingertips and the end of the nose and did not have to attend the hammam until later in the day. Even after menstruation had ceased, sexual intercourse was forbidden until the woman had performed her major ritual ablution. Men, however, were evidently rendered doubly ritually impure from women's menstruation, for they had to attend the hammam, which was always close to the mosque, before the early morning prayer, and perform a major ablution.

Malik relates that when a man asked the Prophet's wife 'A'isha what made ghusl obligatory, she replied:

Do you know what you are like, Ibn Salama? You are like a chick when it hears the cocks crowing and so crows with them. When the circumcised part passes the circumcised part, ghusl is obligatory.[29]

The frankness of these conversations on sexual matters between women and men at that very early period of Islam seems astonishing, and of course it is from men's reports that we hear them.

Menstruation and sexual intercourse were among the principal invalidations of the Fast at Ramadhan. Sickness, pregnancy and breast-feeding also invalidated the Fast, and it goes without saying that large portions of the female population were excluded from strict religious observance at these times. Women were required to make up the days lost to menstruation at some later date, and certain pilgrimage rituals and prayers were also impossible for women in that state. However, it is arguable that there was a concern on the part of the jurists to avoid unnecessary strain on the health of women at particularly vulnerable times of life.

Strictly speaking, a female pilgrim's face should be uncovered during her visit to Mecca. Custom and practice dictated that she should cover it with a mask preventing the fabric from touching her skin. Given the other deprivations of pilgrimage, the discomfort of this face-covering, even during the night, can only be imagined.

The strict observance of religion was difficult for women, and for many there would be a feeling of sadness and exclusion. A childhood memory by a Turkish writer last century described the awe she personally experienced when allowed to worship in public and hinted at an intensely spiritual experience of which many women were deprived.

> It is wonderful to pray led by an *imam*. He chants aloud the verses you usually repeat to yourself in solitary prayer. Each movement is a vast and complicated rhythm, the rising and falling controlled by the invisible voices of the several muezzins. There is a beautiful minor chant. The refrain is taken up again and again by the muezzins . . . The rest belongs to eternal silence.[30]

The lesbian (al-sahhaqa)

We turn now to other categories of women officially categorized as marginal in society, for example lesbians and prostitutes. Homosexuality (*al-lawata*) was discussed in Sura 7, *al-A'raf*, with reference to Abraham's nephew Lot and his family and, together with transvestitism, was forbidden in the *Traditions*. Severe punishment was prescribed for both parties in Sura 4, *al-Nisa*, and marriage was the only legal framework which accommodated sexual relations in the Islamic world. This was the ideal; the reality among mere mortals was frequently somewhat different.

In practice, it must have been well nigh impossible to punish lesbians, since four witnesses, who must have viewed the conduct with their own eyes, were required to testify; this is the case too with adultery. In all other judicial cases only two were needed, and this demonstrates the seriousness not only of sexual transgression and the need for its corroboration, but also the necessity to preclude the likelihood of malicious tittle-tattle. The difficulty was compounded by the fact that these referred to male witnesses; the corresponding number of females would be eight, since the testimony of a man equalled that of two women in Islamic law. Once more one sees evidence of women's perceived 'deficiency'. In great households and palaces there would surely have been a conspiracy of silence at lesbian affairs, even if one personally disapproved. These women offered no serious, permanent competition for the master's attention, and any gossip would probably have been reciprocated in the hothouse atmosphere of the *harim*, with harsh consequences for all.

The following tale illustrates the absolute power of tyrannical rulers and the danger of sexual transgression by women. In the 'Abbasid period, two young maidens from the *harim* of the Caliph Musa al-Hadi, the elder brother of Harun al-Rashid, who were discovered in *flagrante delicto*, were decapitated. The caliph presented their heads, decorated with crowns and perfumed, to his courtiers.[31] Was he a pillar of moral rectitude, or merely aggrieved and insulted that they spurned his advances? This would certainly have been a salutary warning to the ladies, if not some of the men, for Harun al-Rashid's son and successor, Amin, preferred eunuchs to women. His mother attempted to wean him away by dressing slim maidens with very short hair in mannish clothes. They became known as 'boy-girls' and were something of a fashion in the following century or so.

There seems to have been an element of hypocrisy on the part of society regarding lesbianism for although pederasty, for example, was condemned by the orthodox, it was nevertheless acknowledged and practised. The term for lesbian, *sahhaqa*, was defined in medieval dictionaries as 'an epithet of evil import'[32] while al-Mutarrizi's *Mughrib* declared, 'it is said they are cursed by God'.

In the public perception, lesbianism (*musahaqa*) (literally 'rubbing') had connotations of witchcraft. *The Thousand and One Nights*, essentially a popular piece of entertainment, presented a somewhat scurrilous view of lesbians. Shawahi, the 'lady of calamities' was a lesbian witch in the tale of 'Hasan of Bassora'. An ancient witch, Zat al-Dawahi, who was also a wrestler and poisoner was portrayed in an extremely unattractive light. She was a cunning debauchee of none too particular personal habits, with 'red eyelids, yellow cheeks and a dull brown face'.[33] These attributes are all somewhat at odds with the description of 'wanton', which might suggest a contrived attractiveness. Girls in the *harim* found her singularly unappealing. Zat was certainly a prototype for the 'wicked witch' of fairytales, and lesbians may have been popularly demonized for, according to Leo Africanus there was a notorious circle of lesbian witches in late fifteenth-century Fez. In the early 'Abbasid period, and unlike other Arab women, lesbians in Baghdad did not remove their pubic hair. Their sexual predilection would therefore have been very obvious when they visited the *hammam*. In thirteenth-century Egypt a chronicler commented on, 'bawds who corrupt women as well as men'.[34]

There had been a notion in Medina that women turned to other women to avoid being reliant on men for sexual relations. A prostitute, curious, asked a lesbian if this was so. The lesbian replied that preferring her own kind, 'was safer than pregnancy, wherein lies the scandal'. 'Scandal' of course was an illegitimate child, and 'the fear of pregnancy' was mentioned by another lesbian. This may reflect a well-known Arab saying and belief: 'Whenever a man and a woman meet together, their third is always Satan.'[35]

Male homosexuals cited similar reasons for their sexual proclivities, such as, 'safer than pregnancy, childbirth, the burdens of marriage'[36] and so forth. Men were possibly also influenced by the unavailability of women during menstruation or, at court, sated by the superfluity of women vying and plotting for their attention in the *harim*. The institution in the court of *ghilman*, a circle of young male pages, frequently led to the development of close male sexual bonding, and pederasty was tolerated by the upper classes. There is no doubt that the predilection for these same-sex relations could have led frustrated women in the *harim* to turn to other women for emotional and sexual satisfaction. For them the perils, in theory, were no less than for consorting with men outside marriage. The increasing seclusion of women from public life must also have been a consideration for the man in the street.

A female convert to Islam from Judaism reported that among her circle of educated elegant women in the twelfth century, for example scholars, scribes and Qur'an readers, were women who possessed: 'Many of the ways of men so that they resemble them even in their movements, the manner in which they talk, and in their voice.'[37]

One wonders to what extent the effect of the initial upbringing and learning of these women lay in the company of men – grandfather, father and brothers – and whether they were treated as the equals of sons. Did their education alone set them apart from the majority of women in matters of taste and social acceptability, and how relevant was the element of public separation of the sexes? Many men must have felt intellectually intimidated by some of these women. They probably viewed them as subversive to the social order which had been established by Allah and was not subject to change, and in some undefined way 'dangerous'.

The above scholar may have frequented similar circles to those of the poetess Wallada, in eleventh-century Cordova, whom one writer dubbed 'the Sappho of Spain'.[38] As the daughter of the Caliph al-Mustaqfi, Wallada was possibly above reproach. Al-Tayfashi's thirteenth-century work of belles-lettres, Nuzhat al-albab fi ma la yujadu fi kitab, was devoted mostly to forbidden loves, and confirmed that male homosexuality, at least, was fashionable among Egyptian and Syrian intellectuals. Hermaphrodites (singular khuntha') were also included, and al-Tayfashi instructed on how to make the best of their company. It seems that in the medieval period there was no official persecution of lesbians in Muslim society. Was this because their conduct took place 'behind closed doors' and was therefore little spoken of?

The prostitute (al-baghiy)

We turn now to another despised category of woman, the prostitute. Al-baghiy, the term used for the professional prostitute, also covered a woman who commited fornication or adultery. Significantly, its root meaning had connotations both to oppress or treat unjustly and, ironically, to desire. Love played no part. Prostitution has always existed in societies, and the medieval Muslim world was no exception, despite being strictly proscribed by the Qur'an and the Sunna. In Islamic law prostitution was, in principle, likened to adultery and severely punished. A Muslim traveller from Siraf, one Abu Zayd, commented in 912 that: 'God has commended in our country, the land of Islam, one does not levy a tax on such a thing.'[39]

However, there was frequently an element of duplicity on the part of officialdom; moral rectitude in time gave way to pragmatism, and prostitution was legalised and subject to taxation. During the reign of 'Adud al-Dawla, Persian prostitutes were contributing handsomely to the state, and al-Maqrizi reported the imposition of a similar tax in Fatimid Egypt.[40] In Latakia, Syria, prostitutes were taxed according to age, charm and beauty; this implied unveiled faces. It would be interesting to know if these attributes were considered in inverse order, or if age and experience were viewed positively. The client presumably worked out for himself what the scale of charges might be, before making an approach. Tax in Fatimid Egypt was set personally by the superintendent of markets (muhtasib).

Despite the potentially lucrative source of state revenue, it would be wrong to think that all administrations tolerated prostitution. Some rulers were occasionally given to closing down brothels out of personal piety. For example, in 895 in Qayrawan, Ibrahim ibn Aghlab smashed his own wine vessels and rid the city of prostitutes in a public act of contrition, and Baghdad saw a purging and sitting-in demonstrations by the strict Hanbali sect in 934,[41] when women were physically attacked and their homes and furnishings damaged. The Caliph Hakim closed the bath-houses in Egypt in 1014 in an effort to keep prostitutes indoors. Apart from anything else, this would actually have prevented them attending the *hammam* to perform ritual ablutions (assuming that prostitutes did so) and remaining impure, with implications for men desiring sexual relations, if men who patronized prostitutes observed the rules. Sultan Baybars issued an edict banning prostitution, alcohol and other public nuisances; prostitutes' booths were ransacked and their goods seized. These attempts at prohibition were invariably short-lived, lasting days or a few weeks at most, when things continued as before. It is tempting to think that as men were also affected by these ordinances, they may have actively encouraged their flouting.

Discerning well-to-do men, some from foreign lands, patronized gracious establishments. One high-class brothel in Baghdad was described in *The Thousand and One Nights* as, 'A tall and goodly mansion, with a balcony overlooking the river-bank and pierced with a lattice-window'. The riverside situation indicated that it was in a very desirable quarter of the city, beside palaces and other luxurious scented places of entertainment and grand mansions. Prostitutes' charges of between ten and forty dinars a night confirm this. There, good-looking women in perfumed robes, with sprigs of jasmine in their hair, entertained in discreetly furnished surroundings. They were carefully made up, so that their cheeks 'resembled tulips and pomegranate flower' and they set men's hearts a-flutter.[42]

That was the quality end of the trade, for that is what it was, and women were commodities, but prostitutes also found a ready clientele around the caravanserais centred near the *suq*, when traders from all over the empire came into town with their merchandise. They also had willing customers from among the artisans, and some prostitutes solicited in the *hammam*. They plied a trade and charged according to supply and demand.

Procuresses also worked around booths in the *suq* selling alcohol and beer and led clients into a yard, surrounded by rooms. The available women in 'rather mean-looking houses'[43] were generally unattractive, heavily and badly made up and dressed in garish clothes. They sat on divans, chatting among themselves and eating grilled watermelon seeds, spitting out the husks on the floor matting. These establishments catered for working-men, and sailors and soldiers who were necessarily transient. Procuresses were also mentioned in the scabrous shadow-plays. Ports were another obvious situation for brothels, and around 1260, Sultan Qutuz sought to rid Alexandria of its prostitutes.[44] Given the degree of licensing of the trade, it would not be surprising to learn that health regulations covering the women were also in force, although there appears to be no evidence of this to date.

Prostitutes were highly visible throughout Egypt, and particular streets were reserved for them. Al-Maqrizi described their dress as distinctive red leather trousers (red may have been prescribed for prostitutes in the Mamluk era) and a particular kind of wrap, and some had little daggers.[45] Street life, then as now anywhere, could be violent, and men in one small category of homosexuals were known as 'men with short lives', because they ran the risk of attack or murder. Women would feel no less threatened. One wonders about the significance of red, and its use in English at least in 'red light' district, as well as 'red-faced' indicating shame.

There were doubtless wretched women plying their solitary trade in insalubrious byways of the city, in seedy rooms or out of doors. They were probably freelance and unlicensed, and would have been at the mercy of the *muhtasib*, who policed secluded public places for immoral goings-on. One thirteenth century commentator in Egypt deplored, among other things, 'Women who sell depravity to men in broad daylight'.[46] As sodomy was also mentioned in this context, were male prostitutes licensed? Arab writers commented on the extent of depravity in the Mamluk period and noted that fornication among the young was widespread; *plus ca change, plus c'est la même chose*. Wherever prostitutes – female or male – practised, economic circumstances would always have been relevant to their situation, and many must have been desperate.

In the medieval period young men in Cairo organised themselves socially around brotherhoods. Many of the members were not gainfully employed and some were involved in organised crime. Ties of loyalty to 'brothers' were strong, and one fourteenth-century critic alleged that members sometimes even forced their own wives into prostitution to support a fellow-member in financial difficullties.[47] Their concept of honour was not impugned.

Prostitutes went about unveiled. This would of course be useful when they plied their trade, both from their viewpoint if attractive and if, as needed, for identification by regular customers and the authorities. However, it also set them apart from 'respectable' women. Is there any connection here with the concept of 'bare-faced cheek' in English? Historians of Egypt mentioned payment of a tax to *daminat al-maghani*, a house where prostitutes had to register, hence their official recognition by the authorities. There may be connotations of a house of ill repute, as well as an association with singers.

One notes that the penalties for adultery or fornication in thirteenth-century Spain discriminated in favour of the Christian male majority at the expense both of women and Muslims. If the man was Muslim and the woman Christian, both parties were to be burned alive. But, unless a Muslim woman was licensed as a prostitute, her Christian partner went unpunished, while she would be treated under the very harsh Islamic law for adultery or fornication.[48]

Prostitution in Spain, as elsewhere, contributed much to the state treasury; prostitutes may have paid a property tax, as another of their names, '*kharajiyyat*', indicated. It is not clear if this implies that they owned and operated out of their own homes, or whether it referred to their 'outgoings' in taxes.

In seventeenth-century Persia there were apparently fourteen thousand prostitutes on the tax registers; they lived in special lodgings under the supervision of a woman.[49] They plied their trade with their faces covered, but the old woman who stood behind each with bedding allowed potential customers to see their faces by lamplight. (The traveller stressed that this was hearsay as far as he personally was concerned.) The old women would, incidentally, have been able to identify the customers, in case of trouble, and they undoubtedly took a share of the proceeds. It is arguable that many of them were also forced into this position, through widowhood or abandonment. In nineteenth-century Egypt, although prostitutes did not constitute a guild, they sometimes marched at the rear of guild processions. Again they were classified for taxation purposes.

There was evidently some tally of a prostitute's clients for, in the event of her producing a child, all the clients were called and, depending on physical characteristics, one man was named as the father. He had no recourse to a second opinion, and had to take away and support the child.[50] One wonders how much care prostitutes took of their health? It would certainly have been in their interests to do so. Health concerns aside, pregnancy and childbirth obviously curtailed the earning power of the women, as discussed in detail elsewhere here.

One of the nastiest and most offensive slurs against one's parentage was directed at Marwan I, the conqueror of Egypt in the late seventh century. Marwan was taunted by his enemies as the 'child of the woman in blue', a reference to brothels in the 'Period of Ignorance', where his grandmother was allegedly 'one of the women with blue flags'.[51] At that time prostitution (*bigha*) was a type of institutionalised marriage. Entry to the houses of these women was open to all and the women had no right of refusal; one wonders if they had been captured in war and were foreign? The colour blue was also symbolic of marginality, and it is noticeable that the *Maqamat* lutanist (who also sang) in a tavern was unveiled and wore a blue robe. A Danish traveller to Yemen in 1761 noted that the Jews of Arabia were, 'suffered to dress in any colour but blue; all their clothes are of blue cloth'[52] which they must have found shameful, given the norms of society.

Prostitutes in the Greek period dyed their hair yellow (and wore heavy make-up and red lipstick), and it has been demonstrated that in the Near East yellow was also traditionally associated with marginality and the low life, although favoured at court. Yellow garments such as half-silk (*mulham*) were looked upon with disfavour; the disapproval of the refined al-Washsha' was founded on the fact that they were regarded by society as 'the dress of dancing-girls and serving-girls'.[53] Again we have the implicit notion of immorality. At this early period yellow veils were prescribed for Jewish women, (and their menfolk were required to wear a yellow turban), as well as different coloured shoes, one black, one white, and their humiliation was probably intended. Abandoned Muslim women wore white robes, and widows black.

A further association of yellow with marginality is confirmed by the report of the death of the *amir* Sayf al-Dawla Ibn Hamdun, who died in 967. After several washings of the corpse with scents, 'the deceased was then anointed with saffron and camphor'.[54] Saffron, like camphor, was perfumed, but one has to question whether its yellow colour was also significant.

Prostitution was sexual exploitation, a two-way business which aimed to satisfy the man's sexual needs and the economic needs of the woman. Things may have changed with the advent of Islam, but prostitution was never, indeed could never, be eliminated in any country in any era.

The singing-girl (al-mughanniya)

Despite their great success as the paramours of the upper classes, singing-girls in whatever context were perceived by the general public to be morally suspect and somehow 'out of order'. Was this fair? While many probably behaved no better than was expected, they were originally slaves, with little say in their fate, whether they liked it or not. It is arguable that singing-girls had to be sharp-tongued. Because of their generally low status in the public perception and their perceived immorality, they were frequently the target of men's presumptuous lascivious remarks which would have been unthinkable in the company of so-called 'respectable' women.

Al-Jahiz believed that the majority of men who visited drinking-dens were there for sex, and would doubtless have agreed with the *belle-lettrist* al-Washsha' that the greatest catastrophe which could befall a 'virtuous and educated man', a 'person of good morals', was enthralment to singing-girls. Al-Harith, the high-minded narrator of Hariri's *Maqamat* was very loath indeed to enter a tavern in 'Ana to confront his trickster friend who had been masquerading as a 'holy man'. The judge al-Tanukhi repeated an anecdote concerning a father in a debt case who complained that his profligate son wasted his money on 'singing-girls' and that he had been led into trouble by a procurer.[55] Singing-girls were 'treacherous' and their passion rapidly evaporated. While many female entertainers were undoubtedly quite respectable, not all could aspire to the court, and the fate of most was probably not dissimilar to that of prostitutes, and frequently based on economic necessity.

Some, like the celebrated court singer 'Arib, mentioned in the *Book of Songs*, were shockingly outspoken in male company. One admirer asked another, 'What about her desire now?' while his companion tittered. 'Arib demanded to know what had been said, and he reluctantly told her. She riposted cuttingly, 'So what? The desire is quite in order, but the instrument is inactive'.[56] 'Arib boasted that she had slept with eight caliphs; she even managed to slip out of the *harim* to meet a lover, and became pregnant by him. It sounds as if she was extremely fortunate to escape severe punishment, if not with her life. Strictly speaking, it was seemly only for singing-girls to speak in a forthright manner, and in fact they were respected for doing so, such behaviour would never have been tolerated in wives and daughters.

Amber-coloured or yellow clothing was apparently fit for servants or singing-girls; 'yet they may be worn when one is being bled or is undergoing medical treatment'.[57] This is very interesting. The testimony of a phlebo-tomist was reprehensible according to the jurists, and the link with margin-ality is thus established. This seems to corroborate the position of singing-girls in relation to their place on the periphery of society, as well as reiterate the colour symbolism of yellow and its association with marginality.

Slaves

Another category of marginals in society was slaves, who played a major part in the economy of the Muslim world in other occupations in the medieval period, in particular in two major areas, the markets and agriculture. As the following accounts show, they sometimes fetched very low prices indeed in the market place, and were therefore readily affordable to a wide segment of society. It was axiomatic that no Muslim could be enslaved, so slaves were imported from far-off lands and shipped to major centres of trade in the Islamic world. It is apparent from pietist literature from the first five hundred years of Islam that owning slave girls was less deprecated than other luxuries, and this indulgence may well have been a factor in the burgeoning of the slave trade at that period.[58]

In *The Thousand and One Nights*, at the thirty-third tale, a slave broker in the market place harangued potential customers:

> Traders, fortunate men, all which is round is not a nut, all that is long is not a banana . . . Merchants, this unique pearl, for which fortunes will not be sufficient, what value would you put on? Open the bids!

and:

> Merchants, rich men, who among you will be the first to indicate a price for this slave, the queen of full moons, the magnificent pearl, this modest emerald, the object of desires . . .? He who does so will incur neither blame nor reproach.[59]

Another tale mentioned that a woman and her daughter were bought at a market in Kufa for fifty dinars; the daughter, at least, seems to have been marked for higher things, since this was a fair sum of money, however much one deprecated the trade in humans. While in Timbuktu around 1353, Ibn Battuta encountered an Arab slave-girl, from Damascus, who spoke to him in Arabic,[60] so the slave trade was not solely from west to east.

According to al-Maqrizi, janissaries and other Turkish soldiers took negro slaves to Egypt. The negroes had lived in abject poverty in their own countries and wore the minimum of body covering, with leather, iron or other metal nose rings and sundry ornaments. Slaves were of all ages and both sexes, black and white, and caravans from Libya also went down to Africa. Slaves were sold in the Cairo market at the Masrur *khan*; and at the end of the fifteenth century close by the Khalili *khan*. A replacement for the latter was ordered by the Sultan in 1511 on the same spot.[61] Male and female slaves wore only the barest minimum of clothing for modesty; this was apparently to allow potential purchasers to examine their bodies for signs of disease, to assess their strength and so on. It was literally a hands-on approach, to establish the firmness of a breast and strong arms and body in a male. The women, however, were allowed a scrap of linen for modesty and if chosen, were taken away for private examination by a matron under a large coverlet to check if they were virgins, and probably also for disease. This was obviously a factor if men were buying them for sexual purposes, which many did. Such experiences were humiliating, to say the least, and must have left their mark. One observer shockingly noted that slaves achieved very low prices, comparable to those of a herd of animals. Visiting Europeans left accounts of their visits to slave-markets, and one remarked on a market where male and female slaves were sold 'like cattle' at 'a price so low that one might have thought them stolen objects';[62] this is precisely what they were, in a sense.

At a much later Egyptian market, a European traveller reported seeing black and white female slaves on sale, who had been separated as to sex. Some of them, in particular the whites, (who would have been Christians), had face-veils. The reference to veils is curious, since slaves, Jewish and Christian women seem to have been generally exempted from wearing them. Perhaps these women were brought from former Christian lands then under Muslim control, where they conformed to local custom. In a modern setting, national solidarity overrode religious difficulties during the 1936 Rebellion in Palestine, when Christian women veiled in a gesture with their fellow Muslim Palestinians.[63] And Ibn Battuta reported that during a plague epidemic, people of all religions assembled at a richly endowed mosque in Damascus, said to contain a rock with the imprints of Moses' foot.

Christian slaves were largely black, and probably from Ethiopia. Others were classed as 'white slaves', and included Berbers, Greeks and Armenians. They were paraded totally naked, to assess physical defects and were asked to sit, run, speak and sing, and their teeth and breath checked; this was also an extremely humiliating experience. The Christian doctor Ibn Butlan even produced a handbook for those intending to purchase slaves; women slaves (like their male counterparts) were graded according to their proposed occupation and Abyssinians, for example, were excellent cooks.[64] Slave traders 'did them up' before parading them for sale, and after a visit to the *hammam* the women's hair was elaborately braided, while their arms and ankles were adorned with bracelets.

White slaves, particularly Circassian, were highly valued but the black Ethiopian slaves did not fetch high prices. Doubtless market forces came into play here, white slaves being much less usual, and therefore rather exotic. Or was there a particular cachet in owning an infidel? Despite the indignities heaped upon them, another traveller remarked without a trace of irony that slaves did not appear unduly afflicted by their situation, 'they even had a smile for the matrons who came to trade and visit them'.[65] These matrons may have been slave-traders in their own right, but apparently mothers themselves frequently chose slave girls of the household as wives for their sons. Presumably in these cases the slave was freed before the marriage. From the eleventh century onwards sons of slaves – of all races and colours – were able to rise rapidly in Muslim society. Slave women were usually foreigners and from the ninth century onwards it became the custom to grant their offspring equal status with other Muslims. Nor was illegitimacy any barrier to upward social mobility; in the late seventh century, the Caliph Mu'awiya appointed one Ziyad ibn Abihi over Persia and Mesopotamia. Ziyad's second name indicates he was the 'son of his father', that is his father was unknown.

A prospective mother-in-law would have had the opportunity to observe a slave-girl in her household from an early age, a personal relationship would have been formed and – perhaps very important for mothers of sons – the mistress would have trained the girl in her own ways. She therefore ensured that her son would be well looked after and that she had found someone compatible to look after her in her old age. Marriage to a slave was explicitly sanctioned by the Qur'an: 'Marry from among women such as are lawful to you'.[66] One of the names for female servant, *jariya*, has connotations of activity and running about; in other words she was at someone's beck and call.

Ottoman records mentioned the *wakala al-jallaba*, the caravanserai where foreign slaves were lodged before sale; this housed black slaves. This does not necessarily imply racisim, as the term could apply to several commodities from foreign lands which would be sold in their particular markets, and slaves were sadly but other commodity.[67] Slave-dealing was temporarily suspended during a plague outbreak in Egypt in 1437.

Although slaves had personal rights, they had no legal powers. Slaves could not be forced into prostitution, as had happened in the days before the advent of Islam. A slave married to another, slave or free man, could not be taken as a concubine by her master. If a slave woman married a Muslim, her children were themselves slaves; in other circumstances, a slave could marry her master, but he had first had to manumit her. (A free Muslim woman could not have a sexual relationship with her male slave.) If a slave had a child by her master, she could not be used as a pledge. How one's slave dressed reflected on her owner, and there would have been pressure on her to be well turned out. Veiling was not mandatory for slaves, and yet many chose to do so, while others of their class took pleasure in flaunting themselves 'front and back'.[68]

High class Persian families were only too happy to hand over their daughters as slaves to rulers, if asked. This had distinct advantages; they received a stipend and used their daughter as a means to court favours and enhance the family's social status. Furthermore, if a marriage took place, any children became eligible for an inheritance.

Despite the huge prices paid for slave girls in the context of the nobility, the reality was that household slaves were commonplace in town and country, and within the financial scope of many ordinary householders, even those in the most frugal circumstances, as the following tale demonstrates. A traveller in Egypt found an ascetic: 'Reclining upon a felt mat and spitting in a potsherd full of ashes, while a bondwoman sat in his house spinning yarn.'[69]

It is unlikely that the personal treatment of slaves was in any way related to their 'worth' that is, the price paid. Some would be ill-treated, while others would become part of the family, in every sense of the word.

In 1437, during the rule of the Mamluk Sultan Barsbay, female slaves of good character in Egypt were able to do shopping for their mistresses and allowed to appear in public with uncovered faces. The implication may be that they were of no social account. Aged women were also entirely at liberty to go out and about. An old woman was regarded as 'safe' from the viewpoint of sexual danger; she posed no threat, presumably, on the grounds of un-attractiveness or being 'past it'. However, there was a popular male conception that older women were dangerous. Did this suggest that they had nothing better to do than to stir up trouble? Even Tawaddud, the singing-girl in *The Thousand and One Nights*, warned on the peril of sex with old women, 'for they are deadly';[70] perhaps she was in denial concerning her own future. Tawaddud herself surely had nothing to fear from older women as competition. 'Old', of course was relative, particularly in the days before modern medicine; perhaps Tawaddud referred to post-menopausal women. As a doctor, Ibn Qayyim al-Jawziyya cautioned that sex with old women 'shortens the lifespan and makes ill the bodies of healthy people.'[71] Did women believe that the same applied to sex with old men?

The nineteenth-century traveller de Nerval, inspired by Edward Lane's sojourn in Egypt, reported that the slave traders summoned, 'five or six negresses, sitting in a circle on mats, most of whom were smoking, and 'greeted us with bursts of laughter'.[72] They had been made up for sale, their hair parted into hundreds of little rows of tresses and they wore red ribbons.

Their skin gleamed, they wore pewter ankle and arm bracelets, copper earrings, and had tattoos on various parts of their bodies. De Nerval continued touchingly: 'These poor girls . . . they were carefree and *laissez-faire*, most of them laughing almost continuously, which made the scene a little less painful.'

De Nerval also saw about a dozen black male slaves ranged along a wall, with 'more of an air of anxiety than sadness.' The slave-traders called out, 'blacks or Abyssinians'. Although it is possible that they might actually have been better off, materially, than had they remained in their own country, they were going to a fate unknown, without kin or friends.

Non-Muslim women

Turning now to other non-Muslims, the Jews, Christians and Sabeans constituted a class in Muslim society known as *ahl al-dhimma*, 'The People of the Covenant', who were free to practise their own religions and received the protection of the Muslim majority in return for paying a special tax as tribute, and carrying no arms. Marriage or sexual relations between Jewish and Christian men and Muslim women was forbidden and could result in death. A Muslim man, however, could marry Jewish or Christian women, with the proviso that any children would be brought up as Muslims. In Spain and the Maghrib in the twelfth century the zealous Almohads sought to assimilate Jews with Muslims. Ibn Aqnin, a Jew, reported his own personal experiences in al-Andalus, and said that efforts were made to indoctrinate children in Islam. He added that if a Jewish girl had a child by a Muslim, even the man was despised, as was the child.[73] He added that even third-generation Jewish converts to Islam there were subject to restrictions.

There were Jewish and Christian quarters in the cities, and the Jewish population of Baghdad in 1171 numbered some forty thousand.[74] This was not necessarily sinister in the modern sense of ghettoes, for the unarmed minorities were near the citadel for their own protection. It is likely that as their status increased, families moved outside the officially designated quarters; at any rate, some would live at least in the proximity of Muslim neighbours. What contact, if any, did Jewish and Christian women have with their Muslim sisters? For their part, Muslims were in theory officially barred from greeting Jews first, joining Jews at funeral processions or visiting sick Jews. This last-mentioned point appears to be a recognition that there were inter-faith friendships. Business, scholarly and personal relationships were formed in male circles, but it is unclear to what extent this happened among women.

Like their Muslim counterparts, many women from minority religious groups were probably also compelled to supplement the family income. We know that Jewish women ventured outside their homes in a variety of occupations similar to those followed by Muslim women, such as the peripatetic *dallala* or broker. One woman, in Jerusalem, Lifa 'daughter of Ya'qub the Jew', was described as *'al-kahhala'*, one who treated eye complaints.[75] It is unlikely that anyone in business confined their dealings to their own particular religious group, although it is conceded that, for example, marriage-brokers likely did so. Another sixteenth-century deed referred to a Jewish woman who was being sued by a Muslim woman in a dispute over the return of goods as security for a pledge. It is significant that while the Jewish woman represented herself in the Muslim court, the Muslim plaintiff gave a power of attorney to a male to appear on her behalf, but this might only have been an indication of class differences in a tradeswoman/client relationship. Elsewhere, Jewish women were involved in property, and there seems to be no reason why Christian women should not have done likewise, since they presumably were not secluded beyond the restrictions any responsible parent in any community placed upon their young daughters.

However, given the description of the discomfort of the teeming cities, upper class women from the various communities may have chosen to appear infrequently in public, other than to make visits to family and friends. An added disincentive for Jews and Christians for even relatively distant visiting would be the decree, 'that their womenfolk do not ride on padded saddles, but only a pack saddle'.[76] Given the fact that many women from minority groups dressed to all intents and purposes like the Muslim majority, it is likely that many disregarded this and other decrees.

Small, local markets for everyday shopping were found in all quarters in the cities. Maqrizi's mention of the Cairaite Jews in the *suq Hara al-Yahud*[77] does not imply that Jewish women were necessarily confined to their own quarter, for: 'Their residence in the main town and Muslim markets is tolerated and they may buy and sell there, but neither wine nor pigs . . .'

Jewish (and Muslim) women, of course, would have patronised a butcher from their own faith. This was confirmed by an ordinance in Seville around 1100, stating: 'A Jew must not slaughter an animal for a Muslim. The Jews may be authorised to open their own special butcher shops.' Christian women probably used Christian butchers.

A report from early Muslims to 'Umar ibn al-Khattab complained that:
'Several Christians under your jurisdiction have relapsed into the custom of
wearing turbans (and) no longer wear belts at the waist.'[78]

In the early eighth century 'Umar II decreed that the minorities should be
excluded from public appointments and wear distinctive garments indicating
their status; these positions referred to men. Harun al-Rashid ordered the
destruction of churches in the border region and wrote to an official:

> To take measures so that the appearance of the non-Muslims in Baghdad
> should be clearly marked off from that of the Muslims in matters of dress,
> and that neither should they ride horses like them.[79]

The judge Ahmad ibn Talib ordered mandatory discriminatory badges for
non-Muslims in the ninth century; those for Jews showed an ape, while the
Christian versions had a pig. Al-Tabari recorded a decree of the Caliph al-
Mutawakkil dated 850 concerning Christians which mentioned honey-
coloured 'patches', of a different material to that of the garment. 'One of the
patches was to be worn in front on the breast and the other on the back. Each
of the patches should measure four fingers in diameter.'[80]

In other words they had to be readily noticed. Al-Mutawakkil also
prescribed clothing in particular colours for men and women, with mention
of a special belt (*zunnar*). Interestingly, he commanded that the slaves of
Christians also had to wear the *zunnar*. Green would automatically be
proscribed because it is associated with descendants of the Prophet (and
therefore proscribed in any case for the vast majority of Believers) and had
connotations of Paradise and angels. One has to ask just how conversant with
official decrees was the bulk of the population, and would they have cared?
Presumably ordinances on costume referred only to public appearances; away
from the public gaze, did elements of costume distinctive to each community
came to the fore?

In late twelfth-century Morocco Muslim authorities tended to categorize
non-believers by contrasting the colours of clothes with those worn by
Muslims, hence blue (which darkens to black) for non-Muslims, and the white
of the Muslims.[81] Non-Muslim women, no less than their menfolk, also had
to display distinctive signs, for example a yellow wrapper for Jewish women
and blue wrappers for Christians.[82] Al-Hakim ordered *dhimmi* women to
wear one black and one red shoe, while in 1354, the Mamluk regime
prescribed one black and one white shoe. In fourteenth-century Aleppo,
Christians were 'still bound to wear the badge'.

Christians and Jews in Seville around the year 1100 were forbidden to wear aristocratic dress, the garments of scholars, or luxurious fabrics such as silk, or any form of distinctive costume. It was further decreed that: 'It is forbidden to sell a coat that once belonged to a leper, to a Jew or Christian, unless the buyer is informed of its origin.'[83]

Ibn Fadlan wrote to the Caliph Nasr al-Din Allah around 1220, and reminded him that the last time rigorous adherence to the prescriptions had been observed was early in the tenth century in the time of al-Muqtadir bi 'amr Allah. He was anxious that these practices had fallen into disuse and recommended an increase in taxes. Ibn Fadlan pointed out that in most of the Muslim world non-Muslims had to bear distinguishing marks and were 'admitted to none but the most humiliating employments'.[84] This may have been generally true, but brilliant Jews and Christians could and did successfully rise to the very summit of society in the fields of medicine, finance and scholarship, and many Jewish and Christian women must have lived in fine houses. In times of civil crisis or when these minorities were perceived to be 'rising above their station' in some way, there were re-enactments of the laws designed to humiliate and set them apart. Such decrees, certainly in places other than Muslim Spain, apparently rarely rose beyond the 'ink on paper' stage and were a response to popular opinion, which could and did on occasion turn violent.

Around the same time in the early thirteenth century Ibn Aqnin, a Jew living under Almohad rule, said that the purpose of distinctive garments was 'To differentiate us from among them so that we should be recognised in our dealings with them without any doubt, in order that they might treat us with disparagement and humiliation.' He went on:

As for the decree enforcing the wearing of long sleeves, its purpose was to make us resemble the inferior state of women, who are without strength.[85]

Is Ibn Aqnin here speaking of Muslim women, or did Jewish men at that time also regard their women as 'inferior' in some way?

The protected minorities undoubtedly had particular refinements of dress as a proud means of defining their own tight-knit social and religious group. In later Muslim accounts – as well as Jewish writings – the believers were urged to dress in their own distinctive way, lest they become as the infidels. A *hadith* ran, 'He who tries to resemble people becomes one of them', and there must have been occasions when religious leaders urged their communities to display solidarity; one way of doing this could be by costume.

An eleventh-century poll-tax document issued by the famous judge al-Mawardi recommended that non-Muslim subjects wear a distinctive sign (*ghiyar*) on their outer garment, and the *zunnar* was again mentioned. Contemporary dictionaries reiterated that this was a belt worn variously by Christians, Jews, Sabeans and Magians. In the tenth century, Christians were ordered to wear grey or black clothing. Is it not likely that women, particularly young women, would do their best to subvert such rules? Men certainly did. The Almohad al-Mansur was of the opinion that Jewish men in al-Andalus,

> Had become so bold as to wear Muslim clothing and in their dress looked like the noblest among them, mingling with the Muslims in external affairs, without being distinguished from the servants of God.[86]

Their womenfolk probably did likewise, and the Jewish elders also probably feared that in resembling Muslims, they would become 'one of them'.

It is arguable that most women would take an interest in fashion. Even if some did not venture outside their homes, we know that female brokers went around the communities selling clothing and accessories. These brokers all bought their goods in the same *suq*; they would be fully aware of the latest fabrics and fashions, and keep their customers up to date. It is suggested that in many cases edicts were blatantly disregarded and that women pleased themselves, wore clothing similar in pattern and colour across the religious divide and followed the majority, in this case Muslims.

The experience in Sicily certainly bore this out, for Ibn Jubayr saw Christian women in Muslim dress in Palermo, and in Britain today some Muslim girls quarrel with their families over following western fashions. In the fifteenth-century a *shaykh* reported from Tunis:

> It is the custom with us for the women of the Nazarenes to take the veil like unto Muslim women, and most often without any sign of distinction – although some do observe distinction in the manner required of Nazarenes.[87]

We know, too, that bondswomen dressed as free women. If Jewish women did choose to wear the veil in public, they had also to wear a voluminous honey-coloured *izar* or wrap, so there was obviously sometimes an element of choice, depending on time, place, popular sentiment and women's personal whim.

However, those Christian, Nazarene and Jewish women who preferred to veil were not only doing so for fashion, but possibly to avoid the stigma of prostitution. For example, in eighteenth-century Marrakesh and Hamadan, Jewish women had to go unveiled, like prostitutes. This was a great humiliation where all respectable women otherwise covered their faces. Could these measures have been a means to persuade them to convert? But it would be strange that mere conversion could change an oft-despised person into an 'acceptable' person in society.

A report from a modern European traveller told how the Sultan of Tunis possessed:

> More than six hundred concubines, the which he keepeth in his great castle of the Kasba in Tunis, under the eye of a Christian woman and many eunuchs.

She would have been very well dressed, and presumably followed the fashion of the ladies of the *harim*.

A statute demanded that houses of Christians and Jews had to be lower than those of Muslims. Unspecified wooden effigies were to be put on the doors as a distinguishing mark, should any be needed. Al-Mutawakkil's decree spoke of 'wooden images of devils', and non-Muslim homes in the ninth century were compelled to have a board nailed to the door showing a monkey. Jewish homes, of course, would ordinarily have had a *mezuzah* on the right hand doorpost; in the circumstances, this was probably not allowed to be displayed on the outside, but it would be apparent from the inside of the house, and all the other right hand doorposts would have one. The *mezuzah* contained a tiny parchment scroll of the *Shema*, 'Hear, oh Israel' and served both as a distinguishing mark of faith and a reminder from the Book of Deuteronomy of God's presence.

No non-Muslim could enter the public baths on a Friday until after prayers. Was this discriminatory, or pragmatic, given that Friday is the Muslim sabbath, and it is necessary to be ritually pure before worship? The prescriptions of 'Umar ibn al-Khattab concerning Jews stated that they also 'had to wear iron necklaces around their necks' (when they entered the bath-houses.[88]

Women made a great display of going to the baths, and this decree might have been designed particularly to humiliate those who would otherwise have worn silver or gold jewellery, particularly since gold and silver were traditionally given at Jewish weddings.

It is likely that certain Jewish congregations had their own ritual bath (*mikvah*). Some Jewish households had private wells which women used for purification, and these seem to have supplemented visits to the *hammam*. One report told how a Muslim man went to a *hammam* owned by a Jew, although it is not clear if different faiths used the baths at the same time, or even if non-Muslim women used the same bath as Muslim women. Would this really have been likely, given that the rules of female purification are so strict in both Islam and Judaism, and the laws were formulated by males?

Girls (and boys) served in taverns. Because of the connotations of alcohol and its link with perceived licentious behaviour it is likely that they were Christians or Jews. Indeed, contemporary manuscript illustrations of taverns depict women or girls with their breasts uncovered trampling grapes.[89] This would not have been seemly in a Muslim woman, but might have been acceptable from others, who were deemed worthy of no respect.

Ibn Jubayr, travelling between 1183 and 1185, was pleasantly surprised by the generosity shown by the Syrian Christians at grass-roots level to Muslim pilgrims; this was despite the presence of Muslim and Christian armies. It is frequently overlooked that during the Crusading era there were periods of comparative peace. Ibn Jubayr was also impressed by a Christian wedding near Tyre. The bride and groom were together at the bride's door, surrounded by musicians, and went in procession to the groom's home. This custom sounds similar to wedding festivities among Muslims. In the fourteenth century, Ibn Battuta also found a warm Syrian welcome at a monastery at Latakia where all visitors, regardless of religion were entertained.

Interestingly – and reflecting the offence felt by many Muslims at the outward manifestation of another faith – Ibn Battuta was alarmed to hear the sound of bells at the Black Sea port of Kafa, for in Muslim lands bells and the Jews' ram's horn (*shofar*) were not permitted. Jewish women, like Muslim women, also worshipped separately from the men. Curiously, al-Muqtadir's decree obliged Christians to wear 'a cross on their breast'[90] yet they were forbidden to carry crosses on Palm Sunday. On Palm Sunday, Christians elsewhere made conspicuous public displays of Christ's entry into Jerusalem.

The graves of Christians and Jews had to be level with the ground and their tombs quite different to those of Muslims, so that there was no possibility of a Muslim praying beside an infidel's grave. Although Jews elsewhere also had professional wailing women, these were banned at funerals in Muslim areas, and Jews were forbidden to chant in the streets. Nevertheless wailing women probably appeared in private homes.

In the Moroccan folk-tale 'Who's cleverer: Man or Woman?', a prince disguised as a Jewish fish merchant courted an Arab girl, the daughter of a carpenter.[91] This was a variation on the old theme of kings and princes being other than what they seemed, and served to underscore the differences – perhaps only of dress or occupation – in the society of the period. He flirted with 'A'isha, and suggested a kiss on the cheek as payment. She duly obliged.

A Jew was accused of treachery in Baghdad in 1290, imprisoned and faced death; his release was legally bought, and it was reported that in such cases Jewish wives were sometimes also seized.[92] At other times, it has to be said that the minority communities, and rich individuals, offered to and did pay handsomely to be exempted from many of the personal restrictions in force. Others less fortunate had to bear the humiliation themselves.

Women found themselves on the margins of society generally, at different life events, and in some areas of their religious life, and they were subject to official proscriptions and religious prohibition. Therein lies the dilemma; on the one hand, woman was upheld as a paradigm for society; on the other she was a potential source of defilement and danger. Prostitutes were readily identifiable, although they may have exercised some control over their clothing. Many traded their bodies out of dire economic necessity and the lack of social cohesion which might otherwise have helped to define the obligations of their 'betters' in society. Colour symbolism evidently played a significant part in maintaining a particular ideology and defining one's perceptions of 'normality' and marginality in Muslim society, and pertained to Muslim and non-Muslim women alike. In most cases, women's offence, if that is what it was, was involuntary, beyond their control, and ordained by men. Other women, like lesbians, arguably exercised some element of choice in their sexual preference, although the sequestration of many women in a sense facilitated this.

Women in the Jewish and Christian communities were intentionally identified by what amounted to humiliating costume, although it is more than likely that many of these ordinances never progressed beyond the 'ink on paper' stage for much of the time and these women dressed as they pleased. That is not to deny that there were uprisings at the street level from time. Even so, Jews and Christians at least had the benefit of the powerful in their own societies to intercede and mitigate harsh proscriptions.

As for women in Arab lands being perceived as inferior and weak, women in the Middle Ages would undoubtedly have agreed with and been heartened by a modern, enlightened, male opinion of womankind:

He who believes her to be a weak creature is mistaken . . . she who in past centuries bore the age's hardships, the father's oppression, the husband's tyranny, the burden of pregnancy, the pain of menstruation, the bitterness of suckling, in contentment and serenity is no weak creature . . . She is the measure of the community; who wishes to know the secret of a people's progress or backwardness, let him inquire about the woman's influence on the character of their men.[93]

Conclusion

The great desert romances of the Bedouin have long echoed throughout Arabia in a haunting and foreboding refrain. They are valuable as a paradigm for a study of women's private lives as a demonstration of the persistence of tradition and the strength and forbearance of Arab women through the ages. Poets wrote with feeling of the consequences of life in a patriarchal society circumscribed by religion and custom, of arranged marriage, honour and shame and the consequent control of women's sexuality, and women's seclusion. The main themes of the genre were pure, unconsummated love, disapproval of suitors by male relatives, and enforced separation, with the attendant motifs of longing, sadness and frustration.

Arranged marriage was the norm, and girls were frequently married off at a tender age to foster superior social or political alliances, and it has been demonstrated that harsh economic circumstance underlay these motives. Early marriage ensured that girls had no voice, and underlined the subordination of individual wills for the greater good of the tribe. Despite the preference for first-cousin marriage, Jamil ibn Ma'mar al-'Udhri was deemed unworthy of Buthayna. Jamil forlornly sang, 'Shall I ever meet Buthayna alone again, each of us full of love as a cloud of rain?'

Doomed love

Theirs was a star-crossed love bordering on the obsessive. Physical attractiveness was not necessarily a prerequisite; rather it was some inner, deeply spiritual quality which the lover sought to share. The great philosopher al-Ghazali outlined the love of beauty as opposed to sensual desire, 'Everything the perception of which gives pleasure and satisfaction is loved by the one who perceives it'.[1] For many, desire also entered the equation.

Men who were in thrall to their lovers likened their love to enslavement, with underlying notions of women's power to captivate or cast a spell. This much is suggested in the nickname of the lovelorn Qays ibn al-Mulawwah, more popularly known as Majnun, 'possessed', or 'mad'. Majnun sang of his love for Layla bint Sa'd al-Amiriyya:

I did not seek love but it came.
Joy and pain are allotted by Heaven's decree.
None can escape his fate.
I am bound in fetters I would not break, if I could.

The Umayyad poet 'Umar ibn Abi Rabi'a was similarly entrapped:

Quietly with me beside the howdahs stay.
Blame not my love for Zaynab, for to her
And hers my heart is pledged a prisoner.[2]

Yusuf, the Joseph of the Old Testament, and an exemplar for the honourable man, acknowledged that sexuality was ever-present between men and women, that it involved the incitement to sexual indulgence and posed a great threat. It was certainly true of his encounter with the scheming, seductive and duplicitous Zulaykha, the Pharaoh's wife, *femme fatale par excellence*, mad with desire and destructive. He implored Allah:

Unless Thou turn away their guile from me, I might yet yield to their allure and become one of those who are unaware (of right and wrong).[3]

'If it were not for shame, there would be no honest women', so runs an Arabic proverb. There is an element of truth here, for there was a deep underlying fear of pregnancy and the incontrovertible proof of an illicit relationship. One woman sang plaintively:

Long was the night for me, and black
And, without my beloved to play with, I slept not,
This bed would have shaken from our love,
But for fear of Allah, the only God.[4]

Honour and shame

Despite the very harsh penalties and dangers in transgressing sexual codes, it is surprising to find many references to romantic dalliance, even adultery, in Arabic literature. Layla and Buthayna knew full well the perils of a forbidden relationship. Layla bint Lukays, a well-known poetess, was kidnapped by a Persian while en route to Yemen. She had been promised in marriage to her cousin Barraq, a Yemeni nobleman, whom she loved. Layla assured him and her brothers that: 'The foreigner lies, he never touched me and I am still pure, and I'd die rather than share his bed.'[5]

On hearing of her plight, they rescued her, but one wonders what their reaction would have been had she not remained a virgin, and dishonoured her male relatives?

Neither was the faithful Buthayna immune to danger. When Jamil proposed sexual intercourse, Buthayna refused. Jamil, beset by jealousy and insecurity, accepted her decision, but shockingly confessed, 'If you granted it to me, I knew that you would grant it to others also', adding that he would have had to kill her. Buthayna and Jamil defiantly continued to meet in secret for the rest of their lives, at great risk to themselves and their confidants.

> Oh might it flower anew that youthful prime,
> And restore to us, Buthayna, the bygone time!

sang Jamil. Was this what damned them, lovers' trysts, the attendant malicious gossip, the implied loose morals of Buthayna, the consequent slur on her family's honour, and the defiance of authority? Even 'A'isha, the Prophet's young wife, was wrongfully accused of sexual misconduct on the return from a military expedition. The virtuous and much respected 'A'isha was everything Zulaykha was not, and beyond reproach.

The physical manifestations of unfulfilled love in men were the emaciation of self-neglect, perpetual sadness, and copious weeping; these were best exemplified by the wanderer Majnun. From the ninth century onwards pining away even to death became a popular literary theme, but Nizami deplored such sentiments, 'for it rewards the person by relieving him of himself'. Majnun might even have had a death wish. 'Nothing in the world can comfort me but love. Give me Layla or I shall die'.[6]

Although formally rejected as potential husbands, Jamil and Majnun were nonetheless at liberty to express publicly their anguished feelings through their poetry; this was a privilege and a cathartic experience denied the young women. Layla wistfully acknowledged that Majnun:

Does not need to fear anybody.
He can go where he wishes, can shout,
say and put in verse whatever he feels.
But I?
I am a prisoner here.[7]

Tellingly, Layla acknowledged that a woman 'still remains a woman, and cannot act in the same way as he can'.[8] Women were made of sterner stuff, but no less afflicted.

I have been through what Majnun went through,
but he declaimed his love and I treasured mine
until it melted me down.[9]

Was there a death-wish in Majnun's self-neglect and starvation which held out hope of a kind for his future? A widely-contested *Tradition* holds that the Prophet said, 'He who loves, hides his love, waits patiently, and dies, dies as a martyr'; martyrs, of course, go directly to Paradise. In some ways it is difficult to sympathize with Majnun, and there is the suspicion that he exploited his appearance simply to gain sympathy.

Despite their fidelity, and the intensity of their professed love, to say nothing of their fear for their lives – the ultimate penalty for youthful rebellion – Layla and Buthayna did not escape their lovers' blame for their plight; they would have endorsed the words of the noted poet al-Kumayt, who captured well the enchantment and transience of romantic love:

Only he who feels real love,
Knows the joy and sorrow of life,
For in love there is sweetness and bitterness,
And he who has tasted tells you of them.[10]

Majnun petulantly complained:

Silence and night and desert are a vault
In which like winds my passion and verses blow.
You filled the sandy levels, Lord, and the sky
With love, and put all the load on to me.

Buthayna was portrayed as domineering and cruel, and Majnun even had the effrontery to pray to God to:

Forgive Layla for what she burdened me with,
and the ash that clogs the heart.

Here is the enduring allusion to the lover arriving at the cold fire of the
deserted Bedouin encampment, to find once more that the beloved's tribe had
folded up its black hair tents and slipped away into the night. The Umayyad
Caliph Walid ibn Yazid, writing from the comfort of his palace, harked back
to that earlier age:

'Tis grief enough for desperate love to see his love's abodes deserted and
desolate,[11]

On arrival at 'the barren halting-place . . . standing upon the ground' he
wept, 'for I see only ruins' (al-tulul).
Yet Layla wrote to Majnun:

I am with you with all my love
and, tell me, who are you with?
It is true that our bodies are separated,
but my soul does not leave yours for one moment,

which surely gives lie to accusations of female inconstancy. 'I know how you
are suffering and how your heart is breaking'.[12]
From the female lovers we heard relatively little; their voices were muted,
but nonetheless revealing. There was sad resignation and acceptance of
society's norms, perhaps even bewilderment on Layla's part:

Whatever happened to Majnun?
I felt the same as he,
But he could express his love openly,
While I pined in silence away.[13]

Buthayna resignedly lamented Jamil's death:

Never for a single instant have I felt consolation for the loss of Jamil; that
time has not yet come. Whilst thou art absent, O Jamil, son of Ma'amar!
The pains of life and its pleasures are to me equally indifferent,[14]

and she also died of a broken heart.

It is suggested that through their solitary internalization of their plight, women such as Buthayna and Layla were in some way enriched, even ennobled by their experiences. Not so some of the men. This is not to deny that both doomed parties suffered, yet the women did not dwell on their own unhappy plight. Their situations underlined the essential reserve of young Arab women and emphasised the privacy of domestic life and its structured physical space in the Muslim world. It remains relevant in many places today.

Women have always taken risks. Zaynab was but one of several respected women with whom the poet 'Umar ibn Abi Rabi'a consorted. 'Umar was not, however, the most faithful of lovers, but was very attractive to women. Indeed, there is the suggestion that independently-minded and respected women often initiated trysts with him.

In the first half of the eleventh century the daughter of the ruler of Almeria, Umm al-Kiram, wistfully wrote of her love for Assumar, a handsome young man: 'I would give my life if we could meet away from spying eyes and eavesdroppers. Oh how I wish my lap could be his home.'[15]

In such situations the spectres of misunderstanding, slanderous gossip, shame and unfulfilled longing forever loomed. There was no indication of Umm al-Kiram's marital status other than her name indicating that she already had a son, Kiram, but it may be that she was still married, and so it is not surprising that their meetings occasioned scandal. Even 'Ulayya, the sister of Harun al-Rashid, hinted of constraints placed on her freedom. She acknowledged that, 'letters can be read and contacts let you down',[16] echoing Layla's 'I have nobody to whom my heart can talk, whom it can trust.[17] Intermediaries were arguably necessary in these circumstances, but there was an understandable reluctance to be involved.

Women poets

Khansa' of the Bani Sulaym, was arguably the foremost Arab woman poet in the medieval period, Khansa' grieved over the loss of four sons and two brothers on the battlefield, and wrote movingly of her brother Sakhr, 'The rising and setting of the sun keep turning on my memory of Sakhr's death'.[18] Yet even in her grief Khansa' displayed a generosity of spirit noticeably lacking in the self-pitying outpourings of Majnun and his ilk, and shared the sorrow of others, 'And only the host of mourners crying for their brothers saves me from myself'.[19]

In another lament for a brother Khansa' tenderly wrote:

No mother, endlessly circling her foal,
calling it softly, calling aloud,
grazing where the grass was, remembering then,
going unendingly back and forth,
fretting for ever where grass grows new,
unceasingly crying, pining away,
was closer than I to despair when he left –
a stay too brief, a way too long.[20]

Khansa' did not have the solace of a supportive husband; she was married to a ne'er-do-well by whom she had many children, and her heart must have been heavy and any comparison of honourable brothers and sons with her husband odious. Khansa' and other women wrote with feeling of separation and death, but they reiterated the supreme Bedouin principles of liberality and bravery. Umm Khalid Annumayriyya similarly alluded to battle in her eulogy for her son:

I miss him and the thought of him tears my eyes like a prisoner recalling home under the shackles' painful grip, or the cries of a soul away from its love.[21]

The contribution of these poets was considerable, and not only in the literary context; they were the repositories of the tribes' history and lineage and they greatly contributed to the proud collective memory of Bedouin values of succeeding generations. The well-known tenth-century writer and judge al-Tanukhi came from a very modest background. When he was berated for his humble origins, he could do no better than quote a Bedouin, who retorted 'My family line begins with me; yours ends with you'.[22] Even in modern urban society this potent image of a proud tribal heritage endures.

It would be a mistake to imagine that all women's poetry was chaste and restrained; it was not and women were surprisingly frank in sexual matters:

You don't satisfy a girl with presents and flirting, unless knees bang against knees and his locks into hers with a flushing thrust.[23]

Afira bint 'Abbad castigated the lustful third-century Tasmi ruler in a rousing poem for insisting that all new brides spent their wedding night with him. In doing so, he at a stroke traduced the honour of the husbands, made them a laughing-stock, and rendered them politically impotent; an exercising of *droit de seigneur*? Afira also voiced collective values when she incited her own menfolk to:

> Spark the fire of war and kill the tyrant or be killed, or take to the wilderness and starve, for it's better to die honourably than live in shame.[24]

In the latter part of the seventh century Dahna bint Mash'al complained to the governor that her poet husband Ajjaj had not consummated their marriage. Presumably this was in a court of law, as it would be unthinkable for a woman to discuss such an intimate matter with another man. When Ajjaj belatedly became affectionate, Dahna scoffed:

> Lay off, you can't turn me on with a cuddle, a kiss or scent. Only a thrust rocks out my strains until the ring on my toe falls in my sleeve and my blues fly away.[25]

Like Zarqa of the fabled eyesight, Fadl al-Sha'ira was born in Yamama, Bahrain, but brought up in Basra, where she became a highly regarded poet at the ninth-century court of al-Mutawakkil, with a personal retinue of twenty pages. The ungentlemanly and chauvinistic Abu Dulaf impertinently hinted in a poem that Fadl was not a virgin; he personally preferred virgins, referring to them as 'unpierced pearls'. Undaunted, Fadl composed the following riposte:

> Riding beasts are no joy to ride until they're bridled and mounted. So pearls are useless unless they're pierced and threaded.[26]

Although much was made of the wiles of women, their adultery and the like in *The Thousand and One Nights* and elsewhere, there were, in fact, many positive references to the constancy and fidelity of women in affairs of the heart. One Arabic proverb runs, 'The fruit of fidelity grows on the palm of confidence'.

The family

The family, a distinctive cohesive social unit heavily underpinned by economic and political considerations and male honour, was at the heart of Muslim life. This had wide implications for Arab women, who were set apart from the mainstream, male world on psychological, physical and social grounds. However, it has been demonstrated that they rose to the challenge time and time again and carved their own distinctive niche in society through sheer force of character. Arab women were far from the meek and submissive stereotypes portrayed by some. Al-Jahiz conceded that in matters of love, women were the superiors of men in several respects.

> It is they who are wooed, wished for, loved, and desired, and it is they for whom sacrifices are made and who are protected,[27]

and the *Book of Songs* wryly commented:

> So also the women of the Banu Tamim were the most perverse of God's creatures, yet they were the greatest favourite of their husbands.

Notes

A 'short-title' system has been used throughout the notes. For full publishing details of the works mentioned, the reader is referred to the bibliography.

Chapter 1

1. Nawal El-Saadawi, *The Hidden Face of Eve*, p. 141.
2. 'Abdullah al-'Udhari, *Classical Poems by Arab Women*, p. 78.
3. S.24:4, *Al-Nuur*.
4. Studies of the upper classes in nineteenth-century Palestine and Egypt bear this out. Judith E. Tucker, 'The Arab Family in History, "Otherness" and the Study of the Family', in Judith E. Tucker (ed.) *Arab Women, Old Boundaries, New Frontiers*, p. 199.
5. Muhammad Talbi, 'Everyday Life in the Cities of Islam', in A. Bouhdiba and M. Ma'aruf al-Dawalibi, (eds) *The Different Aspects of Islamic Culture: The Individual and Society in Islam*, p. 444, note 259.
6. *op. cit.*, p. 417.
7. S. D. Goitein, 'The Rise of the Near-Eastern Bourgeoisie in Early Islamic Times', in *Journal of World History* (superseded by '*Cultures*'), Vol. III, 3, 1957, p. 602.
8. Albert Hourani, *A History of the Arab Peoples*, p. 121.
9. Ibn Battuta, *Kitab rihlat ibn Battuta al-musamma tuhfat al-nazzar fi ghara'ib al-amsar wa 'aja'ib al-asfar*, tr. H. A. R. Gibb, *Travels in Asia and Africa*, p. 335.
10. *op. cit.*, pp. 131, 149.
11. Tucker, *op. cit.*, p. 200, note 17.
12. Halide Edib, *The Turkish Ordeal: Further Memories*, cited Ruth Roded (ed.) *Women in Islam and the Middle East*, p. 203.
13. Ghassan Ascha, *Du statut interieur de la femme en Islam*, p. 139.
14. Ibn Battuta, *op. cit.*, p. 330.
15. *op. cit.*, p. 108.
16. Al-'Udhari, *op. cit.*, p. 162.
17. Talbi, *op. cit.*, p. 431.
18. Ibn Battuta, *op. cit.*, p. 99.
19. Ibn Jubayr, *Al-Rihla*, tr. R. J. C. Broadhurst, *Travels*, Jonathan Cape, London, 1952, p. 118.
20. Raymond & Wiet, *op. cit.*, pp. 81, 2.
21. *loc. cit.*
22. *loc. cit.*

23. Talbi, *op. cit.*, p. 394.
24. Raymond & Wiet, *op. cit.*, p. 79.
25. *op. cit.*, p. 80.
26. George Makdisi, 'The Topography of eleventh-century Baghdad: Materials and Notes' (1), *Arabica*, 6, 1959, p. 190.
27. Al-Tanukhi, *Nishwar al-muhadara wa akhbar al-mudhakira*, Part II, tr. D. S. Margoliouth, 'The Table-Talk of a Mesopotamian Judge', in *Islamic Culture*, 5 July, 1931, p. 185.
28. Raymond & Wiet, *op. cit.*, p. 82.
29. Makdisi, *op. cit.*, p. 185.
30. Robert Irwin, *The Arabian Nights: A Companion*, Allen Lane, The Penguin Press, London, 1994, p. 174.
31. Talbi, *op. cit.*, p. 420.
32. Al-Ghazali, *Al-adab fi'l-Din*, tr. J. Badeau, 'They lived once thus in Baghdad', *Mediaeval and Middle Eastern Studies in honor of Aziz Suryal Atiya*, (ed.) S. A. Hanna, Brill, Leiden, 1972, p. 43.
33. Talbi, *op. cit.*, p. 420.
34. Al-Ghazali, *op. cit.*, p. 43.
35. Al-'Udhari, *op. cit.*, p. 78.
36. Makdisi, *op. cit.*, , p. 195.
37. Ira Lapidus, 'Muslim Urban Society in Mamluk Syria', in A. H Hourani and S. M. Stern, *The Islamic City*, Bruno Cassirer, Oxford and University of Pennsylvania Press, 1970, p. 196.
38. Talbi, *op. cit.*, p. 424.
39. Robert Irwin, *Night & Horses & The Desert: An Anthology of Classical Arabic Literature*, Allen Lane, The Penguin Press, London, 1999, p. 96.
40. Talbi, *op. cit.*, p. 398.
41. Tariq Wali, *Private Skies: The Courtyard Pattern in the Architecture of the House, Bahrain*, Bahrain, 1992, p. 27.
42. Shirley Guthrie, *Arab Social Life in the Middle Ages: An Illustrated Study*, Saqi Books, London, 1995, illustration 15.
43. Walther, *op. cit.*, p. 83.
44. Rachel Ward, *Islamic Metalwork*, British Museum Press, London, 1993, p. 29.
45. Talbi, *op. cit.*, p. 428.
46. Al-Tha'alibi, *Lata'if al-Ma'arif*, tr. C. E. Bosworth, *The Book of Curious and Entertaining Information*, Edinburgh University Press, 1968, p. 127.
47. Guthrie, *op. cit.*, p. 154.
48. J. Zozaya, 'Material Culture in Medieval Spain', in V. B. Mann, T. F. Glick and J. D. Dodds (eds) *Convivencia: Jews, Muslims and Christians in Medieval Spain*, George Braziller, Inc., New York, 1992, p. 167.
49. Tucker, 'The Arab Family in History ...' in *Arab Women*, p. 204. For example, a relatively modern study in Nablus, Palestine, involved twelve per cent of marriage, while among their social superiors some one quarter of all marriages were between cousins.
50. Again as demonstrated by court records from Nablus. These subsequent unions formed some fifty per cent of all marriages.
51. Talbi, *op. cit.*, p. 420.
52. *op. cit.*, p. 421, note 149.

53. R. Brunschvig, 'Propriétaire et locataire d'immeuble', *Studia Islamica*, Volume LII, 1980, p. 32.
54. Mazaheri, *La vie quotidienne*, p. 68.
55. Talbi, *op. cit.*, p. 428.
56. Al-Tha'alibi, *op. cit.*, p. 135.
57. Mazaheri, *op. cit.*, p. 274.
58. S. B. Samadi, 'Social and Economic Aspects of Life under the 'Abbasid Hegemony at Baghdad', in *Islamic Culture*, 29, 1955, p. 240.
59. Raymond & Wiet, *op. cit.*, p. 97, note 4.
60. Makdisi, *op. cit.*, p.182, citing *Manaqib Baghdad*.
61. Ibn Jubayr, *Al-Rihla*, p. 262.
62. Al-Ghazali, *op. cit.*, p. 43.
63. Talbi, *op. cit.*, p. 421.
64. Talbi, *op. cit.*, p. 402, note 76.
65. Mazaheri, *op. cit.*, p. 67.
66. Al-'Udhari, *op. cit.*, p. 46.
67. Wiebke Walther, *Women in Islam from Medieval to Modern Times*, Marcus Wiener Publishers, Princeton, N. J., Second Printing, 1995, paperback, pp. 107, 8.
68. Ibn Battuta, *op. cit.*, p. 337.
69. Talbi, *op. cit.*, p. 407.
70. Talbi, *op. cit.*, p. 385, note 13.
71. Mazaheri, *op. cit.*, p. 26.

Chapter 2
1. E. W. Lane, *Arabian Society in the Middle Ages: Studies* from *The Thousand and One Nights,* (ed) S. Lane-Poole, Curzon Press, New edition, London, 1971, p. 198, note 1.
2. Abdel Rahim Omran, *Family Planning in the Legacy of Islam*, Routledge, London, 1992, p. 101.
3. Soheir A. Morsy, 'Sex Differences and Folk Illness in an Egyptian Village', in Lois Beck and Nikki Keddie (eds), *Women in the Muslim World*, Harvard University Press, Cambridge, Mass. and London, England, 1978, p. 605.
4. Ibn Qayyim al-Jawziyya, *Tibb al-Nabi*, p. 241.
5. Manfred Ullmann, *Islamic Medicine*, Edinburgh University Press, 1978, p. 108.
6. Lane, *Manners*, p. 267.
7. Evelyn A. Early, 'Fertility and Fate: Medical Practices among *Baladi* Women of Cairo', in Donna Lee Bowen and Evelyn A. Early, (eds), *Everyday Life in the Muslim Middle East*, Indiana University Press, Bloomington and Indianapolis, 1993, paperback, p. 106.
8. The syphilis variant of venereal disease was unknown in the Middle East until the Ottoman period. It was apparently introduced from Europe via Istanbul, and known in the east as 'the Frankish disease'.
9. Ullmann, *op. cit.*, p. 19.
10. Avner Giladi, *Children of Islam: Concepts of Childhood in Medieval Muslim Islam*, Macmillan in association with St. Antony's College, Oxford, 1992, p.77.
11. Mazaheri, *La vie quotidienne*, p. 41.
12. Ettinghausen, *Arab Painting*, p.121, Manuscript *arabe* 5847, Paris, Bibliotheque Nationale, f. 122v, *Maqama* 39 and Guthrie, *Arab Social Life*, Illustration 16.

13. Guthrie, *op. cit.*, p.160, note 15.
14. Lane, *op. cit.*, p. 176.
15. Asad, *The Message of the Qur'an*, Sura 84, *al-Inshiqaq*.
16. *Sura* 18:46, *al-Kahf*.
17. Al-'Udhari, *op. cit.*, p. 94.
18. *ibid*, p. 92.
19. Walther, *Women in Islam*, p. 75.
20. Ar-Raziq, *La femme au temps des Mamlouks*, p. 63.
21. Lane-Poole, *op. cit.*, p. 186.
22. Ibn Qayyim al-Jawziyya, *op. cit.*, p. 281.
23. Waines, *In a Caliph's Kitchen*, p. 23.
24. Rodinson, *Mohammed*, p. 45.
25. M. Z. Siddiqi, *Studies in Arabian and Persian Medical Literature*, Calcutta University Press, Calcutta, p. 3.
26. University of Edinburgh Library, Manuscript 161, al-Biruni's *Athar al-baqiyya*, Dated 1306, Tabriz.
27. Giladi, *Children of Islam*, p. 77.
28. Lane-Poole, *op. cit.*, p. 256.
29. Ar-Raziq, *op. cit.*, p. 53.
30. *ibid.*, p. 83.
31. Lane, *Arabic-English Lexicon*, Volume 2, p. 2418; Avner Giladi, *Infants, Parents and Wet-Nurses: Medieval Islamic views on breast-feeding and their social implications*, Brill, Leiden, Boston, Koln, 1999, p. 45; Ullmann, *op. cit.*, p. 38.
32. Al-Tha'alibi, *Lata'if al-Ma'arif*, p. 145.
33. Youssef Courbage and Phillipe Fargues, *Christians and Jews under Islam*, tr. Judy Mabro, I. B. Tauris, London, 1998, paperback, p. 65.
34. Giladi, *Children of Islam*, p. 74.
35. *ibid.*, p. 116.
36. *ibid.*, p. 88, note 128.
37. Ullmann, *op. cit.*, p. 113.
38. Ibn Qayyim al-Jawziyya, *op. cit.*, pp. 124 and 130 respectively.
39. S.6, *Al-'Anam*: S.18, *Al-Kahf*; S.36, *Ya Sin*; S.44, *Ad-Dukhan*; S.55, *Ar-Rahman*; S.67, *Al-Mulk*; and S.78, *An-Naba'*.
40. S.2, *Al-Baqara*:256; S.12, *Yusuf*, 64, and S.37, *as-Saffat*:7, respectively.
41. Lane, *Manners*, p. 257.
42. S.11:44, *Hud*.
43. Siddiqi, *op. cit.*, p. 3.
44. Ullmann, *op. cit.*, p. 5.
45. Ibn Qayyim al-Jawziyya, *op. cit.*, p. 234.
46. Amnon Cohen and Elisheva Simon-Piqali, (eds.) *Jews in the Moslem Court: Society, Economy and Communal Organization in Sixteenth Century Jerusalem*, Jerusalem, Yad Izhak Ben-Zvi, 1993, in Ruth Roded (ed.) *Women in Islam and the Middle East: A Reader*, I. B. Tauris & Co. Ltd., London and New York, 1999, paperback, p. 137.
47. Ibn Qayyim al-Jawziyya, *op. cit.*, p. 206.
48. *ibid.*, p. 65.
49. Buonaventura, *Beauty and the East*, p. 80.
50. Lane, *Arabic-English Lexicon*, Volume 1, p. 1368.

51. Ibn Qayyim al-Jawziyya, *op. cit.*, p. 220.
52. David S. Margoliouth, 'The Renaissance of Islam: Trade', in *Islamic Culture*, Volume 7, 1933, p. 320.
53. Talbi, 'Everyday Life', p. 431, note 201.
54. *op. cit.*, p. 425.
55. *ibid.*, p. 409, note 105.
56. B.F. Musallam, *Sex and Society in Islam: Birth control before the nineteenth century*, Cambridge University Press, Cambridge, reprint 1986, p. 72, note 74.
57. Guthrie, *op. cit.*, p. 95.
58. Clifford E. Bosworth, *The Mediaeval Islamic Underworld: The Banu Sasan in Arabic Society* and Literature, Part One, Brill, Leiden, 1976, p. 126.
59. Mazaheri, *op. cit.*, p. 269; Lane reported that one remedy for styes was to take a piece of cotton bound to the end of a stick and dip it in a trough out of which dogs drink. The eye was then wiped with this, but – and this almost beggars belief – care had to be taken to preserve the hand from the polluted water if about to apply this to another person. Was this a sort of magic in reverse? It certainly demonstrated the power of ignorance and superstition, and it is likely typical of many age-old so-called remedies from any land. Lane, *op. cit.*, p. 268.
60. William Montgomery Watt, *The Influence of Islam on Medieval Europe*, Edinburgh University Press, reprint, 1984, paperback, p. 38.
61. Al-Ghazali, *Al-adab fi'l-Din*, tr. J. Badeau, p. 47.
62. Chadly Fitouri, 'Childhood and Youth' in A. Bouhdiba and M.M. al-Dawalibi *The Different Aspects of Islamic Culture: The Individual and Society in Islam*, UNESCO, Paris, 1998, p. 213.
63. Giladi, *op. cit.*, p. 78, notes 64, 65.
64. Ar-Raziq, *op. cit.*, p. 53.
65. Lane-Poole, *op. cit.*, p. 201.
66. Gerhard Weiss. 'The Pilgrim as Tourist: Travels to the Holy Land as reflected in the Published Accounts of German Pilgrims between 1450 and 1550', in Marilyn J. Chiat and Kathryn L. Reyerson (eds.), *The Medieval Mediterranean: Cross-Cultural Contacts*, Medieval Studies at University of Minnesota, 1988, p. 126 note 26 and Fig. 14.)
67. Lane, *Manners*, p. 70.
68. Hamilton, *Walid.*, p. 11.
69. Talbi, *op. cit.*, p. 454, note 298; Lane, *Arabic-English Lexicon*, Volume 1, p. 1917, s.v. *damiya*.
70. Talbi, *op. cit.*, p. 456.
71. Fitouri, *op. cit.*, p. 210, note 26.
72. Talbi, *op. cit.*, p. 455, note 306.
73. Talbi, *op. cit.*, p. 451, note 285.
74. Lane, *Arabic-English Lexicon*, Volume 2, p. 2604, s.v. *kurraj*.
75. *op. cit.*, p. 455, note 306.
76. *loc. cit.*, p. 456, note 311.
77. *ibid.*
78. Ibn Hazm, *Tawq al-hamama*, tr. Anthony Arberry, *The Ring of the Dove: Ibn Hazm (994-1069)*, Luzac Oriental, London, 1994, paperback, p. 15.
79. Huda Shaarawi, cited Tove Stang Dahl, *The Muslim Family: a Study of Women's Rights in Islam*, Scandinavian Universities Press, Oslo, Stockholm, Copenhagen,

Oxford, Boston, 1997, p. 105.

Chapter 3
1. Qur'an, S.16, *Al-Nahl*, v.72.
2. Sura 2, *Al-Baqara*, v. 233; Sura 31, *Luqman*, v.14.
3. Lane, *Lexicon*, Volume 2, p. 2319, s.v. *ghayala*.
4. Abdel Rahim Omran, *Family Planning in the Legacy of Islam*, Routledge, London, 1992, p. 172.
5. *loc. cit.*
6. Walther, *Woman in Islam*, p. 61.
7. Omran, *ibid.*, p. 117.
8. *ibid.*, p. 125.
9. B. F. Musallam, *Sex and Society in Islam: Birth control before the nineteenth century*, Cambridge University Press, Cambridge, reprint, 1986, p. 118.
10. Madelain Farah, 'Marriage and Sexuality in Islam: A Translation of al-Ghazali's Book on the Etiquette of Marriage from the *Ihya*', Salt Lake City, The University of Utah, 1984, pp. 106-13, in Ruth Roded (ed.), *Woman and Islam and the Middle East: A Reader*, I. B. Tauris, London & New York, 1999, p. 165.
11. Musallam, *op. cit.*, p. 69.
12. Guthrie, *Arab Social Life*, p. 160.
13. Musallam, *op. cit.*, . 67.
14. *ibid.*, pp. 68, 69.
15. *ibid.*, Table 9, p. 88, from Al-Razi, *Kitab al-Hawi* and *Kitab al-tibb al-Mansuri*, 'Ali Ibn 'Abbas, *Kamil al-sina'a*, and Abu 'Ali Ibn Sina, *Qanun*.
16. *ibid.*, Tables 1-9, pp. 77-78.
17. Mercedes Sayagues, 'Zimbabwe's last sexual taboo', in *Orbit: Views from the developing world*, Voluntary Service Overseas, London, 2000.
18. Musallam, *op. cit.*, pp. 68, 69.
19. *ibid.*, Table 13, p. 103.
20. This practice is confirmed by a graphic painting of a midwife's assistant standing by with a brazier in the famous manuscript of al-Hariri's *Maqamat* illustrated by al-Wasiti, in Guthrie, *op. cit.*, Illustration 16; Richard Ettinghausen, *Arab Painting*, Rizzoli International Publications, Inc., New York, 1977, paperback, p. 121.
21. Musallam, *op. cit.*, Table 9, p. 88, from al-Razi, *Kitab al-Hawi* and *Kitab al-tibb al-Mansuri*, 'Ali ibn 'Abbas, *Kamil al-sina'a*, and Abu 'Ali Sina, *Qanun*.
22. *ibid.*, p. 72.
23. *ibid.*, p. 96.
24. *ibid.*, Table 15, Sha'rani, *Mukhtasar tadkhirat al-Suwaydi*, p. 104.
25. *ibid.*, pp. 94, 103.
26. *ibid.*, pp. 90-1.
27. *ibid.*, p. 94.
28. *loc. cit.*
29. *ibid.*, note 37.
30. *ibid.*, p. 154, note 9.
31. *ibid.*, Table 13, p. 103.
32. Fitouri, 'Childhood and Youth', p. 165.
33. Farah, *op. cit.*, p. 165.
34. Musallam, *op. cit.*, p. 70, note 56.

35. *ibid.*, p. 69.

36. *ibid.*, Table 6, p. 86.

37. *ibid.*, p.155, note 9.

38. Buonoventura, *Beauty and the East*, p. 95.

39. Musallam, *op. cit.*, p. 70, note 57.

40. *ibid.*, p. 94, note 36.

41. Waines, *In a Caliph's Kitchen*, p. 23.

Chapter 4

1. Irwin, *Night and Horses*, p. 208.

2. David Waines, *In a Caliph's Kitchen: Mediaeval Arabic Cooking for the Modern Gourmet*, Riad el-Rayyes, 56, Knightsbridge, London, 1989, p. 15.

3. *ibid.*, p. 32.

4. Guthrie, *Arab Social Life*, p. 118, note 34.

5. *loc. cit.*

6. Waines, *op. cit.*, p. 13.

7. Walther, *Women in Islam*, pp. 151-52.

8. Al-Baghdadi, *Kitab al-Tabikh*, tr. A. J. Arberry, 'A Baghdad Cookery Book', *Islamic Culture*, Volume 13, January 1939, p. 27.

9. Ashtor, *Histoire des prix*, p. 113.

10. George Makdisi, 'An Eleventh-century Historian of Baghdad', 3, *Bulletin of the School of Oriental and African Studies*, Vol. 19, p. 42.

11. Al-Tanukhi, *Nishwar al-muhadara wa akhbar al-mudhakira*, fragmented manuscripts, tr. David S. Margoliouth, 'The Table-Talk of a Mesopotamian Judge', Royal Asiatic Society, London, 1922, p. 66.

12. Lane, *Lexicon*, Vol. 1, p. 1389 s.v. *sakbaja*, citing the *Lughat* of Niamat Allah Khalil Sufi.

13. Thomas Preston, *Makamat or Rhetorical Anecdotes of al-Hariri of Basra*, Cambridge University Press, 1850, p. 41, *Maqama* 48 of the *Bani Haram*.

14. Bernard Lewis, *The Middle East: 2000 years of History from the Rise of Christianity to the Present Day*, Weidenfeld & Nicholson, London, 1996, paperback, p. 158.

15. Al-Baghdadi, *op. cit.*, p. 28.

16. Lane, *Arabic-English Lexicon*, Vol. II, p. 2435, s.v. *falla*.

17. Al-Baghdadi, *op. cit.*, p. 195.

18. Raymond & Wiet, *Les marchés du Caire*, p. 147.

19. Al-Baghdadi, *op. cit.*, p. 195.

20. Waines, *op. cit.*, p. 22.

21. Ibn Qayyim al-Jawziyya, *Tibb al-Nabi*, tr. Penelope Johnstone, *Medicine of the Prophet*, The Islamic Texts Society, Cambridge, paperback 1998, p. 227.

22. *loc. cit.*

23. *ibid.*, pp. 206-207.

24. *ibid.*, pp. 272 and 167, respectively.

25. *ibid.*, pp. 213, 220.

26. Raymond & Wiet, *Les marchés du Caire*, p. 153, note 2.

27. Ibn Qayyim al-Jawziyya, *op. cit.*, pp. 199 and 240, respectively.

28. Al-Miskawayh, *Tajarib al-Umam*, tr. David S. Margoliouth, *The Experiences of the Nations*, London, 1921, p. 77.

29. Talbi, 'Everyday Life', p. 411.

30. E. W. Lane, *An Arabic-English Lexicon*, Islamic Texts Society, Cambridge, reprint 1984, Volume II, p. 2389.
31. *op. cit.*, Vol. II, p. 2514.
32. Ibn Qayyim al-Jawziyya, *op. cit.*, p. 227.
33. The latter is interesting, since in Arabic a honeymoon is 'a month of honey, a month of onions' (*shahr 'asal, shahr basal*), in other words, a return to normal, everyday things, or as the Scots say, 'back to old clothes and porridge'.
34. Margaret Smith, *Rabi'a the Mystic and her Fellow-saints in Islam*, Cambridge University Press, 1984, p. 24.
35. Preston, *op. cit.*, p. 441, note 9.
36. Al-Baghdadi, *op. cit.*, p. 24.
37. Al-'Udhari, *Classical Poems*, p. 78.
38. Lane, *Manners*, p. 539.
39. Ibn Qayyim al-Jawziyya, *op. cit.*, p. 256.
40. *loc. cit.*
41. Gerhard Weiss. 'The Pilgrim as Tourist: Travels to the Holy Land as reflected in the Published Accounts of German Pilgrims between 1450 and 1550', in Marilyn J. Chiat and Kathryn L. Reyerson (eds.), *The Medieval Mediterranean: Cross-Cultural Contacts*, Medieval Studies at University of Minnesota, 1988, p. 129, note 33.
42. Lane, *Manners*, p. 320.
43. George Makdisi, 'The Topography of Eleventh-century Bagdad: Materials and Notes (I), in *Arabica*, 6, 1959, p.194, note 3.
44. Weiss, *op.cit.*, p. 129 note 35.
45. David S. Margoliouth, 'The Renaissance of Islam: Trade', in *Islamic Culture*, Volume 7, 1933, p. 319.
46. David S. Margoliouth, 'Wit and Humour in Arabic Authors', in *Islamic culture*, Vol. I, 1927, p. 528.
47. Al-Baghdadi, *op. cit.*, p. 28.
48. Talbi, *op. cit.*, p. 421, note 154.
49. *ibid.*, p. 430.
50. *ibid.*, p. 428.
51. *ibid.*, p. 450, note 282.
52. R. Hamilton, 'Walid and his Friends: an Umayyad Tragedy', *Oxford Studies in Islamic Art*, Volume VI, 1988, p. 90.
53. Al-Baghdadi, *op. cit.*, p. 199.
54. Al-Tha'alibi, *op. cit.*, p. 141.
55. *ibid.*, p. 134.
56. Ibn Battuta, *Travels*, p. 95.
57. Inea Bushnaq, (tr.) *Arab Folktales*, Penguin Folklore Library, 1986, paperback, p. 254.
58. Manuela Marin, 'Beyond Taste: the complements of colour and smell in the medieval Arab culinary tradition', in Sami Zubaida and Richard Tapper (eds), *Culinary Cultures of the Middle East*, I. B. Tauris & Co. Ltd, London, reprint, paperback, 1996, p. 206.
59. Yedida K. Stillman, 'Costume as Cultural Statement: The Esthetics, Economics, and Politics of Islamic Dress', in D. Frank, (ed.) *The Jews of Medieval Islam: Community, Society and Identity*, International Conference Proceedings, Institute

of Jewish Studies, University College, London, 1992, p. 133.

60. Marin, *op. cit.*, p. 212.

61. Mazaheri, *La vie quotidienne*, p. 211.

62. Ashtor, *Histoire des prix*, p. 107.

63. Lane, *Arabic-English Lexicon*, Volume 2, p. 2732, s.v. *malaha*.

64. Talbi, *op. cit.*, p. 431, note 204.

65. Ibn Qayyim al-Jawziyya, *op. cit.*, p. 163.

66. *ibid.*, p. 164.

67. *ibid.*, pp. 165 and 199, respectively.

68. *ibid.*, p. 162.

69. Al-Ghazali, *Nasihat al-muluk*, translated by F. R. C. Bagley, *Counsel for Kings*, Oxford University Press, London, 1964, p. 58.

70. Lane, *Manners*, p. 109.

71. Guthrie, *op. cit.*, Illustrations 19 and 20.

72. Al-Isfahani, tr. H. Masse, *Conquête de la Syrie et de la Palestine par Saladin*, Librairie Orientaliste Paul Geuthner, Paris, 1972, p. 117.

73. Ibn Khallikan, *Wafayat al-a'yan wa anba' abna' al-zaman*, tr. M. de Slane, (ed.) S. Moinul Haq, Pakistan Historical Society, Karachi, 1961, p. 293.

74. Irwin, *op. cit.*, p. 95.

75. Al-Tanukhi, fragmented manuscripts, tr. David S. Margoliouth, *The Table Talk of a Mesopotamian Judge*, Royal Asiatic Society, London, 1922, p. 24, note 1.

76. Al-Tha'alibi, *Lata'if al-ma'arif*, p. 135.

77. Ibn Qayyim al-Jawziyya, *op. cit.*, p. 199.

78. Maxime Rodinson, *Mohammed*, (translated from the French, Anne Carter) Penguin Books, Harmondsworth, Middlesex, reprint, paperback, 1993, p. 288.

79. Preston, *op. cit.*, p. 247.

80. Al-Tha'alibi, *op. cit.*, p. 127.

81. Ibn Qayyim al-Jawziyya, *op. cit.*, p. 92.

82. Bushnaq, *op. cit.*, p. 44.

83. Ibn Qayyim al-Jawziyya, *op. cit.*, p. 282.

84. Talbi, *op. cit.*, p. 453, note 292.

85. Lane, *Arabic-English Lexicon*, Vol. II, p. 2383, s.v. *faraqa*.

86. Lane, *Manners*, p. 578, note 33.

87. Guthrie, *op. cit.*, Illustration 2; Richard Ettinghausen, *Arab Painting*, Rizzoli International Publications, Inc., New York, 1977, paperback, Plate, p. 118.

88. Mai Yamani, 'You are what you cook: cuisine and class in Mecca', in Sami Zubaida and Richard Tapper (eds), *Culinary Cultures of the Middle East*, I. B. Tauris & Co. Ltd., London, reprint, paperback, 1966, p. 178.

Chapter 5

1. Edward W. Lane, *Arabic-English Lexicon*, Volume II, p. 2194, s.v. *'awira*.

2. Ghassan Ascha, *Du statut interieur de la femme en Islam*, Editions Harmattan, Paris, paperback, 1987, pp. 136-7, reference 47, citing al-Albani, *Hijab al-mara' al-muslima*.

3. Y. K. Stillman, 'Costume as Cultural Statement: The Esthetics, Economics, and Politics of Islamic Dress', *The Jews of Medieval Islam: Community, Society and Identity'*, International Conference Proceedings, Institute of Jewish Studies, University College, London, 1992, p. 135.

4. Tove Stang Dahl, *The Muslim Family: a Study of Women's Rights in Islam*, Scandinavian University Press, Oslo, Stockholm, Copenhagen, Oxford, Boston, 1997, p. 105.

5. Lane, *op. cit.*, Volume II, p. 2648, s.v. *libas*.

6. *ibid.*, Vol. II, p. 2564, s.v. *qamasa*.

7. Muhammad M. Ahsan, *Social Life under the 'Abbasids, 170/289 A.H. – 786-902 A.D.*, Longman, London and New York, 1979, p. 64.

8. Hamda was evidently well regarded as a poet, since she was known as the 'Khansa of Andalus'. This was no mean tribute. Khansa, who died in 646, was the darling of classical Arabic critics and her reputation had already survived in al-Andalus for some six centuries. Al-'Udhari, *op. cit.*, p. 236.

9. Ibn Qayyim al-Jawziyya, *Tibb al-nabawi*, p. 58.

10. Patricia L. Baker, *Islamic Textiles*, British Museum Press, London, 1995, p. 16.

11. Margaret Smith, *Rab'ia the Mystic and her Fellow-saints in Islam*, Cambridge University Press, reissued 1984, paperback, p. 85.

12. Guthrie, *Arab Social Life*, Plate 8.

13. Stillman, *op. cit.*, p. 131.

14. Guthrie, *op. cit.*, Plate 2 and Illustration 3, *Maqamat* manuscripts Paris, Bibliothèque Nationale, *arabe* 5847 and *arabe* 3929 respectively.

15. *ibid.*, Plate 17.

16. R. Hamilton, 'Walid and his Friends: an Umayyad Tragedy', *Oxford Studies in Islamic Art*, VI, 1988, p. 112.

17. Al-'Udhari, *Classical Poems*, p.152.

18. Guthrie, *op. cit.*, p. 133.

19. R. B. Serjeant, *Materials for a History of Islamic Textiles up to the Mongol Conquest*, in *Ars Islamica*, Volumes XV/XVI, reprint, Beirut, 1972.

20. Ibn Qayyim al-Jawziyya, *Tibb al-nabawi*, p. 57.

21. Lucie Bolens, 'The Use of Plants for Dyeing and Clothing', in S. K. Jayyusi (ed.), *The Legacy of Muslim Spain*, Brill, Leiden, 1992, p. 1007.

22. Ibn Qayyim al-Jawziyya, *op. cit.*, p. 57.

23. P. K. Hitti, *History of the Arabs*, Macmillan, Reprint, 1982, paperback, p. 514.

24. S. D. Goitein, 'The rise of the Near-Eastern bourgeoisie in early Islamic times', *Journal of World History*, Vol. III, 3, 1957, p. 589.

25. Ibn Battuta, *Rihla*, p.151.

26. Serjeant, *op. cit.*, pp. 80 ff.

27. Ernst Kuhnel, 'Abbasid Silks of the ninth century', in *Ars Orientalis*, Volume II, 1957, p. 369.

28. Ahsan, *op. cit.*, p. 63.

29. Reuben Levy, 'Notes on Costume from Arabic Sources', *Journal of the Royal Asiatic Society*, 1935, p. 327.

30. Lane, *op. cit.*, Volume I, p. 1355.

31. Al-'Udhari, *op. cit.*, p. 78.

32. Bolens, *op. cit.*, p. 1009.

33. Serjeant, *op. cit.*, pp. 78 ff.

34. S. B. Samadi, 'Some Aspects of the Arab-Iranian Culture from the Earliest Times up to the Fall of Baghdad', *Islamic Culture*, 26, October, 1952, p. 42.

35. Richard Ettinghausen, *Arab Painting*, Rizzoli International Publications Inc., New York, 1977, paperback, p. 111, *Maqamat* manuscript S.23, Oriental Institute,

Academy of Sciences, St. Petersburg.

36. Muhammad Talbi, 'Everyday Life in the Cities of Islam' in A. Bouhdiba and M.M. al-Dawalibi, (eds) *The Different Aspects of Islamic Culture: The Individual and Society in Islam*, UNESCO, Paris, 1998, p. 435.

37. Guthrie, *ibid.*, Plate 5, and p. 178.

38. Talbi, *op. cit.*, p. 390, note 41.

39. Mazaheri, *La vie quotidienne*, p. 73.

40. Guthrie, *op. cit.*, Illustration 17.

41. Ibn Battuta, *op. cit.*, p. 124.

42. Y. K. Stillman, *Encyclopaedia of Islam*, Volume V, Brill, Leiden, 1986, p. 734, s.v. *libas*.

43. Guthrie, *op. cit.*, Plate 17.

44. Hitti, *op. cit.*, p. 334.

45. L. A. Mayer, 'Costumes of Mamluk Women', *Islamic Culture*, Vol. 17, January, 1943, p. 302.

46. Guthrie, *op. cit.*, Plate 18, Paris, B.N. *arabe* 3929.

47. Guthrie, *ibid.*, p.174, note 46.

48. Walther, *Women in Islam*, p. 190.

49. Ashtor, *Histoire des prix et des salaires*, p. 252.

50. Walther, *op. cit.*, p. 191.

51. Guthrie, *op. cit.*, Illustration 17.

52. Preston, *Makamat or Rhetorical Anecdotes of al-Hariri of Basra*, pp.134-5, *Maqama* 18.

53. Lane, *op. cit.*, Volume II, p. 3034, s.v. *nataqa*.

54. Walther, *op. cit.*, p. 194.

55. Hilal al-Sabi, *Rusum dar al-khilafa'*, tr. E. A Salem, *The Rules and Regulations of the 'Abbasid Court*, Beirut, 1977, pp. 75 and 152-3, respectively.

56. Preston, *op. cit.*, p. 402. The 'radiant moon' was her face, the 'pearls' her teeth and the 'ring' her mouth.

57. Lane, *op. cit.*, Volume II, pp. 3053-4, s.v. *wasama*.

58. Guthrie, *op. cit.*, p. 260.

59. Stillman, *op. cit.*, Volume V, Brill, Leiden, 1986, p.733, s.v. *libas*.

60. Bolens, *op. cit.*, p. 1003.

61. Ibn Battuta, *op. cit.*, p. 79.

62. Guthrie, *op. cit.*, Illustration 15.

63. Al-'Udhari, *op. cit.*, p.184.

64. Al-Tha'alibi, *Lata'if al-Ma'arif*, p. 129.

65. Bolens, *op. cit.*, p. 1008.

66. Mazaheri, *op. cit.*, p. 252.

67. Serjeant, *op. cit.*, p. 77.

68. Ashtor, *op. cit.*, pp. 153, 165.

69. *ibid.*, p. 153.

70. *ibid.*, p. 54.

71. Mazaheri, *op. cit.*, p. 199.

Chapter 6

72. Ashtor, *Histoire des prix*, p. 53.

73. Mazaheri, *op. cit.*, p. 199.

74. Ibn Battuta, *op. cit.*, p. 165.
75. Talbi, *Everyday Life*, 433, note, p. 219.
76. Baker, *Islamic Textiles*, p. 40.
77. Mazaheri, *op. cit.*, p. 198.
78. Ibn Battuta, *op. cit.*, p. 335.
1. Al-'Udhari, *Classical Poems*, p. 146.
2. *ibid*, p. 144.
3. R. Hamilton, 'Walid and his Friends: an Umayyad Tragedy', *Oxford Studies in Islamic Art*, VI, 1988, p. 123.
4. E. W. Lane, *Arabian Society in the Middle Ages*, (ed) S. Lane-Poole, New edition, Curzon Press, London, 1971, p. 214.
5. Norah M. Titley, *Plants and Gardens in Persian, Mughal and Turkish Art*, The British Library, London, 1979, paperback, p. 5.
6. Ibn Khallikan, *Wafayat al-a'yan wa anba' abna' al-zaman (Biographical Dictionary)*, tr. M. de Slane, (ed) S. Moinul Haq, Pakistan Historical Society, Karachi, 1961, p. 224.
7. W. Buonaventura, *Beauty and the East: A Book of Oriental Body Care*, Saqi Books, London, 1998, paperback, p. 35.
8. *ibid.*, p. 115.
9. *ibid.*, p. 42.
10. Malise Ruthven, *Islam in the World*, Penguin Books, London, 1984, paperback, p. 54, note 1.
11. Ibn Qayyim al-Jawziyya, *Tibb al-Nabawi*, p. 281.
12. Al-'Udhari, *op. cit.*, p. 180.
13. R. A. Nicholson, *A Literary History of the Arabs*, Cambridge University Press, Cambridge, 1930, p. 310.
14. Ibn Qayyim al-Jawzia, *op. cit.*, p. 205.
15. Chenery, *The Assemblies of al-Hariri* (translated from the Arabic), Williams and Norgate, London and Edinburgh, 1867, p. 296, citing Arabic proverb I, 192.
16. Al-'Udhari, *op. cit.*, p. 28.
17. Buonaventura, *op. cit.*, p. 95.
18. Hamilton, *op. cit.*, p. 168.
19. Ghazi al-Gosaibi, *Wa'l-lawn min al-awarid, (Dusting the Colour from Roses: A Bilingual Collection of Arabic Poetry)*, Echoes, London, 1995, paperback, p. 65.
20. Al-'Udhari, *op. cit.*, p. 112.
21. Clifford E. Bosworth, *The Mediaeval Islamic Underworld: The Banu Sasan in Arabic Society and Literature*, Part One, Brill, Leiden, 1976, p. 126.
22. Ibn Sirin, *The Interpretation of Dreams*, Dar al-Taqwa, London, 1996, paperback, p. 48.
23. Walther, *Woman in Islam*, p. 176.
24. Hamilton, *op. cit.*, p. 168.
25. Ibn Qayyim al-Jawziyya, *Tibb al-Nabi*, p. 207.
26. Preston, *Makamat*, p. 248.
27. Fatima Mernissi, *Beyond the Veil: Male-Female Dynamics in Muslim Society*, Saqi Books, London, 1985, paperback edition, p.190, note 9.
28. Bolens, 'The use of Plants for Dyeing', p. 1002.
29. Lane, *Manners*, p. 568.
30. Buonaventura, *op. cit.*, p. 6.

31. Ibn Qayyim al-Jawziyya, *op. cit.*, p. 65.
32. *ibid*, p. 260.
33. Hamilton, *op. cit.*, p. 78.
34. Ibn Qayyim al-Jawziyya, *op. cit.*, p. 259.
35. Al-Tanukhi, fragmented manuscripts, tr. D. S. Margoliouth, *The Table Talk of a Mesopotamian Judge*, Royal Asiatic Society, London, 1922, p. 184.
36. Walther, *op. cit.*, p. 207.
37. Aida S. Kanafani, 'Rites of Hospitality and Aesthetics', in Donna Lee Bowen and Evelyn A. Early, (eds), *Everyday Life in the Muslim Middle East*, Indiana University Press, Bloomington and Indianapolis, 1993, paperback, p. 128.
38. Lane, *Lexicon*, Volume II, pp. 2288-9.
39. Margoliouth, *Table Talk*, p. 192.
40. Guthrie, *Arab Social Life*, p. 174, citing Ibn 'Abd Rabbih's *The Unique Necklace*.
41. Erika Friedl, 'Traditional Songs from Boir Ahmad', in Bowen & Early (eds), *Everyday Life*, p. 19.
42. Irwin, *Night and Horses*, p. 246.
43. Ibn Sirin, *op. cit.*, p. 68.
44. Al-Tha'alibi, *Lata'if* , p. 132.
45. Walther, *op. cit.*, p. 199.
46. Walther, *op. cit.*, p. 200, note 18:53.
47. Raymond & Wiet, *Les marchés du Caire*, p. 80.
48. Lane, *Manners*, p. 571.
49. Ibn Hazm, *Tawq al-hamama*, p. 122.
50. Lane, *Lexicon*, Volume II, p. 2517, s.v. *qarrat*.
51. Lane, *op. cit.*, Volume I, p. 1464, s.v. *sawara*.
52. Ashtor, *Histoire des prix et des salaires*, p. 220.
53. Walther, *op. cit.*, p. 194.
54. Lane, *Lexicon*, Volume I, p. 779, s.v. *khalla*.
55. Isaiah 3:16.
56. Preston, *Makamat*, p. 402.
57. Ibn al-Jawziyya, *op. cit.*, p. 65.
58. Ar-Raziq, *La femme*, p. 76.
59. Lane, *Manners*, p. 56.
60. Ahsan, *Social Life*, p. 279, citing al-Muqaddasi.
61. Mazaheri, *La vie quotidienne* , pp. 205, 6.
62. Franz Rosenthal, *Four Essays on Art and Literature in Islam*, Brill, Leiden, 1971, p. 97.
63. *ibid*, p. 68.
64. *loc. cit.*
65. *ibid*, p. 69.
66. Ibn Battuta, *Rihla*, p. 128.
67. Rosenthal, *Four Essays*, p. 95.
68. Irwin, *Night and Horses*, p. 184.
69. Rosenthal, *Four Essays* , p. 72, note 3.
70. Bernard Lewis, 'Islam from the Prophet Muhammad to the Capture of Constantinople, II', in *Religion and Society*, Volume I, London, 1974, p. 127.
71. *ibid.*, pp. 94, 5.
72. Rosenthal, *op. cit.*, p. 95, citing al-'Ayni.

73. Irwin, *op. cit.*, p. 253.
74. Lane, *Lexicon*, Volume II, p. 3030.
75. Rosenthal, *Four Essays*, p. 89, note 8.
76. Buonaventura, *op. cit.*, p. 29.
77. Ibn Battuta, p. 335.
78. Al-'Udhari, *op. cit.*, p. 144.

Chapter 7
1. Walther, *Women in Islam*, p. 123.
2. *ibid.*, p. 124.
3. Al-Mawardi, *al-Ahkam al-sultaniyya*, p. 61, cited Roded, *Women in Islam and the Middle East: a reader*, p. 113.
4. *loc. cit.*, cited Roded, *op. cit.*, p. 113.
5. Nizam al-Mulk, *The Book of Government or Rules for Kings: The Siyasat-nama or Siyar al-Muluk*, trans. Hubert Dark, Routledge & Kegan Paul, London, 1960, cited Roded, *op. cit.*, p. 121.
6. Al-Mawardi, *al-Ahkam*, pp. 61, 2, cited Roded, *op. cit.*, p. 113.
7. Sura 4, *Al-Nisa'*:34.
8. Nizam al-Mulk, *The Book of Government*, cited Roded, *op. cit.*, p. 126.
9. *The History of al-Tabari*, Volume XXX, *The 'Abbasid Caliphate in Equilibrium*, trans. C. E. Bosworth, Albany: State University of New York Press, 1989), cited Roded, *op. cit.*, p. 85.
10. Hitti, *History of the Arabs*, p. 467.
11. Al-Tabari, *History*, cited Roded, *op. cit.*, p. 88.
12. Hitti, *op. cit.*, pp. 531, 2.
13. Walther, *op. cit.*, p. 121.
14. Al-Suyuti, *Husn*, Vol. ii, p. 39, cited Hitti, *op. cit.*, p. 671.
15. Walther, *op. cit.*, p. 122.
16. Al-'Udhari, *Classical Poems*, p. 80.
17. Margoliouth, 'Wit and Humour', p. 527.
18. Hitti, *op. cit.*, p. 560, note 5.
19. Walther, *op. cit.*, p. 146.
20. *ibid.*, p. 145.
21. *ibid.*, pp.146-147.
22. Hitti, *op. cit.*, p. 274.
23. Walter, *op. cit.*, p. 118.
24. Hamilton, 'Walid and his Friends', p. 44.
25. Hitti, *op. cit.*, p. 275.
26. Ar-Raziq, *La femme au temps des Mamlouks*, p. 69.
27. Al-Mas'udi, *Muruj al-dhahab wa ma'adin al-jawhar*, Vol. viii, p. 299, cited Hitti, *op. cit.*, p. 342.
28. Lane, *Arabian Society*, pp. 211, 2.
29. Guthrie, *Arab Social Life*, p. 128.
30. *ibid.*, p. 129.
31. Hamilton, *op. cit.*, p. 64.
32. Ar-Raziq, *op. cit.*, , p. 68, citing al-Maqrizi.
33. *ibid.*, pp. 66, 67.
34. *loc. cit.*, citing al-Qalqashandi.

35. *ibid.*, p. 57, citing Ibn Taghribirdi.
36. *ibid.*, p. 61.
37. *loc. cit.*
38. Walther, *op. cit.*, p. 111.
39. Marmaduke Pickthall, *The Meaning of the Glorious Koran*, Dorset Press, n.d., cited Roded, *op. cit.*, p. 28.
40. Guthrie, *op. cit.*, p. 166.
41. Al-Bukhari, *The Translation of the Meanings of Sahih al-Bukhari*: Arabic-English, trans. Muhammad Muhsin Khan, al-Medina al-Munawwara: Islamic University, 1973-76, 2nd revised edition, cited Roded *op. cit.*, p. 49.
42. Muhammad ibn 'Abd al-Rahman al-Sakhawi, *Al-daw' al-lami' li ahl al-qarn al-tasi'*, cited Roded, *op. cit.*, p. 134, note 6.
43. Francis Robinson, (ed) The *Cambridge Illustrated History of the Islamic World*, Cambridge University Press, 1996, p. 190.
44. *ibid.*, p. 191.
45. *loc. cit.*
46. *ibid.*, p. 110.
47. Hitti, *op. cit.*, p. 302.
48. St. H. Stephan, trans. 'An Endowment Deed of Khasseki Sultan, Dated the 24th May 1552', in *The Quarterly of the Department of Antiquities in Palestine*, 10, 1944, cited Roded, *op. cit.*, pp. 141, 2.
49. Salah al-Din al-Munajjid, 'Women's Roles in the Art of Arabic Calligraphy', in George N. Atiyeh, (ed) *The Book in the Islamic World: the Written Word and Communication in the Middle East*, State University of New York Press, 1995, paperback, p. 142.
50. Walther, *op. cit.*, p. 78.
51. Atiyeh, *op. cit.*, p. 146.
52. *loc. cit.*
53. *ibid.*, 144.
54. *loc. cit.*
55. Walther, *op. cit.*, p. 94.
56. *Sura 4:32, Al-Nisa'* and Sura 3:195, *Al-'Imran*.
57. J. Sadan, 'Kings and Craftsmen: a Pattern of Contrasts on the history of a medieval Arabic Humoristic Form', Part II, in *Studia Islamica*, LXII, 1985, p. 111.
58. Ar-Raziq, *op. cit.*, p. 48.
59. S. D. Goitein, *Letters of Medieval Jewish* Traders, Princeton University Press, 1973, p.122.
60. *ibid*, p. 262.
61. Guthrie, *op. cit.*, p. 130.
62. Al-Tha'alibi, *Lata'if*, pp. 140-141.
63. Amnon Cohen and Elisheva Simon-Piqali, 'Jews in the Moslem Court', cited Roded, *op. cit.*, p.139.
64. *op. cit.*, pp. 136-7.
65. Guthrie, *op. cit.*, Illustration 17, Paris, Bibliotheque Nationale ms. *arabe* 5847, f.25r, *Maqama 9*, Abu Zayd's wife in court in Alexandria.
66. Ar-Raziq, *op. cit.*, , p. 59.
67. Walther, *op. cit.*, p. 81.
68. *ibid*, p. 115.

69. Guthrie, *op. cit.*, p. 110.
70. Ar-Raziq, *op. cit.*, p. 44.
71. *loc. cit.*
72. Ar-Raziq, *op. cit.*, p. 82.
73. C. E. Bosworth, *The Mediaeval Islamic Underworld: The Banu Sasan in Arabic Society and Literature*, Part One, Brill, Leiden, 1976, p. 209.
74. Guthrie, *op. cit.*, Illustration 1, Bib. Nat. ms. arabe 5847, f.18v, *Maqama 7*.
75. Cohen and Simon-Piqali, in Roded, *op. cit.*, p. 138.

Chapter 8
1. Barbara F. Stowasser, 'Women's Issues in Modern Islamic Thought', in Judith E. Tucker, (ed.), *Arab Women: Old Boundaries, New Frontiers*, Indiana University Press, Bloomington and Indianapolis, 1993, paperback, p. 15 note 58.
2. *Leviticus* 12:2,4,5.
3. Mazaheri, *La vie quotidienne*, p. 42.
4. E. S. Drower, 'Woman and Taboo in Iraq', *Iraq*, 1938, Volumes 5-6, p. 106.
5. Lane, *Manners*, p. 388.
6. Ar-Raziq, *La femme au temps des Mamlouks*, p. 81.
7. Drower, *op. cit.*, p.105.
8. Lane, *Arabic-English Lexicon*, Vol. II, p. 2864.
9. Talbi, 'Everyday Life', p. 458, note 320.
10. Al-'Udhari, *Classical Poems*, p. 48.
11. *ibid.*, p. 120.
12. Ar-Raziq, *op. cit.*, p. 86 citing Ibn Taghribirdi and al-Yununi.
13. *ibid.*, p. 86.
14. Guthrie, *Arab Social Life*, p. 133.
15. Ibn Munqidh, (Usama ibn Murshid) (Mu'ayid al-Dawla called Ibn Munqidh), *Kitab al-I'tibar*, tr. P. K. Hitti, *An Arab-Syrian Gentleman and Warrior in the Period of the Crusades: Memoirs of Usamah ibn Munqidh*, I. B. Tauris, London, 1987, p. 145.
16. Ashtor, *Histoire des prix*, p. 233.
17. Al-'Udhari, *op. cit.*, p. 212.
18. *ibid.*, p. 122.
19. Smith, *Rabi'a the Mystic*, p. 124.
20. *ibid.*, p. 24.
21. Ruthven, *Islam in the World*, p. 166, note 17.
22. Malik ibn Anan, al-Muwatta, tr. Aisha Abdurrahman Bewley, *An Early Legal Compendium: Purity, Legal Competence and Property Ownership*, Kegan Paul International, London, 1989, cited Roded, *Women in Islam*, p. 99.
23. Lane, *Manners*, p. 94.
24. Guthrie, *op. cit.*, Plate 5; Walther, *Women in Islam*, Ill. 12.
25. *Leviticus* 12:4.
26. Sura 2 (*Al-Baqara*):222.
27. Bewley, *op. cit.*, p. 100.
28. *ibid.*, p. 98.
29. *loc. cit.*
30. Walther, *Women in Islam*, p. 53.
31. *ibid.*, p. 174, citing al-Tabari.

32. Lane, *Arabic-English Lexicon*, Volume I, p. 1319, citing the 13th-century '*Ubab* of al-Saghani and the 14th-century *Qamus*.
33. Irwin, *The Arabian Nights*, p. 171.
34. Bouhdiba, *Sexuality in Islam*, p. 189.
35. El Saadawi, *The Hidden Face of Eve*, p. 136.
36. Musallam, *Sex and Society*, p. 154, note 8.
37. Walther, *op. cit.*, p. 174.
38. Hitti, *History*, p. 560.
39. Mazaheri, *La vie quotidienne*, p. 64.
40. *loc. cit.*, citing Maqrizi, *Khitat*, 1, p. 89.
41. Bouhdiba, *op. cit.*, p. 192.
42. Mazaheri, *op. cit.*, p. 65.
43. Bouhdiba, *op. cit.*, p. 190.
44. Ar-Raziq, *op. cit.*, p. 46.
45. Irwin, *The Arabian* Nights, p. 174.
46. Bouhdiba, *op. cit.*, p. 189.
47. Irwin, *op. cit.*, p. 148, note 16.
48. Mark D. Meyerson, 'Prostitution of Muslim Women in the Kingdom of Valencia: Religious and Sexual Discrimination in a Medieval Plural Society', inMarilyn J. Chiat & Kathryn L. Reyerson, (eds) *The Medieval Mediterranean: Cross-Cultural Contacts*, Medieval Studies at University of Minnesota, 1988, p. 88.
49. Walther, *op. cit.*, p. 99.
50. Bouhdiba *op. cit.*, p. 187.
51. Guthrie, *op. cit.*, p. 129, note 66.
52. Bat Ye'or, *The dhimmi: Jews and Christians under Islam*, Associated University Press, London, U.S.A. and Canada, 1985, revised and enlarged English edition, p. 213.
53. Serjeant, 'Islamic Textiles', p. 77.
54. Talbi, 'Everyday Life', p. 458, note 327.
55. Guthrie, *op. cit.*, p. 129.
56. Walther, *op. cit.*, p. 168.
57. Reuben Levy, *A Baghdad Chronicle*, Cambridge University Press, 1929, pp. 122,123.
58. S. D. Goitein, 'The rise of the Near-Eastern bourgeoisie in early Islamic times', *Journal of World History*, Volume III, 3, 1957, p. 590.
59. Raymond & Wiet, *Les marchés du Caire*, p. 38.
60. Ibn Battuta, *op. cit.*, p. 334.
61. Raymond & Wiet, *op. cit.*, p. 224.
62. *loc. cit.*
63. Julie M. Peteet, 'Authenticity and Gender: The Presentation of Culture' in Tucker, *Arab Women*, p. 60.
64. Guthrie, *op. cit.*, p. 101.
65. Raymond & Wiet, *op. cit.*, p. 228 note 4.
66. Sura 4:3, *al-Nisa'*.
67. Raymond & Wiet, *op. cit.*, p. 271, note 111.
68. Talbi *op. cit.*, p. 436 note 23.
69. *ibid.*, p. 387, note 27.
70. Irwin, *op. cit.*, p. 175.

71. Ibn Qayyim al-Jawziyya, *op. cit.*, p. 284.
72. Raymond & Wiet, *op. cit.* , p. 229.
73. Ye'or, *op. cit.*, p. 350.
74. Talbi, *op. cit.*, p. 388.
75. Cohen & Simon-Piqali, 'Women in Court: Economic Transactions', in Roded, *Women in Islam*, p. 137.
76. Ye'or, *op. cit.*, p. 169.
77. Raymond & Wiet, *op. cit.*, p. 231 note 38.
78. *ibid.*, p. 231, note 38.
79. Talbi, *op. cit.*, p. 389.
80. Ye'or, *op. cit.*, p. 186.
81. Eliahu Ashtor, *The Medieval Near East: Social and Economic History*, Variorum Reprints, London, 1978, p. 77.
82. *Ibid.*, p. 80.
83. Ye'or, *op. cit.*, p. 187.
84. *Ibid.*, p. 192.
85. *Ibid.*, p. 350.
86. Jerrilynn D. Dodds, 'Mudejar Tradition and the Synagogues of Medieval Spain: Cultural Identity and Cultural Hegemony', in (eds) Vivian B. Mann, Thomas F. Glick, Jerrilynn Dodds, *Conviencia: Jews, Muslims, and Christians in Medieval Spain*, George Braziller in association with the Jewish Museum, New York, 1992, paperback, p. 119, note 2.
87. Talbi, *op. cit.*, p. 390, note 41.
88. Ye'or, *op. cit.*, p. 191.
89. Guthrie, *op. cit.*, Illustration 18.
90. Ye'or, *op. cit.*, p. 191.
91. Roded, *op. cit.*, p. 173.
92. Yeor, *op. cit.*, p. 209.
93. Stowasser, 'Women's Issues', in Tucker, *Arab Women*, p. 23, note 91.

Conclusion
1. Gulru Necipoglu, *The Topkapi Scroll – Geometry and Ornament in Islamic Architecture*, The Getty Center for the History of Art and the Humanities, Santa Monica, California, 1995, p. 192.
2. R. A. Nicholson, Nicholson, *A Literary History of the Arabs*, Cambridge University Press, Cambridge, 1930, p. 237
3. Sura 12:33, *Yusuf.*
4. Walther, *Women in Islam*, p. 164.
5. Al-'Udhari, *Classical Poems*, p. 17.
6. P. J. Chelkowski (ed) Mirror of the Invisible World: *Tales of the Khamseh of Nizami*, New York, 1975, p. 61.
7. Walther, *op. cit.*, p. 179.
8. *loc. cit.*
9. Al-'Udhari, *Classical Poems*, p. 76.
10. Walther, *op. cit.*, p. 155.
11. Hamilton, 'Walid and his Friends', p. 73.
12. Walther, *op. cit.*, p. 180.
13. *ibid.*, p. 179.

14. Ibn Khallikan, *Wafayat*, p. 153.
15. Al-'Udhari, *op. cit.*, p. 164.
16. *ibid.*, p. 112.
17. Walther, *op. cit.*, p. 179.
18. Nicholson, *op. cit.*, p. 127.
19. Al-'Udhari, *op. cit.*, p. 60.
20. Irwin, *Night & Horses & the Desert*, p. 26.
21. Al-'Udhari, *op. cit.*, p. 48.
22. Irwin, *op. cit.*, p.155.
23. *ibid.*, p. 56.
24. Al-'Udhari, p. 32.
25. *ibid.*, p. 84.
26. *ibid.*, p. 132.
27. Walther, *op. cit.*, p. 163.

Bibliography

M. M. Ahsan, *Social Life under the 'Abbasids, 170/289 AH – 786-902 AD*, Longman, London and New York, 1979.

Ghazi Algosaibi, *Dusting the Colour from Roses: A Bilingual Collection of Arabic Poetry*, Echoes, London, 1995.

Muhammad Asad, *The Message of the Qur'an*, Dar al-Andalus, Gibraltar, 1980.

Ghassan Ascha, *Du statut intérieur de la femme en Islam*, Editions Harmattan, Paris, 1987.

E. Ashtor, *Histoire des prix et des salaires dans l'Orient Médiéval*, Touzot, Paris, 1969.

G. N. Atiyeh (ed.), *The Book in the Islamic World: the Written Word and Communication in the Middle East*, State University of New York Press, 1995.

Al-Baghdadi, *Kitab al-Tabikh*, tr. A. J. Arberry, 'A Baghdad Cookery Book', *Islamic Culture*, 13, 1939, pp. 1-47; 189-214.

Patricia L. Baker, *Islamic Textiles*, British Museum Press, London, 1995.

Lois Beck and Nikki Keddie (eds), *Women in the Muslim World*, Harvard University Press, Cambridge, Mass. and London, England, 1978, p. 605.

Lucie Bolens, 'The Use of Plants for Dyeing and Clothing', in S. K. Jayyusi, *The Legacy of Muslim Spain*, Brill, Leiden, 1992.

C. E. Bosworth, *The Lata'if al-Ma'arif of Tha'alibi*, Edinburgh University Press, 1968.

—— *Mediaeval Arabic Culture and Administration*, Variorum Reprints, London, 1982.

—— *The Mediaeval Islamic Underworld: The Banu Sasan in Arabic Society and Literature*, Part One, Brill, Leiden, 1976.

A. Bouhdiba, *Sexuality in Islam*, Saqi Books, London, 1998.

A. Bouhdiba and M. M. al-Dawalibi (eds), *The Different Aspects of Islamic Culture: The Individual and Society in Islam*, UNESCO, Paris, 1998.

Donna Lee Bowen and Evelyn A. Early (eds), *Everyday Life in the Muslim Middle East*, Indiana University Press, Bloomington and Indianapolis, 1993.

R. Brunschvig, 'Propriétaire et locataire d'immeuble', in *Studia Islamica*, Vol. LII, 1980.

W. Buonaventura, *Beauty and the East: A Book of Oriental Body Care*, Saqi Books, London, 1998.

R. Burton (tr.), *The Book of the 1,001 Nights*, (ed.) P. H. Newby, London, 1968.

Inea Bushnaq (tr.), *Arab Folktales*, Penguin Folklore Library, Harmondsworth, Middlesex, 1986.

P. J. Chelkowski (ed.), *Mirror of the Invisible World: Tales of the Khamseh of Nizami*, New York, 1975.

Thomas Chenery, *The Assemblies of al-Hariri*, tr. from the Arabic, Williams and Norgate, London and Edinburgh, 1867.

Marilyn J. Chiat and Kathryn L. Reyerson (eds), *The Medieval Mediterranean: Cross-Cultural Contacts*, Medieval Studies at University of Minnesota, 1988.

Amnon Cohen and Elisheva Simon-Piqali (eds), *Jews in the Moslem Court: Society, Economy and Communal Organization in Sixteenth Century Jerusalem*, Jerusalem, Yad Izhak Ben-Zvi, 1993.

Youssef Courbage and Phillipe Fargues, *Christians and Jews under Islam*, tr. Judy Mabro, I. B. Tauris, London, 1998.

Tove Stang Dahl, *The Muslim Family: A Study of Women's Rights in Islam*, Scandinavian Universities Press, 1997, Oslo, Stockholm, Copenhagen, Oxford, Boston.

Al-Dhahabi, *Kitab Duwal al-Islam* (tr. A. Negre), *Les dynasties de l'Islam: traduction annotée des années 447/1055-6 à 656/1258*, Institut Français de Damas, Damascus, 1979.

E. S. Drower, 'Women and Taboo in Iraq', *Iraq*, Vols 5-6, 1938, pp. 105-117.

Richard Ettinghausen, *Arab Painting*, Rizzoli International Publications Inc., New York, 1977.

Evelyn A. Early, 'Fertility and Fate: Medical Practices among Baladi Women of Cairo', in Donna Lee Bowen and Evelyn A. Early (eds), *Everyday Life in the Muslim Middle East*, Indiana University Press, Bloomington and Indianapolis, 1993.

Madelain Farah, 'Marriage and Sexuality in Islam: A Translation of al-Ghazali's Book on the Etiquette of Marriage from the *Ihya*', The University of Utah, Salt Lake City, 1984, pp. 106-13, in Ruth Roded (ed.), *Woman and Islam and the Middle East: A Reader*, I. B. Tauris, London, 1999.

Chadly Fitouri, 'Childhood and Youth' in A. Bouhdiba and M.M. al-Dawalibi, *The Different Aspects of Islamic Culture: The Individual and Society in Islam*, UNESCO, Paris, 1998.

Al-Ghazali, *al-Adab fi'l-din*, tr. J. Badeau, 'They lived once thus in Baghdad', *Mediaeval and Middle Eastern Studies in honor of Aziz Suryal Atiya*, (ed.) S. A. Hanna, Brill, Leiden, 1972.

—— *Nasihat al-muluk*, translated by F. R. C. Bagley, *Counsel for Kings*, Oxford University Press, London, 1964.

Avner Giladi, *Children of Islam: Concepts of Childhood in Medieval Muslim Islam*, Macmillan in association with St. Antony's College, Oxford, 1992.

—— *Infants, Parents and Wet-Nurses: Medieval Islamic views on Breast-feeding and their Social Implications*, Brill, Leiden, Boston, Koln, 1999.

S. D. Goitein, *Letters of Medieval Jewish Traders*, Princeton U.P., 1973.

—— 'The Rise of the Near-Eastern Bourgeoisie in Early Islamic Times', *Journal of World History*, Vol. III, 1957.

Shirley Guthrie, *Arab Social Life in the Middle Ages: An Illustrated Study*, Saqi Books, London, 1995.

R. Hamilton, 'Walid and his Friends: an Umayyad Tragedy', *Oxford Studies in Islamic Art*, Vol. VI, 1988.

P. K. Hitti, *History of the Arabs*, Macmillan, London, reprint, 1982.

Albert Hourani, *A History of the Arab Peoples*, Faber and Faber, London, 1991.

A. H. Hourani and S. M. Stern (eds), *The Islamic City*, Bruno Cassirer, Oxford and the University of Pennsylvania, 1970.

Ibn Battuta, *Kitab rihlat ibn-Battuta al-musamma tuhfat al-nazzar fi ghara'ib al-amsar wa-'aja'ib al-asfar*, tr. H. A. R. Gibb, *Travels in Asia and Africa, 1325-1354*, Routledge and Kegan Paul, London, reprint 1984.

Ibn Hazm, *Tawq al-Hamama*, Tr. A. J. Arberry, *The Ring of the Dove: A Treatise on the Art and Practice of Arab Love*, Luzac Oriental, London,1994.

Ibn Munqidh, (Usama ibn Murshid) (Mu'ayid al-Dawla called Ibn Munqidh), Kitab al-I'tibar, tr. P. K. Hitti, *An Arab-Syrian Gentleman and Warrior in the Period of the Crusades: Memoirs of Usamah ibn Munqidh*, I. B. Tauris, London, 1987.

Al-Isfahani, tr. H. Masse, *Conquête de la Syrie et de la Palestine par Saladin*, Librairie Orientaliste Paul Geuthner, Paris, 1972.

Ibn Jubayr, *al-Rihla*, tr. R. J. C. Broadhurst, *Travels*, Jonathan Cape, London, 1952.

Ibn Khallikan, *Wafayat al-ay'an wa anba' abna' al-zaman*, I, tr. M. de Slane, (ed.) S. Moinul Haq, Pakistan Historical Society, Karachi, 1961.

Ibn Qayyim al-Jawziyya, *Tibb al-Nabi*, tr. Penelope Johnstone, *Medicine of the Prophet*, The Islamic Texts Society, Cambridge, 1998.

Ibn Sirin, *The Interpretation of Dreams*, Dar al-Taqwa, London, 1996.

R. Irwin, *The Arabian Nights: a Companion*, Allen Lane, The Penguin Press, London, 1994.

—— *The Middle East in the Middle Ages: the Early Mamluk Sultanate, 1250-1382*, Southern Illinois University Press, Carbondale and Edwardsville, 1986.

—— *Night and Horses and the Desert: An Anthology of Classical Arabic Literature*, Allen Lane, The Penguin Press, London, 1999.

Al-Jahiz, *Risalat al-qiyan*, tr. A. F. L. Beeston, *The Epistle of Singing-girls of Jahiz*, Aris and Phillips, Warminster, 1980.

M. Jastrow, 'Dust, Earth and Ashes as Symbols of Mourning among the Ancient Hebrews', *Journal of the American Oriental Society*, Vol. 20, 1899.

Aida S. Kanafani, 'Rites of Hospitality and Aesthetics', in Donna Lee Bowen and Evelyn A. Early (eds), *Everyday Life in the Muslim Middle East*, Indiana University Press, Bloomington and Indianapolis, 1993.

E. Kuhnel, 'Abbasid silks of the Ninth Century', in *Ars Orientalis*, Vol. II, 1957, pp. 367-371.

—— *Catalogue of Dated tiraz fabrics: Umayyad, 'Abbasid, Fatimid'*, Textile Museum, Washington, 1952.

E. W. Lane, *An Arabic-English Lexicon*, Islamic Texts Society, Cambridge, reprint 1984, 2 vols.

—— *Manners and Customs of the Modern Egyptians*, Alexander Gardner, Paisley and London, 1895.

—— *Arabian Society in the Middle Ages: Studies from The Thousand and One Nights*, (ed.) S. Lane-Poole, New edition, Curzon Press, London, 1971.

Ira Lapidus, 'Urban Society in Mamluk Syria', A. H. Hourani and S. M. Stern (eds), *The Islamic City*, Bruno Cassirer, Oxford and the University of Pennsylvania, 1970.

Bernard Lewis, *The Middle East: 2000 years of History from the Rise of Christianity to the Present Day*, A Phoenix Giant, London, 1996.

George Makdisi, 'The Topography of eleventh-century Baghdad: materials and notes', in *Arabica*, Vol. 6, 1959, pp. 178-197.

Malik ibn Anan, *al-Muwatta*, tr. Aisha Abdurrahman Bewley, *An Early Legal Compendium: Purity, Legal Competence and Property Ownership*, Kegan Paul International, London, 1989.

David S. Margoliouth, 'Meetings and Salons under the Caliphate', *Islamic Culture*, Vol. 3, January 1929, pp. 1-17.

—— 'The Renaissance of Islam: Trade', *Islamic Culture*, Vol. 7, 1933, pp. 309-323.

—— 'The Table-Talk of a Mesopotamian Judge', Part II, tr. D. S. Margoliouth, *Islamic Culture*, Vol. 5, July, 1931, pp. 169-193.

Idem, 'Wit and Humour in Arabic Authors', *Islamic Culture*, Vol. 1, 1927, pp. 522-534.

Manuela Marin, 'Colour and Smell in the Medieval Arab Culinary Tradition' in Sami Zubaida and Richard Tapper (eds), *Culinary Cultures of the Middle East*, I.B. Tauris, London, 1996.

S. Masliyah, 'Mourning Customs and Laments among the Muslims of Baghdad', *Islamic Culture*, Vol. 54, January, 1980, pp. 19-29.

L. A. Mayer, 'Costumes of Mamluk Women', *Islamic Culture*, Vol. 17, January, 1943.

Aly Mazaheri, *La vie quotidienne des musulmans au moyen age*, Librairie Hachette, Paris, 1951.

Miskawayh, *Tajarib al-Umam*, tr. D. S. Margoliouth, *The Experiences of the Nations*, Blackwell, Oxford, 1921.

Soheir A. Morsy, 'Sex Differences and Folk Illness in an Egyptian Village', in Lois Beck and Nikki Keddie (eds), *Women in the Muslim World*, Harvard University Press, Cambridge, Mass. and London, England, 1978, pp. 599-616.

S. al-Din al-Munajjid, 'Women's Roles in the Art of Arabic Calligraphy', G. N. Atiyeh (ed.), *The Book in the Islamic World: the Written Word and Communication in the Middle East*, State University of New York Press, 1995.

B. F. Musallam, *Sex and Society in Islam: Birth control before the nineteenth century*, Cambridge University Press, Cambridge, reprint, 1986.

Gulru Necipoglu, *The Topkapi Scroll: Geometry and Ornament in Islamic Architecture*, The Getty Center for the History of Art and the Humanities, Santa Monica, California, 1995.

R. A. Nicholson, *A Literary History of the Arabs*, Cambridge University Press, Cambridge, 1930.

Abdel Rahim Omran, *Family Planning in the Legacy of Islam*, Routledge, London, 1992.

Julie M. Peteet, 'Authenticity and Gender: The Presentation of Culture' in Judith E. Tucker, *Arab Women: Old Boundaries, New Frontiers*, Indiana University Press, Bloomington and Indianapolis, 1993.

Thomas Preston, *Makamat or Rhetorical Anecdotes of al-Hariri of Basra*, Cambridge University Press, 1850.

A. Raymond and G. Wiet, *Les marches du Caire: Traduction annotee du texte de Maqrizi*, Institut Francais d'Archeologie Orientale du Caire, *Texte Arabes et Etudes*

Islamiques, Tome XIV, 1979.

Ahmad 'Abd ar-Raziq, *La femme au temps des Mamlouks en Egypte*, Institut Francais d'Archéologie Orientale du Caire, 1976.

Ruth Roded (ed.), *Women in Islam and the Middle East: A Reader*, I. B. Tauris, London, 1999.

Maxime Rodinson, *Mohammed*, tr. Anne Carter) Penguin Books, Harmondsworth, Middlesex, reprint, 1993.

Franz Rosenthal, *Four Essays on Art and Literature in Islam*, Brill, Leiden, 1971.

Malise Ruthven, *Islam in the World*, Penguin Books, London, 1984.

Nawal El Saadawi, *The Hidden Face of Eve: Women in the Arab World*, Zed Books, London, fourth reprint, 1985.

Fatna A. Sabah, *Woman in the Muslim Unconscious*, Pergamon Press, The Athena Series, New York, 1984.

Hilal al-Sabi, *Rusum dar al-Khilafa*, tr. E. A. Salem, *The Rules and Regulations of the 'Abbasid Court*, American University of Beirut, 1977.

J. Sadan, 'Kings and Craftsmen: a Pattern of Contrasts on the history of a medieval Arabic Humoristic form', Part 1, in *Studia Islamica*, Vol. XVI, 1982, pp. 5-49; Part II, in *SI*, Vol. LXII, 1985, pp. 89-120.

S. B. Samadi, 'Some Aspects of the Arab-Iranian Culture from the Earliest Times up to the Fall of Baghdad', in *Islamic Culture*, Vol. 26, October, 1952, pp. 32-49.

R. B. Serjeant, *Islamic Textiles*, Librairie du Liban, Beirut, 1972.

M. Z. Siddiqi, *Studies in Arabian and Persian Medical Literature*, Calcutta University Press, Calcutta, 1959.

Margaret Smith, *Rabi'a the Mystic and her Fellow-saints in Islam*, Cambridge University Press, 1984.

Yedida K. Stillman, 'Costume as Cultural Statement: The Esthetics, Economics and Politics of Islamic Dress', in *The Jews of Medieval Islam: Community, Society and Identity*, International Conference Proceedings, Institute of Jewish Studies, University College, London, 1992.

—— 'libas', *Encyclopaedia of Islam*, Vol. V, Brill, Leiden, New Edition, pp. 733-751.

Barbara F. Stowasser, 'Women's Issues in Modern Islamic Thought', in Judith E. Tucker, (ed.) *Arab Women: Old Boundaries, New Frontiers*, Indiana University Press, Bloomington and Indianapolis, 1993.

Muhammad Talbi, 'Everyday Life in the Cities of Islam' in A. Bouhdiba and M. M. al-Dawalibi, (eds) *The Different Aspects of Islamic Culture: The Individual and Society in Islam*, UNESCO, Paris, 1998.

Al-Tanukhi, fragmented manuscripts, tr. David S. Margoliouth, *The Table Talk of a Mesopotamian Judge*, Royal Asiatic Society, London, 1922.

idem, 'The Table-Talk of a Mesopotamian Judge', Part II, tr. D. S. Margoliouth, in *Islamic Culture*, Vol. 5, July, 1931, pp. 169-193.

Al-Tha'alibi, *Lata'if al-Ma'arif*, tr. C. E. Bosworth, *The Book of Curious and Entertaining Information*, Edinburgh University Press, 1968.

Judith E. Tucker, *Arab Women: Old Boundaries, New Frontiers*, Indiana University Press, Bloomington and Indianapolis, 1993.

—— 'The Arab Family in History: 'Otherness' and the study of the family', in Judith

E. Tucker (ed.), *Arab Women: Old Boundaries, New Frontiers*, Indiana University Press, Bloomington and Indianapolis, 1993.

—— *Women in nineteenth-century Egypt*, Cambridge University Press, 1985.

'Abdullah al-'Udhari, *Classical Poems by Arab Women: A Bilingual Anthology*, Saqi Books, London, 1999.

M. Ullmann, *Islamic Medicine*, Edinburgh University Press, 1978.

David Waines, *In a Caliph's Kitchen: Mediaeval Arabic Cooking for the Modern Gourmet*, Riad El-Rayyes Books, London, 1989.

Tariq Wali, *Private Skies: The Courtyard Pattern in the Architecture of the House, Bahrain*, Bahrain, 1992.

W. Walther, *Woman in Islam: from Medieval to Modern Times*, Markus Wiener Publishers, Princeton, N.J., 1993.

William Montgomery Watt, *The Influence of Islam on Medieval Europe*, Edinburgh University Press, reprint, 1984.

Gerhard Weiss, 'The Pilgrim as Tourist: Travels to the Holy Land as reflected in the Published Accounts of German Pilgrims between 1450 and 1550', in Marilyn J. Chiat and Kathryn L. Reyerson (eds), *The Medieval Mediterranean: Cross-Cultural Contacts*, Medieval Studies at University of Minnesota, 1988, pp. 119-131.

Mai Yamani, 'You are what you cook: cuisine and class in Mecca', in Sami Zubaida and Richard Tapper (eds), *Culinary Cultures of the Middle East*, I. B. Tauris, London, reprint, 1996, pp. 173-84.

Bat Ye'or, The *dhimmi: Jews and Christians under Islam*, Associated University Press, London, U.S.A. and Canada, 1985, revised and enlarged English edition.

J. Zozaya, 'Material Culture in Medieval Spain', in V. B. Mann, T. F. Glick and J. D. Dodds (eds) *Convivencia: Jews, Muslims and Christians in Medieval Spain*, George Braziller, New York, 1992.

Sami Zubaida and Richard Tapper (eds), *Culinary Cultures of the Middle East*, I. B. Tauris, London, 1996.

Index of Names

Ibn Bassam 183
Ibn Battuta, Muhammad ibn 'Abdallah
 (*Tuhfat al-nuzzar fi ghara'ib al-amsar wa
 'aja'ib al-asfar*) 15, 16, 17, 18, 39, 51, 94,
 97, 99, 107, 119, 123, 128, 130, 135,
 138, 158, 184, 205, 206
Ibn Baytar al-Maliki, Treatise on Simples
 (*Al-jam'i li mufradat al-adwiya wa'l-
 'aghdhiya*) 74
Ibn Butlan 60, 206
Ibn Daniyal 8, 58, 144, 155, 182
Ibn Durayd 89, 102
Ibn Fadlan 212
Ibn al-Faqih 84
Ibn al-Furat, Muhammad ibn 'Abbas 172
Ibn al-Hajj 8, 17, 19, 20, 21, 44, 47, 136,
 151
Ibn Hanbal 7, 16, 162, 200
Ibn Hawqal 116
Ibn Hazm, The Ring of the Dove (*Tawq al-
 hamama*) 'Ali 64, 151, 159
Ibn Irshad 132
Ibn Iyas 20
Ibn Jarir al-Tabari 163
Ibn al-Jassas 105
Ibn al-Jawzi, The Gleaning of Benefits
 (*Kitab iltiqat al-manaf'i*) 74, 76
Ibn Jubayr, Abu al-Husayn Muhammad
 ibn Ahmad, *Al-rihla* 19, 20, 24, 213,
 215
Ibn Khaldun 23, 30, 40, 60, 63
Ibn Khallikan, Ahmad ibn Muhammad,
 Biographical Dictionary (*Wafayat al-
 'ayan wa-anba' abna' al-zaman*) 8, 80,
 105
Ibn Qayyim al-Jawziyya, Medicine of the
 Prophet (*Tibb al-nabawi*) 52, 54, 58, 59,
 87, 88, 92, 108, 118, 129, 141, 147, 155,
 208
Ibn Mammati 105
Ibn Munqidh, Usama 172, 192
Ibn al-Quff 47, 69
Ibn Qutayba 77
Ibn Razin al-Tujibi, *Fadalat al-khiwan fi
 tayyibat al-ta'am wa'l-alwan* 98
Ibn al-Rumi 91
Ibn Sahnun 57, 109
Ibn al-Sa'i 88
Ibn Salama 195
Ibn Sina, Care of the Newborn 55, 66, 69,
 70, 76
Ibn Sirin 144, 150
Ibn Taghribirdi, Chronicles of Egypt
 (*Husn al-muhadara fi akhbar misr w'al-
 qahira*) 84
Ibn Taymiyya 53, 170, 171
Ibn Zaydun, Abu al-Walid Ahmad 166
Ibn Zuhr, Abu Marwan, Book of Diet
 (*Kitab al-aghdiya*) 86
Ibrahim, the Prophet's infant son 46, 51
Ibrahim ibn Aghlab 200
'Id al-Adha, the celebration at the end of
 the Pilgrimage 111
'Id al-Fitr, the celebration at the end of
 Ramadhan 111, 156, 185
Imad al-Isfahani 105,
Ibn Sa'd 171
India 24, 84-5, 102, 119, 125, 128, 176
Iraq 9, 26, 33, 81, 84, 88, 92, 100, 102, 117,
 128, 132, 137, 140, 158, 165, 188, 192,
 194
Isfahan 142
Italian 178
Ittifaq 169

Al-Jahiz 8, 24, 32, 34, 57, 63, 73, 74, 94, 95,
 97, 102, 104, 116, 142, 150, 169, 177,
 204, 226
Ja'far, vizier of Harun al-Rashid 50
Jahiliyya, the 'period of ignorance' before
 Islam 7, 167, 190, 203
Jamil ibn Ma'mar al-'Udhri, 218, 220, 222
Jamila, 'Fount and Origin of Song' 167
Jamila bint Nasir al-Dawla 102
Jawhara 142
al-Jazira 50
Jerusalem 60, 181, 186, 210
Jesus 187
Jews, the People of the Book (*ahl-al-
 dhimma*) 14, 15, 52, 54, 60, 68, 81, 85,
 92, 100, 115, 117, 122, 124, 125, 179,
 180, 181, 186, 187, 209-217
Jinn, evil spirits 62
Joseph (see Yusuf)
Judaism 87, 198
Juha 98
Juhamiyya, poetess 165
Jur 108, 149

Al-Kayyim 115

General Index

bracelets (*asawir*) 146, 150, 151, 153, 154, 181, 209
brazier 27, 107, 157
bread 30, 47, 82, 87, 88, 89, 90, 91, 92, 94, 96, 97, 109, 174
breast-feeding 47-50, 66-68, 70, 115, 144, 195, 217
bride 47, 61, 62, 134, 141, 149, 160, 184, 188, 215, 224
bridegroom 215
brocade 127, 134, 136, 137, 157
broker, female (*dallala*) 27, 75, 136, 137, 180, 181, 182, 210, 213
bronze 156
brothel 200, 201, 203
brother 22, 79, 165, 198, 223-4
brown 147, 197
bughlutaq 113
buqayra, a children's game 63
buran, sweet date sauce 82
burda, an outdoor wrap 130
burghul, cracked wheat 91
burqu', outdoor veil 122
butchers 83, 88
butter 89, 91, 92, 93, 100, 109, 110, 130, 178

cabbage 71
calf 135
calligrapher, female (*al-khattata*) 176-177
calligraphy 174, 176
cambric (finely woven white linen or cotton) 131
camels 38, 74, 83, 84, 90, 111, 148
camomile 182
camphor 24, 85, 117, 157, 158, 203
candles 27, 176
candlesticks 27, 107
caravan
cardamom 75
carpets 29, 105, 106, 121
carrier-pigeon 159
carrot 75, 76
celery 55
cemeteries 20, 215
cereals 91
charcoal 95, 96
charlatans 57, 144
charms 43, 75, 115, 160
cheese 93
chick peas 47, 91, 92, 93, 97, 102
chicken 37, 82, 93, 101

child, children 33, 41-64 passim, 65, 66, 67, 77, 100, 101, 109, 114, 130, 132, 152, 153, 171, 173, 174, 175, 179, 202, 207, 209, 215, 224
childbirth 43-47, 53, 65, 66, 70, 109, 110, 187-189, 193, 198, 202
children's games 61-64
childcare and health 47-56 passim, 188
cinnamon 71, 72, 82
circumcision 60, 109, 119, 188, 195
citrus 55, 58, 121
city 7, 11, 16-35 passim, 66, 114
clerk, female 178
cloak 115-116
clove 55
coconut 147
colocynth (a type of cucumber) 75, 76
colour symbolism (and see individual colours) 130, 137, 188, 204, 216
consolation treatises 51
combs 39, 146
concubine 12, 13, 14, 15, 16, 21, 113, 119, 164, 174, 214
confectionery 101
consanguinity 48-50, 123
contraception 65-78 passim
contraception, male 71-73
cookery 9, 79-112 passim
cooking oil 92, 178, 179
cooking utensils 97
cooks 95, 180, 206
cook-shops 94
copper 97, 98, 209
copyists 176
coral 144
corn 91, 166
cosmetics 70, 139-150 passim, 155, 161
costume 7, 8, 20, 32, 79, 113-138 passim, 150, 151, 165, 209-217
cotton 28, 32, 72, 115, 118, 130, 131, 132, 136, 137, 157, 158
counsellor 178
countryside 35-37, 66, 89, 101, 103, 114, 132, 134, 140, 155
court, royal 26, 30, 34, 79-88 passim, 91, 95, 97, 106, 117, 118, 119, 121, 124, 125, 126, 129, 132, 134, 136, 137, 140, 141, 143, 146, 147, 148, 150, 155, 157, 159, 162, 165, 167-170, 171, 176, 177, 180, 181, 192, 193, 194, 197, 198, 200, 203, 204, 208